Conrad Wilson,
1986

Sibelius

VOLUME II

by the same author

SIBELIUS
Volume I
1865–1905

SIBELIUS

VOLUME II
1904–1914

Erik Tawaststjerna
translated by Robert Layton

faber and faber

LONDON · BOSTON

This translation first published in 1986
by Faber and Faber Limited
3 Queen Square London WC1N 3AU

Photoset by Parker Typesetting Service Leicester
Printed in Great Britain by Richard Clay Limited
Bungay Suffolk

Originally published in Finnish as *Jean Sibelius 3*
by Octava, Helsinki 1972

British Library Cataloguing in Publication Data

Tawaststjerna, Erik
Sibelius
Vol. 2
1. Sibelius, Jean — Criticism and interpretation
I. Title
780'.92'4   ML410.S54
ISBN 0–571–08833–3

Contents

Illustrations

Translator's Foreword

Erik Tawaststjerna's study of Jean Sibelius runs to five volumes in Finnish. Although these have been the first to appear in print, they are in fact translations from the author's original Swedish. This is often forgotten even in Scandinavia where the assumption is not unnaturally made that the original must be in Finnish. The dimensions of the book differ in the two languages: the first volume in Swedish comprises the first two Finnish volumes. Perhaps the diagram below will make the relationship between the editions clear. The present volume encompasses Volume 3 of the Finnish edition together with a few pages of Volume 4, and covers the crucial period from 1904 and the beginning of the Third Symphony to the outbreak of the First World War ten years later.

Finnish edition, translated from the Swedish original under the guidance of the author	Author's original text (Swedish)	English edition, translated by RL from Swedish original
PUBLISHER Otava, Helsinki	Volumes I and II: Bonniers, Stockholm Volume III: Almqvist & Wiksell, Stockholm	London: Faber and Faber California University Press
Jean Sibelius 1 (1965) translated by Tuomas Anhava Jean Sibelius 2 (1967) translated by Tuomas Anhava	Volume I (1968)	Sibelius, Volume I, 1865–1905 (1976)
Jean Sibelius 3 (1972) translated by Erkki Salmenhaara	Volume II (in preparation)	Sibelius, Volume II, 1904–1914 (1986)
Jean Sibelius 4 (1977) translated by Erkki Salmenhaara Jean Sibelius 5 (in preparation)	Volume III (in preparation)	

During the years covered by this volume Sibelius began keeping a diary. These diary entries as well as the letters he wrote to his wife, Aino, and his friend and confidant, Axel Carpelan, call for some comment. The letters are the more straightforward, although their prose, though characteristically personal, is not always finished, but the style of the diaries is very difficult to convey. They make even fewer literary aspirations and convey the feeling of an informal dialogue with an *alter ego*; they are cryptic jottings, highly idiosyncratic in their vocabulary and more often than not unsyntactical and badly punctuated. Indeed, at times they are difficult to make much of and in order to convey what Sibelius's intentions are, I have found myself drawing on idioms that may not have enjoyed currency in English in the early part of the century. However, I hope that something of their flavour and also what he is trying to say to himself comes across. One example may suffice. During the gestation of the Fourth Symphony, Sibelius uses the not inappropriate image of an ironsmith, since this is a work that was (to quote the Oxford Dictionary definition) 'shaped by beating in fire and hammering'. Yet, a diary entry such as 'Forged a little', which would be the literal translation, makes a somewhat bizarre impression on the present-day reader.

Of course, perspectives differ from country to country and assumptions that one can take for granted in one cultural background cannot necessarily be made in another. In the English-speaking world there is a vast literature on the music of the period covered by Sibelius's lifetime, and one can assume that the more specialist reader of Tawaststjerna's *Sibelius* will be familiar with it. Similarly in England and America, the lending-library systems, record libraries and organizations such as the BBC equip the English reader with a more informed view of the musical-historical background than is possible in remoter parts of Scandinavia. Hence, for the English reader, some of the general musical background in Volume I was supererogatory, but in the present instance the Swedish text has required altogether minimal adaptation. Conversely the historical background, which the educated Finnish reader will take for granted, will not be familiar to most readers in the English-speaking world, and the developments that took place both in the political sphere and the arts other than music need the fullest exegesis for the non-Scandinavian reader. Finnish and Swedish readers will probably recognize allusions to the poet Johan Ludvig Runeberg, but the vast majority of English-speaking readers are little acquainted with his work. In many instances in the course of the diaries, Sibelius apostrophizes himself in a way that sounds distinctly self-regarding without some background knowledge of Runeberg. When he is talking to himself Sibelius uses the term 'Wonderful Ego' or 'Glorious Ego' and I have spent some time pondering how best to render this or whether to omit it altogether. The expression is not, however, as narcissistic as it seems, for it derives from Runeberg's epic poems, which Sibelius knew well and ultimately, of course, has Homeric origins. Thus, in referring to one of his daughters, Sibelius could – and very often did – write, 'Ruth, the Glorious Maiden' or 'Katarina, the Proud Damsel'. As far as the author's own text is concerned, I see it as my function to try and envisage the way in which he might have expressed himself were English his first tongue. For, as anyone who has done any translation knows, if the text is to read well in the new language, it must be free from the thought processes that go to structure the original.

A note about the source material may also be in order. The Sibelius family carefully preserved letters, diaries and other documents. Erik Tawaststjerna has had unrestricted access to them and during the course of his work this Archive has been in his possession. It would be tedious to repeat footnotes referring to letters in the possession of the Sibelius Estate, and I have, for the most part, embedded the date of a letter or diary entry in the body of the text.

R. L.

CHAPTER ONE

Pelléas et Mélisande

My inner self is in the grip of change. I have observed it
with feelings of melancholy and concern. Let me not
become cold and hard, for that would be the end of
happiness.

Sibelius to Axel Carpelan, June 1904

Now that he was approaching his forties, Sibelius sensed that he stood on
the threshold of the most decisive change in his whole artistic career. Ever
since *Kullervo*, he had worked within a stylistic framework whose premises
he had not questioned or sought to change. This first flowering with its aura
of late romanticism and strongly national overtones with its flavouring of
the *Kalevala*, had produced such personal utterances as *The Four Legends* and
the First Symphony, and had culminated in the Second, which already
points the way to a new classicism. It is not surprising that the first fully
realized masterpiece that an artist produces brings special anxieties in its
wake. Can its achievement be sustained and is it real or illusory? Does it lay
the foundations for further artistic growth? After the Second Symphony,
Sibelius seems to have been the victim of such doubts, which grew in
strength as his struggles with the Violin Concerto progressed. In its first
version, the Concerto did not satisfy him at all and demanded a thorough-
going revision. Similarly, after the Fourth, another peak in the symphonic
range, comparable doubts assailed him, while after the Fifth, which seems
to have posed special difficulties for him, he was satisfied only after two
revisions, one the following year and a second in 1919. One can only
speculate about his state of mind after the climactic achievement of the
Seventh Symphony and *Tapiola*. Was the reaction so strong that the resul-
tant anxieties even inhibited him from completing the Eighth Symphony,
let alone working and reworking it?

In the spring of 1904, before he wrote the lines to Axel Carpelan that
stand at the head of this chapter, Sibelius was poised on the brink of his
'second period'. The Violin Concerto, a transitional work, still made its
claims on his energies, and its revision weighed heavily on his spirits. In an

earlier letter to Carpelan, he confides that he is reading a fair amount of history and indulging in philosophical musings. 'All the same life is wonderful, even if we are sent here to suffer. In my view he is the richest in spirit who can suffer most. My *Alleingefühl* is stronger than ever. Death draws near . . . I have many new ideas.'[1] Sibelius sensed his future potential and glimpses of his stylistic path in the coming years floated across his field of vision. As had been the case when he had just finished the *Karelia* music, he was seized by fears that he would die before accomplishing all that awaited him. No doubt some of his sense of change was generated by an awareness of all that was happening in Europe, but there is no doubt that the greater part of it sprang from inner sources. His *Alleingefühl* made it difficult for him to attach himself to any special stylistic trend, but it would be equally wrong to think of him as working wholly in isolation, for his evolution prompts a number of parallels with developments on the Continent.

By the middle of the first decade of the present century, the impetus behind art nouveau began to slacken. Waterlilies, the wings of Osiris, nocturnal hallucinatory vampires and other ornate patterns began to lose their expressive vitality as symbols of the unconscious. Out of a bold stillness of surface planes, stretching into infinity like the sea (the image is Proust's), a new style was born from the world of silence and night. From this cool yet highly charged atmosphere, full of electricity and a mystic sense of expectation, emerged Debussy's *La Mer*, the *chef d'oeuvre* of musical impressionism. But in Germany, Wilde's moon still shone over the palace terraces in Strauss's *Salome*. Schoenberg was in the throes of developing his own distinctive contribution to the breakdown of tonality, while Skryabin, fertilized by the chromaticism of Wagner and Liszt on the one hand, and Chopin's sound world on the other, began to move away from classical major-minor tonality. Glazunov and Rachmaninov were both present in Paris when, in 1907, the year before his death, a bewildered Rimsky-Korsakov played stretches of *Poem of Ecstasy*, wondering whether Skryabin had taken leave of his senses. Neither Glazunov nor Rachmaninov lost their heads in the wake of ever-increasing chromaticism and maintained a solid tonal stance. Indeed, Rachmaninov thought Rimsky-Korsakov's *The Golden Cockerel* the fount of modernism, and it was from its springs that the young Stravinsky was to drink, even if his early Symphony shows some traces of Glazunov as well. In Busoni's remarkable Piano Concerto with its Lisztian sweep and range, as well as its final choral peroration in the manner of the *Faust Symphony*, one can discern an Italianate simplicity and a Faustian complexity which were to be assimilated in his dawning *junge Klassizität*. Reger was working towards his late-romantic, neo-baroque style with its richly chromatic polyphony, while, in his Sixth

1 Written on 8 March 1904.

Symphony, Mahler was adding a new dimension to his expressive language.

It was through these composers that Sibelius encountered the music of his time. They formed the magnetic field that bounded his horizon, and acted as poles by which he was either drawn or repelled. It should be stressed that he was far better informed about them than many observers would have us believe, preferring to think of him as an isolated figure without real contact with the European tradition. In 1905 the other arts were also witnessing the emergence of new forces. In Picasso, national Spanish symbols were being transformed into a universal, geometric style: the cubist *Les demoiselles d'Avignon* comes from 1907. In architecture, art nouveau crumbled before the onslaught of Frank Lloyd Wright's 'free-flowing space', while as a counter-balance to the naturalistic world of the senses, Freud and Bergson explored the depths of the psyche, the unconscious and the intuition. Parallel trends or 'correspondences', in Baudelaire's sense, however vague they may be, are undoubtedly to be found in Sibelius's development: his growth from a partly nationalistic, representational style to a more supra-national 'abstract' outlook. The freer organic metamorphosis technique suggests a sense of 'free-flowing space' while in a few years' time he was to explore the inner world of the psyche in the Fourth Symphony.

In Finland itself, architecture was the art form that offered the most striking parallels with Sibelius's emergence from late romanticism. When, in 1902, Sibelius's friend, the architect Eliel Saarinen built a villa complex at Hvitträsk, not far from Helsinki, together with his colleagues Armas Lindgren and Hermann Gesellius, they reflected something of the spirit of art nouveau that had moved Sibelius in the *Lemminkäinen Legends* and the First Symphony.

Among the earliest visitors to Hvitträsk were Sibelius, Maxim Gorky and Gustav Mahler. Later, in his sketches for the new Helsinki railway station, Saarinen departed from his art-nouveau conception and was criticized by Sigurd Frosterus and Gustav Strengell, fellow members with Sibelius of the Euterpist circle, who were more classical in outlook. 'Bears and plant-like ornamentation are scarcely representative of an age distinguished by the locomotive and by electricity.' The station finally emerged as purer and more classical in style. But musical life still retained a strong parochial stamp. Among the new rising generation, Selim Palmgren, Erkki Melartin and Erik Furuhjelm, there was no one who could be remotely thought of as radical. True, Palmgren's First Piano Concerto, which had been given its first performance in December 1904, showed some faint traces of impressionism, and his later work surprises with some harmonic audacities. In time, Melartin was to reveal some impressionist (and expressionist) traits but basically these composers, and their contemporaries elsewhere in Scandinavia, were all too heavily embedded in the romantic tradition to be able to create a new style. It was not from them that the renewal of Scandinavian music was to come, but from two composers in their forties: Sibelius and his great Danish contemporary, Carl Nielsen.

Sibelius's musical crisis coincided with a change in his attitude to the world around him. Up to the age of 40, he had to a large extent lived gregariously and responded to the world of nature; lived, as he put it, 'among people and animals'. Indeed, there was something of a restiveness in his quest for new impulses and experiences, and perhaps in his search for human sympathy and understanding. But now he began slowly to turn away from the world, at first almost imperceptibly, and then more noticeably.

This inner development is matched by an outward change in his life: he made up his mind to leave Helsinki and settle in the country. As he told Karl Ekman, 'My art demanded a different environment. In Helsinki all melody died within me.'[1] As early as 1903 he had purchased a plot of land at Järvenpää, some 30 kilometres north of Helsinki. There on the eastern shore of the long, thin lake of Tusby, some artists had formed a colony. Juhani Aho had led the way in making his home there in 1897, and his example was soon followed by the painters, Pekka Halonen and Eero Järnefelt. Sibelius's own land was beautifully situated on a woodland slope facing south-west, some 200 metres from the lake itself. It had originally comprised a half-hectare, but subsequently through various transactions and donations grew to be 4 hectares. The villa itself was designed by Lars Sonck, one of Finland's best architects, who gave his services free. At this time Sibelius had no capital at his disposal, and borrowed money both for the land and the villa. The foundations were laid in the autumn of 1903 and the actual building work was well under way in the following spring. Sibelius was torn between pessimism and a cautious optimism: he wrote to Carpelan,

> The villa has its foundation stone together with five oak beams. If only I can get it up; fight for it with muscle and might. I long to get it all in order, as well as to work without planks, etc. I have drunk nothing now for a whole month. So you see, I am gradually getting things back to shape.

Carpelan sent him his quarterly cheque from his group of patrons, whom he had mobilized on Sibelius's behalf since the autumn of 1901; and 100 marks were invested in a porcelain Dutch-oven fireplace. Sibelius was still impatient: 'At times during these months it has seemed that the house would never be ready. This home is a necessity for my art, which is why it is so important.'[2]

Sibelius was fairly active in the concert hall during the spring of 1904.

1 Ekman, *Jean Sibelius: his Life and Personality*, London, 1936, p.177.
2 Written on 3 June 1904.

After the first performances of the Violin Concerto in its first version on 8 and 10 February, he conducted the Philharmonic Orchestra lottery concert on 5 March in some music to a tableau under the title, *Ein Fichtenbaum – träumt von einer Palme* (A pine-tree dreaming of a palm) (Heine). Later the same month he conducted another novelty in Turku, dedicating it to the conductor of the orchestra there, José Eibenschütz: the piece was an Andante for strings, which he later decided to call Romance in C for strings. Then in April came a couple of concert appearances in Vaasa in aid of the Helsinki orchestra's pension fund at which Sibelius conducted his new 'Andante' and, for the first time in a concert hall, *Valse triste*.

War clouds darkened the horizon and the outbreak of the Russo-Japanese conflict is touched on in his correspondence with Carpelan. 'What do you think about the war, and the official communiqués? Japan possesses 23 battleships, and according to Bobban (Bobrikov) 40 have been destroyed. *Sic itur ad gehennam!*'[1] However, as Sibelius wrote these words, Bobrikov's days were already numbered. In June, Eugen Schauman fired three shots at the Tsarist Governor-General, killing him, and then committed suicide on the spot. Richard Faltin's son, who had been a member of the quartet in which Sibelius himself played during his student years, performed the operation on the mortally wounded Governor, and subsequently showed the composer two of the bullets that had buried themselves in his body. Apparently, the main theme in the tone poem *In Memoriam* (1909) was originally conceived in tribute to Eugen Schauman.

Later during the summer Sibelius made a concert tour of the Baltic states, and in Dubbeln, a resort in the bay of Riga, he conducted a mammoth three-part concert of his own music, comprising two of the *Lemminkäinen Legends*, *Spring Song*, *En Saga*, the Second Symphony, four movements from the *King Christian II* music, the new 'Andante' for strings, and *Valse triste*. The concert ended with *Finlandia*, again presented under its uncontroversial title, *Impromptu*. Not only were the Riga critics impressed by the music, but they were electrified by his performance as a conductor. Even before he had left on his Baltic tour, Sibelius had told Carpelan, 'As you see, I want to conduct as much as possible, since in the last and final resort, one does one's own things best.' Also on this Baltic trip, he was welcomed at the quayside at Reval by one of the leading champions of Finnish civil rights, R. A. Wrede, who had been banished to the Estonian capital. 'I was really delighted to see Wrede, and talked to him for a long time, which resulted in my being shadowed. It was not really troublesome except in Reval itself where it became really rather embarrassing.'

During the summer Sibelius had hoped to compose in earnest, but his concert tour and the new villa consumed all his time. In order to keep a watchful eye on the progress of the villa, which he called Ainola, Sibelius

1 Written on 8 March 1904.

rented a farmhouse near by in Tuomala (Tomasby). Here he was visited by his childhood friend, Walter von Konow, who had since become Intendant of Turku Castle. Von Konow worshipped Sibelius, and his letters bear such superscriptions as 'your lonely friend' or 'your eternal Walter', and so on. When Sibelius omitted to visit him on one occasion when he was in Turku and von Konow was in bed with influenza, he was roundly reproached: 'Did you not even have ten minutes for me? You were with the Holms for *hours!*' In this respect he reminds one of Carpelan who also played on his frail health, though he lacks Carpelan's more searching mind in musical matters. A streak of sentimentality runs through all his letters: 'Do not leave me without some words of warmth. You know what they mean to me.' Sibelius undoubtedly regarded Walter as a relic of his school years, but treated him with consideration, gentleness and a certain sympathy. Perhaps he thought Walter, like his brother Christian, had retained his 'youthfulness with all its qualities untarnished'.

At the beginning of the autumn, Sibelius was plagued by worries about his hearing, and was admitted to a private clinic in Helsinki. He mentions it in a letter to Carpelan on 4 September 1904, though his mood seems predominantly optimistic.

> My hearing is very bad. We'll see how things go. As far as the new works I am working on are concerned, I rely on the inner ear . . . ! I have sunny thoughts, and am going home now, with the doctor's permission, to Järvenpää. This month we move into our new home.

The prospect seems to have stimulated an outburst of creative energy, for later the same month he wrote to Carpelan:

> My hearing is much better, thank God! I have just begun my Third Symphony, and there are new songs ['The harper and his son' and 'I would I were in India', both from Op. 38]. I am also working on a piano piece in three movements [*Kyllikki*] which should be finished the day after tomorrow. I have other new plans too. Of course, I have not been able to resist composing something for the theatre, a bad habit of mine! *Pelléas et Mélisande*. Our new home ought to be finished this week. You must come and see it.[1]

But even if his head was full of new plans, he did not forget to express due concern about Carpelan's health even to the extent of reinforcing his martyr's complex:

> Try now and keep up your courage. Aino and I often think of you and your miserable fate. I have thought a lot about your financial problems. When I have my own economy sorted out, I shall take yours in hand. Forgive my presumption in saying so, but it springs from purest egotism.

1 Written on 21 September 1904.

Carpelan readily forgave, particularly as he was the privileged observer of Sibelius's creative process: Sibelius opened his mind to few other people as he did to Carpelan.

On 24 September, the Sibelius family moved into Ainola, and the Järnefelts and the Ahos celebrated the occasion in style. The villa seems to grow out of the surrounding countryside, and comprises two log storeys. With its sharp sloping roof, it recalls a Swiss chalet, though the windows in the library constitute a Karelian element. In the basement there were originally four rooms while, in 1911, the attic was converted into a study cum bedroom. Sonck's architectural skill can be seen even in the interior detail and layout. The rooms are beautifully proportioned.

When Sibelius first left Helsinki, Järvenpää was to a large extent untouched countryside. Foals and sheep almost nosed their way into the house, and from time to time an elk majestically bestrode the grounds. Even by Nordic standards, Sibelius responded with exceptional intensity to the moods of nature and the changes in the seasons: he scanned the skies with his binoculars for the geese flying over the lake ice, listened to the screech of the cranes, and heard the cries of the curlew echo over the marshy grounds just below Ainola. He savoured the spring blossoms every bit as much as he did autumnal scents and colours. With the exception of an occasional stay in Helsinki, Sibelius lived at Ainola for the remaining years of his life, more than a half-century in all.

No one had imagined that his move to Ainola would automatically resolve the problems that had beset Sibelius in Helsinki. His journeys into the capital 'to go the bank' became unnecessarily prolonged at times, and this heavy drinking posed problems for the marriage. On his way to a concert in Uleåborg, an angry letter from Aino must have reached him since he answered by telegram appealing for another chance and promising improvement. By the time he had arrived in Uleåborg he saw the comic side of his telegram, and wrote in encouraging terms:

> Don't worry so much, all will turn out for the best. If only you could be more cheerful and 'not sulky', that gets one nowhere. I have just ordered sour milk! Have been ordained! I will bring Kaj (Katarina) something very nice from the far north. Remember to take care of yourself. Read memoirs when dark thoughts assail you. Do not attach any significance to my hand, other than that the pen is poor, and my arm tired from too much conducting.[1]

Sibelius seems intent on protesting his innocence against the unworthy thought that his handwriting should betray symptoms of the morning-after-the-night-before! However this may be, the fact remains that already, at the age of 39, he evinced symptoms of tremor. This grew in severity

1 Written on 8 December 1904, his thirty-ninth birthday!

over the years, so that it finally impeded both his conducting and his ability to write. He had shown a predisposition towards this during his youth: an eye-witness account of the première of the *Kullervo* Symphony mentions the tremulous baton. At the same time it is only fair to say that conditions in the concert halls of Finnish provincial towns were hardly such as to soothe his (or any other conductor's) nerves. In Uleåborg the cello section consisted of one single player, who did not deign to attend rehearsals.

During the first autumn at Ainola, he made scant progress with the Third Symphony and *Pelléas*. The change in his life-style that his new circumstances entailed naturally called for a period of psychological adjustment. Although his ear trouble had cleared up, he was not enjoying perfect health: indeed, his doctors were beginning to suspect that he might be suffering from diabetes. 'When I heard this,' he told Carpelan, 'I realized that at last, only now, am I really grown up. Thirty-nine years old! In all events, I think that the illness will, if I may say so myself, be of benefit to my music. My art will go deeper, and at the same time, I shall write more.' Needless to say, he was put on a strict diet, but somewhat later the diagnosis was modified, and it was decided that Sibelius had a propensity for diabetes rather than the illness itself. At Christmas he was plagued by a heavy cold and an attack of rheumatism. Some weeks later, while on a visit to Berlin, he consulted a distinguished specialist, Professor Klemperer about his possible diabetic condition. After making all the appropriate tests Klemperer was led to express his surprise at Sibelius's 'fine physical condition and outstanding hypochondria'. He gave him dietetic advice that 'would enable him to live to a hundred'.[1] A few days later he wrote to Aino that he was still worried and that Klemperer's advice was 'the usual old story', but he subsequently cited Klemperer's exact words 'My wine, he said, should be lemonade.' Of course, it is possible that Sibelius dwelt on his illnesses as a means of attracting sympathy, and that basically his condition throughout the autumn of 1904 could be thought of as a phantom illness. The year 1904 had been exacting, full of unfinished artistic enterprises and burdened with countless practical problems. It is arguable that he took refuge from this pressure in illness, and of course constant alcohol only served to weaken his powers of resistance. Indeed, his drinking *was* the major problem; the other symptoms were of minor significance, a fact that Professor Klemperer was quick to grasp.

After the Berlin performance of *En Saga* in 1902, Ferruccio Busoni had written in the *Allgemeine Musik-Zeitung* of the vivid impression Sibelius had made as a conductor-composer, and he made up his mind to re-engage him for his next series of concerts. In the summer of 1903 he wrote inviting Sibelius to return: 'You know, I need strong weapons in my fight against

---

1 A letter to Carpelan dated 16 January 1905.

the Berlin critics, and in planning my orchestral concerts. I am very much relying on you.'¹ At the time Sibelius was far too preoccupied with his Violin Concerto to accept but Busoni did not give up and when, just after the Christmas of 1904, he wired Sibelius asking him to conduct his Second Symphony, the invitation came at the right psychological moment. Sibelius was in need of a change of scene, and Aino was quick to give her blessing to the enterprise. 'It would be good in more ways than one if Janne refreshed himself,' she wrote to Carpelan in the new year. And so, on 5 January 1905, Sibelius arrived in Berlin. The very next day he went to a rehearsal of a new work; Felix Weingartner was preparing his new symphony at the Royal Opera House, though it left Sibelius unmoved. A wholly different experience was to follow however: Richard Strauss conducting a concert comprising his *Sinfonia domestica* and *Ein Heldenleben*, both of which delighted him. He learned a great deal from them, he told Aino in a letter home. A few days later, on 9 January, he was invited to dinner at Busoni's home. 'He was very warm, even though there were twenty-odd people present,' he told Aino.

He has become a shade self-aware. He has had so many setbacks and so much trouble on account of these concerts. Early this morning comes the first rehearsal. Busoni is totally enamoured of my symphony and understands its [here he turns to Swedish] chaste concentration. [Back to Finnish] In particular, he thinks the second movement the best music in existence. He hasn't said a word about the finale. [Again Swedish] You realize that Busoni cannot understand its significance.

At the rehearsal Sibelius was in a state of some tension: 'I turned some ladies (English) out; they belong to Busoni's court and I can't bear them!' He thought that both Hans Pfitzner and Albéric Magnard, who were represented by a scherzo and a symphony respectively, behaved more and more distantly towards him. He took this (or pretended to take it) as a good omen: 'thus, I am in the ascendant!' Christian Sinding ('that wonderful man') gave him moral support and came to the rehearsals. Sibelius prepared himself carefully for the event. He went to bed early; he took his valerian drops, and did not mix any wine with his mineral water! At seven o'clock he wrote to Aino, 'The barber will come soon. At 8.30 I will perform. My evening dress is spruced up. Goodbye now, you are all I have in the world.' In the artists' room, he was so nervous that he scarcely knew whether he was coming or going. As white as a ghost, he mounted the rostrum, but suddenly regained his composure and conducted excellently. When it was all over he reported, 'I have scored a great success. Am so tired, so tired. After the concert I went with Busoni and others to an Italian restaurant. I asked [Adolf] Paul to send a telegram about my great success.'²

1 Written 25 August 1903.
2 Letters to Aino written on 6, 8, 9, 11 and 12 January 1905.

Overnight, Sibelius became one of the most controversial names in German musical life. 'Here I am at the centre of battle. Fired at or praised. Mostly the latter.' Sibelius did not exaggerate: the favourable reviews outnumbered the negative ones. In the *National-Zeitung*, Wilhelm Altmann called the Second Symphony 'a grandiose work which Weingartner and [Artur] Nikisch ought to have presented for us'. Otto Taubmann in the *Berliner Börsen-Courier*, though not particularly impressed by the quality of the thematic substance, praised Sibelius's capacity for developing his ideas and building up powerful climaxes, as well as his feeling for sonority. The *Tägliche Rundschau* called the Symphony 'a source of renewal' but the *Berliner Tagesblatt*'s Paul Schmidt thought the composer had only partly mastered the larger forms. Comparisons with other Scandinavian composers, such as Grieg and Sinding, were unavoidable; more surprisingly, Strauss came into the picture. Sibelius was thought to lack the rich contrapuntal textures of Strauss but to surpass him in the quality of his invention! *Die Musik* thought Sibelius one of the great creative figures of his day, but the *Neue Zeitschrift für Musik*, while recognizing his distinctive personal profile, hesitated before ranking the work in the great line of symphonies from Haydn to Bruckner. But as far as the general public was concerned, Sibelius was undoubtedly a big name. When he went to see Professor Klemperer the second time, after the concert had taken place, the latter told him, 'I had no idea I was dealing with someone so famous, being myself sceptical of the reputations of others.' Sibelius felt as if he had been given a blood transfusion.

If I get back to normal – and the Professor thinks I will get completely better – life will be worth living again for you, my only great love in life. And my great art, as I gradually realize. You must write about the children and, above all, yourself. You know that our life will acquire greater richness and meaning. One thing is clear for me: I must come here and listen to more music at the height of the season. Two or three months in the year. Otherwise I shall get out of touch. I am studying as best I can, Mahler's Fifth Symphony and Sinding's new quartet, which he gave me as thanks for my powerful symphony.[1]

Ever since his fine Piano Quintet, which had inspired Sibelius during his Berlin years, Sinding's art had paled and settled into a kind of late Nordic romanticism, so that it is hardly likely that Sibelius should have been particularly taken with the new string quartet. On the other hand, one would have imagined Mahler to have acted as a magnetic antipole. When one thinks of the line Sibelius pursued from the Second to the Third and Fourth Symphonies, it is difficult to conceive of him responding to the blend of irony, tragedy, the grandiose, the emotional complexity and the

1 Letter written to Aino on 22 January 1905.

passionate intensity of Mahler. But, at the same time, he could not help being impressed with the opening funeral march, which possibly has echoes in his own *In Memoriam*. With Strauss it was another matter. True, the German master had disappointed him by not conducting the Second Symphony for some reason that is not clear, a fact that drew unworthy comments from Sibelius's German friends. But this did not blind him to Strauss's greatness. They were somewhat distant friends, openly contesting their supremacy in the field of the symphonic poem.

Something of the rhythmic thrust and drive of the cello theme in *Ein Heldenleben* is echoed in Sibelius's next tone poem, *Pohjola's Daughter*, which he had at one time even thought to call 'l'Aventure d'un héros'. But every bit as important was another discovery. Busoni had conducted *Nuages* and *Fêtes* the previous month, and it is reasonable to assume that he showed the scores to Sibelius, since we find the latter writing to Robert Kajanus recommending him to study and perform them. This was probably the first time he had encountered an important large-scale Debussy score, and Debussy's influence, along with that of Strauss, manifests itself already in *Pohjola's Daughter*.

But if he encountered three of the leading composers of the day in Berlin, thanks to the initiative of Busoni, the latter's own art appears to have made scant impression on him. Sibelius heard the second of Busoni's legendary Liszt recitals, and recorded that he played 'like an angel'. Busoni's Piano Concerto had only recently received its first performance in the previous November and had generally met with hostility. 'Höllenspektakel' was what Adolf Weissmann called it. The beginnings of Busoni's ill-fated career as a composer, at least ill-fated in terms of public and critical response, were being laid, and it is characteristic of their relationship that Sibelius, who had discussed a number of important new works in his letters home, at no point even mentions Busoni's latest work. Indeed, one is left wondering whether he even saw the score. It was his earthy, Nordic *joie de vivre* and its complementary pantheistic melancholy that drew Busoni to Sibelius, but his affection for him was undoubtedly tinged with an element of nostalgia for their time together in the 1880s. Throughout his stay in Berlin, Sibelius lived in a state of euphoria: conducting, composing, negotiating. Busoni was engrossed in practising for his Liszt recital and in giving concerts with the Sgambati Quartet. The two friends did not get a great deal of time together, except meeting between various musical events. But perhaps this was the most stimulating aspect of their encounter.

There are some striking resonances in Sibelius's diaries of an article that Busoni published in *Die Musik* in 1905. They may even spring from their exchange of ideas when they met during these January days. In his article, which was prompted by Strauss's revision of Berlioz's *Treatise on Orchestration*, Busoni touched on a number of orchestral parallels to the effect produced on the piano by the sustaining pedal.

At times one plays the piano without the pedal, but for the most part, the right foot is continually active, helping, filling out the tone, binding the texture together; not to mention the typically big pedal effects. This 'right foot' is also indispensable in the orchestra.

Similar thoughts recur in Bengt von Törne's portrait of Sibelius:

The orchestra, you see, is a huge and wonderful instrument, that has got everything – except the pedal. You must always bear this in mind. You see, if you don't create an artifical pedal for your orchestration, there will be holes in it, and some passages will sound ragged.[1]

Sibelius goes on to give von Törne practical advice on how to sustain sonority, how a transition from one woodwind group to another can be effected by neutral strings – and how one can obtain a dying-away, *morendo* effect in the orchestra, one of the great pedal effects. He also reverts to this subject later on in his diaries (see Chapter Six).

Also, as far as the geniuses of the orchestra are concerned, Busoni and Sibelius seem of like mind. Busoni numbered among the absolute masters, whose instrumentation is matched by comparable musical inspiration, Mozart, Weber, Berlioz and, with a few reservations, Wagner. Sibelius's list also included Mozart and Weber, but added Mendelssohn, omitting no doubt on account of his own complexes both Berlioz and Wagner, but more surprisingly Beethoven, the central figure in his musical world. Sibelius's great admiration for Beethoven's symphonic genius and his whole ethos did not prevent him from criticizing his technique, evidently just his orchestration, which he thought a little 'dated and wanting in brilliance'. Busoni's list also omits Beethoven. Oddly enough, when he first visited England in 1905, Sibelius surprised Ernest Newman when he voiced these sentiments and maintained that a certain composer, usually regarded as 'a master of the orchestra' thought basically in pianistic terms. 'I found it impossible to agree with him on that occasion', wrote Newman, 'but after *Tapiola* and the Seventh Symphony I understood much better what he meant.'[2] Strauss in the first edition of his Berlioz *Treatise* argues on much the same lines: 'More than with Haydn and Mozart, the spirit of the keyboard impregnates Beethoven's symphonies, just as it was to do to an even greater extent with the orchestral works of Schumann and Brahms, not always to their advantage or the listener's pleasure.' Perhaps Busoni also discussed with Sibelius the *junge Klassizität*, which was forming in his mind during these years. Not to be confused with neo-classicism, it should be thought of as the complete antithesis of late romanticism, expressionism and impressionism. As he put it himself in *Entwurf einer neuen Ästhethik der Tonkunst*, 'There is greater depth in the so-called "champagne aria" from *Don Giovanni* than in many a

1 von Törne, *Sibelius: A Close-up*, London, 1937, pp.30–1.
2 Newman, *More Essays from the World of Music*, London, 1958, pp.119–20.

funeral march or nocturne.' Something of this outlook undoubtedly rubbed off on to Sibelius in his next symphony.

After his successful appearance in Berlin, Sibelius turned his attention to the reworking of the Violin Concerto but suddenly broke off to compose the incidental music to *Pelléas*. On 31 January he wrote a midnight letter to Aino:

All day I have laboured over *Pelléas*. I am also making a piano reduction of the score as I go along, and that takes time. It has been difficult to work entirely in one's head without the aid of a keyboard, but I shall make a success of it. Here I have the chance to hear what I like and meet anyone I want to, but I don't force myself to go to concerts, but only go when I feel like it. I'm glad that you went to hear Levertin [Oscar Levertin, the Swedish author who had given a lecture in Helsinki]. Tomorrow I will hear what you have been doing and how things are. Try and enjoy yourself. At times I feel so miserable that I cry out for you. How are the walls in my room? See that they are properly done [sound-proofed]. Now I am so tired that I'm dizzy. But I will continue all the same. Paul has been full of consideration for me and my work. Not at all as he was in the past. Aunt Speckman [his landlady] is a character, and I am thoroughly happy here. This letter is hardly a work of literature, as you see, but it's good to talk to you like this in the middle of the night. I'm feeling very well and working at a good pace.

Work on *Pelléas* proceeded well, and by the middle of February eight orchestral numbers were ready. Originally Sibelius had intended to go direct to England in response to an invitation from Granville Bantock, who at this time was in charge both of the Music School in Birmingham and of the Liverpool Philharmonic. He was to have conducted some of his own works in Liverpool on 18 March and, as he spoke no English, he began to take lessons together with Adolf Paul and his wife. But his plans changed from day to day; Busoni noticing his indecision promised him letters of introduction in England, and was at pains to stress that he ought to establish a foothold there.

For all that, Sibelius returned instead to Helsinki, from where he wired a last-minute withdrawal from the concert. His cancellation caused something of a stir: the Liverpool press concluded that an all-too-paternalistic regime had simply not allowed him to leave Finland. Granville Bantock stepped in at short notice and conducted the First Symphony and *Finlandia*, and the atmosphere was undoubtedly heightened when Ada Crossley sang the solo part in *Song of the Athenians*, scored for boys' and men's voices, wind and percussion, though under the title 'War Song of Tyrtaeus'. The concert drew a penetrating notice from the *Manchester Guardian*, in all probability represented by Ernest Newman, which stressed the difficulties for a composer working within a strongly nationalist idiom to reconcile the needs of colour with the claims of form. In Norway, he argued, Grieg had not been successful in this respect, whereas in Finland, Sibelius had. Two weeks earlier, when Hans Richter had conducted the Second Symphony at a Hallé concert in Manchester, Newman had written enthusiastically, and hailed a new voice in music.

On 17 March, at the Swedish Theatre in Helsinki, Sibelius raised his baton for the prelude to his incidental music to *Pelléas et Mélisande*, which was to accompany Bertel Gripenberg's translation of Maeterlinck's play. Karl Flodin wrote that Sibelius had with limited means achieved 'the most powerful and compelling effects without ever having recourse merely to the endless pianissimos that by all accounts distinguish Debussy's setting of the play'. In Helsinki, Maeterlinck's play was given fifteen times and Sibelius himself conducted the majority of the performances.

Where Debussy's opera with its dreamlike atmosphere makes the most of the impressionist possibilities offered by the play, and Schoenberg's tone poem can be thought of as an expressionist vision where a Tristanesque dusk descends over Arkel's castle, Sibelius, one could say, sees *Pelléas et Mélisande* in terms of a legend played out against an art-nouveau backcloth. The various numbers – the seven interludes, two *mélodrames* and a song – follow each other like a series of Flemish Gobelins, in which figures, trees and castles are woven in delicately shifting grey-blue colours. Maeterlinck's play poses the eternal question, perhaps best expressed in Arkel's words on the death of Mélisande: 'C'était un pauvre petit être mystérieux, comme tout le monde . . .'

The action takes place in mythical Allemonde; the very décor itself reflects the various levels of consciousness at play, while the protagonists, their past background and possible fates all remain shadowy. Sibelius's intimate sonorities call for limited orchestral resources (as for that matter had Fauré's): a flute doubling piccolo, an oboe doubling cor anglais, two each of clarinets, bassoons and horns; timpani, bass drum and strings. The prelude, *At the castle gate*, has epic overtones, and its recitative-like line suggests narration. The horn cries and the growing string tremelo over a timpani roll in the closing bars would seem to relate to the servants' words: 'The sun rises over the sea.'

Mélisande herself is pictured in a melancholy waltz for cor anglais, though the response from flute and clarinets, accompanied by *pizzicato* strings *à la Valse triste* is in danger of bordering on the banal. Fortunately, a descending clarinet figure in thirds evokes the more mysterious and elusive side of Mélisande's personality:

Ex 1

The first of the *mélodrames*, *By the seashore*, begins at Pelléas's words: 'One sees nothing the sea no more.' Against a motionless string background, the woodwinds gradually unleash their bird cries. The tonal effect is reminiscent of *Nuages*; the violins' rapid figuration begins with the same motive as the cor anglais call in the Debussy. Suddenly, the monotony is broken by a *fortissimo* outburst with a string tremolo in the uppermost register:

Ex 2

By the seashore is the first real instance of impressionist tone-painting in Sibelius, albeit one where shadows can be said to outweigh light.

After this portrait of the sea, the waltz-like entr'acte, *By a spring in the park*, seems relatively conventional. *Mélisande at the spinning-wheel* has none of the touching, young girl's reveries of Fauré's beautiful piece. Sibelius senses darkness and tragedy: against the viola trills, there is an anxious string figure which emerges in the clarinets:

Ex 3

Mélisande's song, 'The three blind sisters', conjures up the atmosphere of a medieval ballad. The phrases in the vocal line all follow the same rhythmic outline, though in the concert version the vocal part is omitted. Like Maeterlinck, Sibelius seems touched by their fate, and brings to this music simple but genuine feeling. The *Pastorale* comes after Golaud's final lines in Act 3, scene 4. Over a cello ostinato *pizzicato* and a sustained horn, we hear a delightful idea from the clarinets in thirds:

Ex 4

The major mode leans gently towards an Aeolian minor.

The drama culminates in Act 4, for which Sibelius composed a festive introductory overture *alla gavotta*. An A minor episode in which there is a typical mediant pedal is thoroughly characteristic, and the whole piece generates an air of expectancy. In the second scene comes Golaud's brutal outburst of jealousy. Sibelius's prelude to this scene begins with a somewhat Tchaikovskian dialogue in D minor between solo cello and cor anglais:

Ex 5

At the time of writing, this powerful piece remains unpublished.

The Death of Mélisande is the final number: she dies without disclosing the exact nature of her feelings for Pelléas. In Debussy's opera, the music itself maintains a poignant reticence, while in the Sibelius, the strings well up passionately in D major leaving no doubts whatever about the matter, before the melody ebbs slowly away.

★

The Romance in C, Op. 42, is a charming piece whose sonorities occasionally call to mind Tchaikovsky's Serenade for strings. The tonal ambiguity of the opening bars serves to heighten tension: the recitative-like line is in E minor, while the persistent return of the first-position C major chord lends some ambivalence to the tonality:

Ex 6

Sibelius is generous with his invention in this piece: its thematic substance could have supported a bigger edifice.

The piece Sibelius had conducted in the Helsinki Philharmonic concert on 5 March, the tableau, *Ein Fichtenbaum – träumt von einer Palme* is clearly identical with *Musik zu einer Scène*. This comprises an introduction and a waltz for full orchestra and survives in autograph. The introduction, *Andante di molto*, begins with an idea that reminds one of the beginning of Beethoven's C minor Sonata, Op. 13:

Ex 7

This idea also returns in the waltz itself. As early as 1897 Sibelius was working on a tone poem called *The Tree of the North* which, based on the Heine poem, dreams of a southern palm. It is possible that the introductory motive is related to a 'Forest Song', which Sibelius mentions in a letter to Aino on 25 August 1897. But later in the spring of 1904, Sibelius reworked his *Musik zu einer Scène* and sold the new version in a piano reduction to Fazer under the title, *Dance-Intermezzo*. Later on the orchestral score was published by Breitkopf und Härtel in 1907, as Op. 45, No. 2. The pageant's

31

introduction has been cut down to a mere four bars with a harp glissando added.

The piano suite, *Kyllikki* is among the best pieces Sibelius wrote for the piano even if the last movement is perhaps wanting in weight and substance. The latter is in places quite elegantly written for the instrument, while the middle movement, an *Andantino*, has something of the spirit and atmosphere of such early works as *Kullervo*, *En Saga* and the Piano Sonata in F. Each of the four phrases comprising the main idea of this movement is based on a similar pattern:

Ex 8

The first movement is of special interest in one respect: the opening *largamente* idea

Ex 9

is later used as a bridge passage between the first and second groups, and its first three notes presage the reprise; while in the coda it appears in a number of variants. All in all, it serves as a powerful unifying factor. The first subject itself is well laid out for the piano and acquires a dramatic character thanks to the Neapolitan sixth of the second bar:

Ex 10

Kyllikki was Sibelius's second – and last – attempt at a keyboard work in more than one movement and its success, for all its positive qualities, is only partial.

The success of the Second Symphony in Berlin had fired his spirits. 'I have been thinking about things', he told Aino,[1]

> and come to the conclusion that this is the crucial hour, the last chance to make something of myself and achieve great things. My youth has now gone for ever. And I must learn, despite my thirty-nine years, really to work. I want my work to meet with appreciation so that I can achieve financial independence. In this respect, I have everything working in my favour, after this performance. Now the important thing is not to let up but to sustain this momentum. You, my angel Aino, shall see. We must come to that point in life, you know, when we can be happy. I am not now sure if you understand me. When we have, then themes and inspiration will come.

Sibelius was looking for more income from his published works, and to this end he was in touch with the head of Schlesingersche Buch- und Musikhandlung, Robert Lienau. 'An important publisher, Schlesinger, is showing strong interest in me, and I have retrieved the score of my Violin Concerto from Burmester and will start work on the revision,' he told Aino in a letter from Berlin. He asked Aino to send him Willy Burmester's letter of praise about the Violin Concerto together with the postcard he had received from Edvard Grieg, in which the Norwegian master had written of his 'beautiful songs which I admire much and love'. In 1902, Grieg had accompanied Ida Ekman in a couple of Sibelius songs. No doubt Sibelius wanted to make an impression on Lienau so as to get the best possible terms for his most valuable property, the Violin Concerto. Busoni had advised him not to part with it for less than 5,000 Reichsmarks.

Sibelius was feeling some measure of discontent with his present arrangement with Fazer and Westerlund and through them, Breitkopf und Härtel. Fazer had been his main publisher in Finland up to this time and had not treated him unreasonably by Scandinavian standards. His Second Symphony had even earned him between 1,500 and 2,000 marks, but on the other hand, he received only 100 Finnish marks for every 3,000 copies of the piano transcription of *Valse triste* and 300 Finnish marks for an edition of 500 copies of the orchestral version. The song, 'Sigh, rushes, sigh' again yielded only 100 marks, so that with his mounting international reputation he was anxious to find a Continental publisher of repute with whom he could deal direct. He might have been better advised to turn direct to Breitkopf und

---

1 In a letter dated 19 January 1905.

Härtel in Leipzig, for the negotiations with Lienau, in which Adolf Paul acted as an adviser, were something of a strain on his nerves. On 13 February he wrote to Aino that he had definitely decided 'to leave Fazer (and B & H)', and on the 22nd he signed a contract with Lienau that was to decide his working pace for a number of years ahead. On his side he bound himself to deliver four major works a year for a minimum of 8,000 Reichsmarks. Even if Lienau was prepared to accept chamber works, sets of songs and piano pieces as well as symphonies and symphonic poems, these were demanding terms.

When he broke the news to Aino, it was not with unqualified enthusiasm:

> I have been in such a state of anxiety about our affairs at home. Now I feel that up to a point I can put my mind at rest. [. . .] We have had so many difficult years during the last decade. Now at least we have some security. I am by no means an optimist, but I believe some good will come of this.

In any event his optimism stretched as far as deciding to build himself a sauna.

The contract with Lienau was due to run until May 1909, some four years, but during this time he made only three 'deliveries'; in short, Sibelius was unable to meet the pace that the terms of the contract had imposed. The advantages of the arrangement were obvious: that he was forced to maintain a high degree of professional efficiency, and to compose with a sophisticated, international public in mind. In Finland he had fobbed off his publishers with the occasional trifles, among them small piano pieces and the like, when circumstances forced him to do so. With Lienau, things were different and, even when pressed, he hesitated to send slighter pieces and postponed doing so until the last possible moment. In time, however, the pressure proved irksome and in the end counter-productive. The spur that gave him security turned into a thumbscrew that deadened his spirits. Although he served his one-year periods to the end, the terms of the contract hung over him like a Damoclean sword, and his four years with Lienau reduced him to a nervous pulp.

At the beginning of April, Lienau wrote to K. G. Fazer asking whether he would be willing to act as his representative in Finland and Sweden for Sibelius's new works. Only three months later, however, Fazer sold the complete rights in the Sibelius works he owned, whether published or unpublished, together with the plates, to Breitkopf und Härtel. The agreement covered the bulk of Sibelius's output up to that time: the two symphonies, *En Saga*, the *Karelia* Suite, *Spring Song*, *The Ferryman's Brides*, *Finlandia*, some songs, piano pieces and smaller works, among them *Valse triste*. The price was 30,000 Reichsmarks (about 37,000 Finnish marks): Fazer had paid Sibelius about 10,000 Finnish marks all told for these works. For Fazer and Westerlund it was undoubtedly a foolish move: had they retained this repertoire, it could have served as the basis of a publishing venture of international proportions. What were Fazer's motives? One possible factor in his thinking may well have been that his Sibelius publications, which had been published in the Russian Grand Duchy of Finland, were not protected by copyright outside Russia since the latter was not a signatory of the Berne Convention. Hence, strictly speaking, they did not enjoy copyright protection in Europe. Accordingly, Fazer needed the protective cover that Breitkopf und Härtel provided and this in turn reduced the attractions of Sibelius as a publishing proposition.

Personal factors could also have coloured the situation. Fazer himself was kindly, reticent, an accomplished amateur violinist and a skilful businessman, who never really understood Sibelius's impulsive and extravagant nature. Sibelius on his side feared Fazer's powers of persuasion in business matters. He had little grasp on the realities of the situation, and regarded the publication of Sibelius's music as an act of charity. It is possible that Fazer acted partly in pique. Sibelius had left him for another publisher, evidently without a word of warning; so that when an opportunity arose of disposing of him lock, stock and barrel, he seized it with alacrity. Moreover, it was important to act before news of Sibelius's new contract with Lienau reached Breitkopf in Leipzig.

For Breitkopf, on the other hand, this gamble was a safe investment. Newly published works of Sibelius would serve to stimulate interest in the already existing catalogue and gradually build up his image. Unaware that Sibelius was already tied hand and foot by the terms of his contract with Lienau, the head of Breitkopf, O. von Hase wrote asking the composer to send him his work then in progress so that a new contract could be drawn up. Von Hase's feelings may well be imagined when one day in November 1905, he opened his newspaper to read that Sibelius's Violin Concerto and incidental music to *Pélleas and Mélisande* had just been published by his rival, Lienau of Schlesinger. However, he managed to contain his feelings and decided to postpone raising the matter until he met the composer personally. Certainly, Sibelius's position was strengthened in so far as Breitkopf were energetic in promoting his compositions in Germany and through their agents in England, America, Belgium and even other countries. Of course, it must have grieved him to see an important part of his life's work slip out of his hands in this way. Breitkopf had offered to honour Fazer's obligations 'after each edition of the various works had been exhausted'. But these obligations were by no means onerous for Breitkopf. Some works had been sold outright and, in other cases, the first edition was so large that it would be a long time before a reprint was necessary. Moreover, for new editions derisory terms had often been agreed and, in accordance with the practice of the day, the publisher retained the rights to make any arrangements without the obligation to give the composer anything. At least one of the works affected by this clause would have made Sibelius a fortune: namely *Valse triste*.

CHAPTER TWO

Pohjola's Daughter

In August 1905 came news of the sudden death of the artist Albert Edelfelt. A figure of European vision and standing, he had made a coloured crayon sketch of Sibelius in profile, and it seems that he and the composer had drawn closer during the last year or so of his life. Edelfelt's harmonious nature seems to have drawn out the serenity and balance in Sibelius's features, and one can well think of his sketch as a contrast to the darker overtones of Axel Gallén-Kallela's demonic watercolour made in 1893. Edelfelt had also given Sibelius's features to one of the main figures in his large canvas depicting the inaugural procession of the Åbo Academy in 1640, a painting that was, alas, destroyed during the last war. In any event Edelfelt's passing came as a blow to Sibelius, and a letter to Carpelan conveys his sense of loss. For the funeral he composed a setting of lines from Runeberg's *The Clouds' Brother*:

Ex 11 'Not with lamenting shall your memory be celebrated . . .'

36

Carpelan perhaps summed up a more general feeling when he wrote to Sibelius at the beginning of September: 'Our great link with Europe has gone. Now our great hopes and pride reside in *you*.' Although this was all very well, bearing a national mantle posed its problems: his work on the revision of the Violin Concerto had been interrupted not only by a concert in Viipuri but also by a commission for a Cortège for a festivity to honour two prominent figures in Finnish theatrical life, Kaarlo and Emilie Bergbom. He was also planning a work in a quasi-oratorio format to honour the centenary of J. V. Snellman's birth, which was due in May 1906. However, his inspiration did not catch fire, and instead he turned to a new symphonic poem that he planned to call *Luonnotar*; this never assumed its final form in this purely orchestral guise. The Third Symphony in the meantime seems to have receded from the foreground: indeed, the Symphony as such seemed less close to him than the tone poem if one is to judge from a letter to Aino written in January 1905. 'I'm no longer writing a symphony, rather [in Swedish] a symphonic fantasy for orchestra. [In Finnish] This is my genre!! Here I can move freely without feeling the weight of tradition.'

Money continued to trouble his long-term plans. In April, Carpelan had told him that he could no longer expect support from the private sources for whom he had acted as an intermediary over the past few years. Although the news was unwelcome, it seems to have depressed Carpelan rather more than it did Sibelius himself. The summer found Carpelan in the depths of despair: 'For me, life is a nightmare at present,' he wrote. No doubt he entertained fears that his role in Sibelius's life was becoming played out.

> You blush, you say, at not having written to me for the whole summer; I blush to receive any letters at all. Why should you concern yourself with someone who has not really been alive for the last twenty years. I have never chosen to weep on your shoulder as I remember how this cost me A. T.'s [Axel Tamm's] friendship and help.[1]

Sibelius answered Carpelan's letter by promptly inviting him to Ainola.

The political situation was also becoming a cause for greater anxiety. At first, Carpelan had rejoiced at the news of the Japanese victory at Tsushima and interpreted the subsequent unrest as evidence of the death throes of Tsarism. However, as events took their course, it became clear that there was scant chance of the collapse of the Tsarist tyranny, and he advised Sibelius not to allow himself to become side-tracked by what was going on but rather to concentrate on his work. Not that it was entirely possible for him to do so. In July he saw the devastation in the Senate Square in Helsinki after the attempt on the life of the Governor-General's Deputy: 'There was a powerful explosion, which broke the windows of three houses, among

1 Written on 3 September 1905.

them the police station and the Town Hall,' he reported in a letter to Aino, though he went on to express the suspicion that it was all the work of police *agents provocateurs*. For all Carpelan's words, he clung to the hope that the Tsarist regime was on the point of collapse, and news reports of troubles at a Russian garrison bolstered his spirits: 'These really are epic times.'

At the end of October, a general strike was called in Finland, a few days after its outbreak in Russia itself. It found the unfortunate Carpelan on a train bound for his home in Tampere; it never arrived. In recounting the event Carpelan tells of his fears of revolution and of 'jumping out of the frying pan into the fire'. Certainly there were grounds for anxiety: tension between armed student groups and the workers' Red Guards was growing and there were fears of civil war. The Finnish resistance movement was already splitting along class lines into a right- and left-wing phalanx, and Sibelius had an instinctive foreboding about this class division. A year later there was a bloody incident between Reds and Whites in Helsinki that had been triggered off after a mutiny in the Russian garrison at Sveaborg. Writing to Aino on 9 August 1906, he described the atmosphere thus: 'Here it is – and has been – very calm on the surface, but it strikes me as being very much the "calm before the storm". Feelings run so high that I have difficulty in recalling such strong class hatred. Eyes literally blaze.' The storms he sensed ahead were to erupt twelve years later.

The strike achieved one of its aims: the February Manifesto of 1899 was substantially modified even if it remained on the statute book. Exiles were allowed to return home and a government reshuffle took place, which strengthened the hands of the moderates. For example, R. A. Wrede, whom Sibelius had met on the quay at Reval the previous summer closely watched by plain-clothes detectives, suddenly became Vice-Chairman in the Justice Department of the Senate.

In Liverpool, Sibelius's cause had a strong advocate in Granville Bantock, and no doubt Ernest Newman's excellent reviews strengthened his resolve to persuade the Finnish composer to come to England. Bantock even considered going on to Helsinki to see him, as he was spending part of the summer in Sweden. However, he had not appeared in the Finnish capital by 20 August, and the date for Sibelius's concert appearance was finally agreed by letter (2 December). Bantock's attitude, like that of Newman and Henry Wood, was symptomatic of the outgoing and welcoming attitude that the English had shown to foreign composers since the days of Handel, Haydn and J. C. Bach, Clementi and Mendelssohn. Admittedly, circumstances were beginning to change: in the past foreign creative talent had filled a vacuum; now the English musical renaissance had become a reality.

By 1905 there was what one could already call the older Establishment, whose most powerful luminaries were Hubert Parry and Charles Stanford; the younger generation, composers roughly contemporary with Sibelius, or, in the case of Elgar, slightly older, Delius, Holst, Vaughan Williams, were at various stages of their careers and were to establish their names outside their native country in a way that their senior colleagues had failed to do. Even if England possessed a long and rich musical tradition, this younger generation still confronted problems similar to those faced by the nationalist composers from younger cultures. They had to overcome prejudice both at home and abroad, and in this they were often given German support. Richard Strauss's famous toast to 'Meister Edward Elgar', occasioned by the success of *The Dream of Gerontius* at Düsseldorf in 1902, was an important step in winning Elgar wider recognition and success. German recognition had come to Sibelius at Heidelberg in the preceding year, and was an even greater factor in Delius's case.

There are other points of contact between Sibelius and Delius: a highly developed feeling for nature, a youthful admiration for Grieg, and a subsequent predisposition towards impressionism, though Delius had some years still to wait until his Kajanus was to emerge on the scene in the form of Sir Thomas Beecham. Moreover, in England, Sibelius could count on some intuitive understanding of his musical objectives, and the way in which he had chosen to evolve the European tradition would not be condemned out of hand. Ernest Newman had accepted his individual approach to the symphony without arrogant eyebrow-raising such as had characterized the responses of so many of the German critics. Awareness of the achievements of their own rising generation of composers also sharpened English interest in a Scandinavian musician who faced similar – or nearly similar – isolation.

In November, Sibelius undertook his first visit to England. His journey took him first to Copenhagen and then Berlin, where Adolf Paul and Robert Lienau took care of him. His concert at Heidelberg was cancelled as he was not ready to present the new work he had promised, *Luonnotar*. Indeed he was beginning to doubt its feasibility in its present form and wrote to Aino to that effect. But the same letter, written while a storm was raging in the Baltic, recounts his shock at the thought of reaching 40, which brought him up with a jolt as well as a sudden realization of life's seriousness and brevity.

Sibelius landed at Dover on 29 November and underwent a body search on the part of His Majesty's Customs and Immigration who promptly fined him two pounds six shillings for trying to smuggle in some cigars. At Victoria he was met by Bantock for whom he felt an immediate sympathy.

Bantock has made an extraordinarily good impression on me: he is totally English, even in the way that he remains unruffled. Today he is going to introduce me to Wood (England's Nikisch), and others. Hans Richter is said to be very taken with my music. He has said [in Swedish] that I have struck on a new path in the symphony! In fact, the path of the future. [In Finnish] I behave here just as I am. [In Swedish] I believe that is the best thing in the long run. I often think of you, darling. Nothing will come, I think, of our mutual creation, *Luonnotar*. Things don't work just by will-power or under pressure.

Writing a few days after his arrival, Sibelius spoke of Bantock as 'a good person': they had read through the score of the Second Symphony together. Carpelan's anxious promptings to display tact and fine breeding – 'don't forget that their etiquette is rigorous' – rang in his ears, but Bantock's sensitivity to his feelings enabled him to overcome his inhibitions. Bantock's thoughtfulness stretched even to practical matters. He took care of his guest's expenses, so much so that Sibelius never learned to distinguish the different kinds of English coins. Sibelius wrote of his extraordinary generosity:

> I have never experienced his like. Perhaps they are all like him here – I don't know – but such things always make a strong impression on me. He has introduced me into many splendid homes. Tells me that I should just be myself and not try to ape English manners. Truly, this is an old culture.

Bantock was, of course, a many-sided and prolific composer whose interests ranged over the widest area: Hebridean folk music, Celtic lore, the *Kalevala*, Persian, Indian and Chinese art and literature. His greatest success as a composer still lay before him: *Omar Khayyám*, the first part of which received its première in 1906. He strikes one as a Kiplingesque figure with something of Yeats about him and his music combines a vein of mysticism with the conventional post-romanticism. He used to call Sibelius 'Dear Väinämöinen', and in their correspondence he reported the strong impression made by *En Saga* on the musicians at Liverpool, and 'on Mr Wood, Mr Newman and [Fritz] Kreisler, who chanced to be in the audience. The public response on this occasion was not as warm as I could have wished but one must not expect too much of an English audience at a first performance.'[1] On another occasion he mentions that both he and Newman often spoke of him with undivided admiration for his mastery and genius. Throughout their correspondence he rarely touches on his own work except in passing.

Bantock also introduced Sibelius to Wood, as he mentions in his letter home to Aino. Henry Wood was founder and conductor of the Proms whose first wife was Princess Olga Ouroussoff and related to the Naryshkin family, a fact that Sibelius by no means neglected to report to Aino, Christian and Carpelan. Even if Wood lacked Nikisch's strong musical personality, he was a dynamic figure whose most recent achievement had been to put an end to the deputy system that had so much undermined standards in the Queen's Hall Orchestra. Even before they had met, Henry Wood had conducted the *King Christian II* Suite and the First Symphony, while his pioneering work on behalf of new music from Debussy, Strauss, Skryabin and Schoenberg is far too well known to relate here. His letters to

1 Written on 29 March 1906.

Sibelius leave the impression of an impulsive and highly practical man, not without vanity perhaps, particularly when he felt threatened by Beecham's fame. Sibelius also paid his respects to Sir Alexander Mackenzie, then Principal of the Royal Academy of Music, who was quite outspoken in his insistence that there were no younger composers worth hearing nowadays. That same evening he attended an operetta by Sidney Jones, the composer of *The Geisha*, in the company of Bantock and Kling, the head of Breitkopf und Härtel's London office. After that he made the rounds of the music-halls. He wrote to Aino, 'You simply cannot imagine the endless noise of seven million people, their passions and religions.'

For Sibelius, England, in the persons of Bantock, Wood and their circle, was 'pleasing and aristocratic', and he in his turn won full acceptance. There had been fears that the new star of the north would be 'the uncombed German type of musician invariably associated with the concept of genius', but instead came a full-blooded Viking with golden hair, ice-blue eyes and perfect deportment. He was moreover eminently well groomed. As far as dress was concerned, Sibelius was careful to observe etiquette: a brown suit in the morning, a long coat, green waistcoat, grey-striped trousers to lunch, and evening dress with a white silk scarf for dinner. He bought dress shirts with only one button on the front, which was the latest fashion; he engaged in polite conversation, and never permitted his expression to betray his thoughts. In English society he was able to develop his feeling for ceremonial and to learn to behave exactly as was expected of him.

Sibelius made his headquarters during his first visit to England at Bantock's home in Broad Meadows, Birmingham. In the studio, he could rest in the comfortable chair that had come from Napoleon's residence in St Helena, and admire Bantock's collection of orientalia, including Buddhas, shepherd's pipes and various other folk instruments. The room seemed loudly to dispute Kipling's famous *bon mot* about East and West not meeting. Hokusai woodcuts hung over the bookshelves, whose contents revealed many areas of common interest and taste. Through the windows, a pathway lined with beeches and elms led on to a Purcellian park-like landscape.

While in Birmingham, Sibelius chanced to meet Busoni who told him that *The Ferryman's Brides*, with Maikki Järnefelt as soloist, had scored a great success in Berlin, and been greeted more warmly than a Mahler work in the same programme. Needless to say, he went to Busoni's concert and yet again was overcome by admiration for his genius. On 2 December, he conducted his First Symphony and *Finlandia* in Liverpool; such was the success of the latter that it had to be immediately repeated. In the *Manchester Guardian*, Ernest Newman restated his admiration for the way Sibelius's music succeeded in evoking an entirely new sound world.

The impression it [the First Symphony] makes on one is the same as that made by the Second Symphony – that here we have a man really saying

POHJOLA'S DAUGHTER

things that have never been said in music before. [. . .] I have never listened to any music that took me away so completely from our usual Western life, and transported me into a quite new civilization. Every page of it breathes of another manner of thought, another way of living, even another landscape and seascape than ours.

Coming back on the train from London to Birmingham, Bantock had introduced Sibelius to a lady in her fifties with a somewhat imposing, almost masculine bearing. This was Rosa Newmarch, and soon they were engaged in animated conversation in a mixture of French and German. Mrs Newmarch had spent some time in St Petersburg and indeed opened their conversation in fluent Russian, assuming that Sibelius spoke it. She knew many of the young Russian composers as well as such important figures as Mily Balakirev and Vladimir Stasov. She had already published her study of Tchaikovsky and was to become widely known to the music-loving public as the annotator of the Proms. She generally preferred masculine company to *femmes en bloc*, and possessed an inexhaustible fund of idealism and love of music. An effective and knowledgeable advocate of his music, she was a sensitive and faithful friend. Mrs Newmarch's letters to Sibelius show us something of the composer himself: Carpelan's warnings about the English social code and Bantock's advice to relax and be himself seem to have made Sibelius more correct and buttoned-up than usual.

Even in the 1920s Sibelius remained eminently correct. In her monograph on her father, Myrra Bantock writes:

When I was about 15 Sibelius stayed with us . . . and I was now old enough to form a clear impression of that great man. He arrived on a winter evening and I have a vivid impression of his being ushered into the dining room by my father. [. . .] Although vain of his appearance, Sibelius was really an ugly man but he was undeniably striking. The great domed head, which he kept shaved so that it should not be said of him that he was going grey or bald, was the first thing one noticed. Then one became aware of his thin-lipped mouth, down-curving and with deep lines running from the sides of the nose, which gave his face its severe expression and a look of great suffering. A thick, short neck and very strange, large ears with long lobes made me think at once of a Nordic troll. He radiated force and power; without knowing why, you felt awed in his presence.

Sibelius came forward and shook hands with us, bending over my mother's hand in the Continental manner. His suit (like my father's) was too large, but the remaining details of his dress showed a fastidious neatness – he would never have appeared with his coat unbuttoned or in anything but the most correct of collars and ties.[1]

1 *Granville Bantock*, J. M. Dent, London 1972, p.126.

42

Some years later, when Mrs Newmarch was describing Rachmaninov to him she could write, 'He is so reserved, almost as reserved as you.'[1] Sibelius could relax into nonchalance: 'Je suis absolument sans moralité.' But Mrs Newmarch was not deceived: 'When next you find yourself confronted by a crisis, we shall see whether you are without morality – and the best moral standards into the bargain.' Behind his dandyism she discerned his uncertainty and indecisive nature without ever being deceived as to his basic strength. 'I know you are a little *stimmungsvoll* in small matters but very certain in the important things of life,' she wrote in December 1910.

Mrs Newmarch herself was nothing if not decisive: after her husband had mismanaged their financial affairs, she took them into her own hands. But her sense of reality in her practical dealings did not stand in the way of genuine imaginative insight and a sense of mystery. She had a genuine feeling for nature, and her descriptive writing, the coming of spring in the English countryside, could have been penned by Sibelius himself. She certainly had the measure of his finest work: for example, of the Violin Concerto she wrote,

> Why aren't all the virtuosi falling over themselves to be the first to play it? [. . .] In fifty years' time, your concerto will be as much a classic as those of Beethoven, Brahms and Tchaikovsky. I burn with impatience to hear it again immediately.

Sibelius's first visit to England had gone well, and it served to put Berlin in a wholly new perspective. What Berlin was to Hämeenlinna, so London was to Berlin, or so it seemed to him at the height of his enchantment with England.[2] Yet he did not prolong his stay and only two days after his concert he made his farewells in London to Henry Wood and took the Paris train the same evening. A couple of months later, Mrs Newmarch gave a lecture on him at the Concert Goers' Club: 'Everyone there was interested to hear some of the songs given in Finnish,' she told him; Breitkopf und Härtel published her lecture both in German and English together with a list of Sibelius's works. That selfsame year Bantock conducted *En Saga*, the new *Pelléas et Mélisande* suite and the Second Symphony in Liverpool. Henry Wood included *En Saga* and *Finlandia* at the Proms, and 'despite her noble birth', as Sibelius put it, 'Madame Wood announced her intention of singing *Autumn Evening* or *The Ferryman's Brides*.'

In Paris, Sibelius booked himself into a hotel of royal lineage, Pavillon Henri IV, the birthplace of Louis XIV, at Saint-Germain, where from his window he had a commanding view of the city. A month earlier, Camille Chevillard had conducted *The Swan of Tuonela* with the Lamoureux Orchestra and according to the concert announcements *Finlandia* was in

1 Letter dated 5 November 1910.
2 A letter to Aino dated 13 March 1912.

preparation. At the beginning of the year, the American singer Minnie Tracey accompanied by an orchestra conducted by Alfred Cortot had given *Autumn Evening*. 'So you can see the way things are moving,' wrote an encouraged Sibelius to Carpelan. However, this proved a false dawn. Paris, which Sibelius always thought of as 'the city of cities', did not open its doors for him or his music. Yet it must be stressed that Paris was far from provincial or closed to new music during the first decade of the century. On the contrary it was the leading musical centre of the world. Diaghilev was to introduce such composers as Rimsky-Korsakov, Skryabin, Rachmaninov and Stravinsky (not to mention Nijinsky, Benois and Bakst); Parisians willingly succumbed to heady draughts of Wagner and Strauss, the charm of Italian *verismo*, and the exotic colours of Grieg and Falla. But there was strong resistance against the epic Teutonic symphony and in particular Brahms and Bruckner. When Mahler conducted his Second Symphony at a concert given under the patronage of the Countess of Greffulhes (the model for Proust's Duchess of Guermantes in *A la recherche du temps perdu*) a number of distinguished French musicians, among them Debussy, ostentatiously walked out after the first movement. Mahler never made headway in Paris; nor in the end did Sibelius. Breitkopf had no offices in the French capital, nor was there a Busoni or Bantock to conduct and promote, or an Otto Lessmann or Rosa Newmarch to champion his cause. No countess held receptions for him where Ysaÿe and Cortot could have played the Violin Concerto.

Moreover, Sibelius always felt himself something of an outsider in Paris. In Vienna things were different: he felt deeply involved in the tension between the rival Bruckner and Brahms factions; in Bayreuth he had come to terms with Wagner, and in Berlin experienced the impact of Busoni's championship of the new music. But in Paris he was scarcely even aware of the strong tension between the followers of Debussy (the 'Pelléasters', as he called them) and the more conservative Schola cantorum centred on Vincent d'Indy. Later he was to deplore (not without some justice but more with a touch of sour grapes) that so many fifth-rate composers seemed to score such successes in Paris.

At the turn of 1905–6, Sibelius was consumed by the feeling that the musical world was expecting something from him. But he was more depressed than elated, more weighed down than inspired: 'One should take life as it is, with all its demands on one's talent.' His birthday on 8 December served to dampen his spirits, 'It is difficult to accept the fact that I am now 40. But there is nothing one can do about it. Nothing other than gritting one's teeth and just getting on with it.'[1]

Sibelius was grappling with the difficulties of his new tone poem *Luonnotar*, which had at one time threatened to turn into a complete symphony.

1 Letter to Aino on 18 December 1905.

He longed for Aino's moral support, but plans for her to join him fell through because of money difficulties. His letters became all the more slovenly; his countrymen were constant visitors to his flat and he thoughtlessly lent them the money Lienau had sent him. As his purse shrank, he left Paris for Berlin to sort out various contractual matters with Breitkopf und Härtel. He began to think that Fazer's stupidities could still be turned to his advantage, and up to a point his optimism seemed to be justified. Breitkopf wanted to acquire the rights of several works, including *The Swan of Tuonela* and *Lemminkäinen's Homeward Journey*, which still remained in the possession of two Finnish publishers, Wasenius and Lindgren. The Leipzig management of Breitkopf was urging Sibelius to bring pressure to bear on Wasenius to release these scores, and offered in return favourable terms.

Back in Finland, however, Sibelius's spirits sank. He wrote to Lienau that it was not now possible to save his earlier catalogue except on 'highly idiosyncratic terms', a fact to which Lienau resigned himself. Sibelius's attempt to sort out Fazer's 'lunacy' got nowhere: for example, as far as *Valse triste* was concerned, Breitkopf insisted on clinging firmly to the old Fazer agreement. For every 3,000 copies of the piano arrangement sold, Sibelius would receive 100 Finnish marks or 80 Reichsmarks. By comparison Breitkopf und Härtel agreed the sum of 400 Reichsmarks for an edition of 1,000 copies of the piano arrangement of *The Swan of Tuonela* and a similar sum for *Lemminkäinen's Homeward Journey*.[1] For a piano reduction consisting of eight pages of the tone poem *The Dryad*, they agreed a fee of 300 marks per edition of 1,000 copies.[2] As far as the full scores were concerned, the composer's royalty was up to 33⅓ per cent while, in the draft contract proposed in 1906, the royalty was proposed at 20 per cent for piano arrangements – in both cases of the counter price in music shops.

But as far as *Valse triste* was concerned, it was highly disadvantageous in two important respects. The cover price of *Valse triste* in Finland was 2.50 Finnish marks and had Sibelius received the normal royalty of 15 per cent (the sum Lienau agreed for the violin and piano arrangement of *Mélisande*) on an edition of 3,000 copies, it would have amounted to 1,125 Finnish marks. As it is, the contract gave him a mere 100 Finnish marks, per edition, which works out as a royalty of derisory proportions: 1.33 per cent! The extent of his loss can be seen by the simple calculation that by the outbreak of the First World War, when *Valse triste* had gone into sixteen editions, Sibelius had received 1,600 Finnish marks as opposed to 18,000!

The second disadvantage was that the 100 Finnish marks per edition (all of 3,000 copies each) took no account of inflation, whereas a royalty is always related to the cover price, which can and is adjusted. During the years 1914–20, *Valse triste* ran through a further thirteen editions during

1 Letter from Breitkopf und Härtel to Sibelius, 16 January 1907.
2 Letter from Breitkopf und Härtel to Sibelius, 1 March 1910.

which time the Finnish and German currencies both lost value, the latter much faster than the former. Hyperinflation in Germany during the early 1920s reduced his royalty to insignificance. In 1924 Breitkopf und Härtel did at least compensate Sibelius for his losses by calculating the value of the Finnish mark at 80 per cent of the newly stabilized Deutschmark, which had been the pre-war relationship.

By the 1930s *Valse triste* had reached sixty-seven editions, just over 200,000 copies, to which must be added a further 20,000 sold during the war years by Wilhelm Hansen of Copenhagen and another 11,000 which were sold by J. & W. Chester in London. The royalty on such numbers, had it been 15 per cent, can readily be calculated and it must be borne in mind that the 1.33 per cent that he received at the beginning of the agreement soon fell as inflation took its toll. The orchestral score too brought in totally insignificant sums, while for new arrangements, for practically all conceivable kinds of salon combinations, military bands of various shapes and sizes, he received not a single penny. The other older pieces taken over by Breitkopf seem to have yielded the composer no appreciable return either, with the sole exception of the popular Romance in D flat, Op. 24, for piano.

Sibelius in his straitened economic circumstances must have taken scant pleasure in the eager rivalry of two leading publishers for the spoils. Robert Lienau took the view that he had a right to every composition Sibelius had not sold to Fazer, while Breitkopf und Härtel stuck their ground and patiently bided their time. As a result of Breitkopf's energetic publicity, Sibelius's name was becoming more and more familiar in German programmes, particularly after the autumn of 1906. The Leipzig Gewandhaus Orchestra at last decided to put *The Swan of Tuonela* into their repertory, while, at the beginning of 1907, some eighty orchestras had *Valse triste* in their programmes. It appeared that at last the wind was blowing in Sibelius's favour.

On 1 February 1906, three days before Sibelius's return from Berlin, an unusual literary and musical evening took place in the Finnish National Theatre. Maxim Gorky and Eino Leino read excerpts from their works, and Kajanus conducted Tchaikovsky's Serenade for strings and Sibelius's *Spring Song* and *The Ferryman's Brides* while the proceeds went to those who had suffered during the recent unrest in Russia, i.e. the revolutionaries. The thought of Tchaikovsky and Sibelius as symbols of the bond between Finnish intellectuals and Russian radicals is not a little bizarre. After the general strike, many Russian revolutionaries took refuge in Finland where police vigilance was less strict, and where they could count on the support of both the bourgeois and socialist elements in society. Gorky's journey had been organized on the Finnish side by Gallén-Kallela who was an active supporter of the resistance movement, even to the extent of hiding smuggled arms in his drawing-room sofa, and receiving Russian revolutionaries in his home. However, his ardour was somewhat cooled by the plans for a bank robbery that were mooted by some of the group, and he quietly withdrew to his country retreat!

Some days later Eero Järnefelt gave a dinner party at their home in Järvenpää for Gorky and Gallén, at which the Sibeliuses were also present. Aino records the event in a letter to her mother, but Sibelius himself makes no mention of his meeting with Gorky, whose work, it would seem, did not particularly appeal to him. His reticence is in marked contrast to Eero Järnefelt's keen enthusiasm for him and his strongly radical sympathies. For his part, Gorky hailed Gallén, Sibelius and Leino as 'the fathers of Finnish culture' and wrote enthusiastically of Saarinen as 'a genius, whose buildings are miracles of beauty'. He spoke of Axel Gallén as 'a great artist, and even in other respects this little country is a land of great men'.[1] When the gendarmes' interest in Gorky became too keen for comfort, Gallén, Saarinen and Bertel Gripenberg helped to keep him hidden and smuggled him with an escort of Red Guards out of the country, to the undoubted relief of the Tsarist authorities. None of these conspirators would have dreamt that in 1918 they would be in completely different camps; Gallén and Gripenberg with the Whites, and Gorky in the circles close to Lenin.

Even if Sibelius did not take an active part in his friends' actions, he was in close contact with them and undoubtedly sympathized. However, he largely managed to avoid being drawn into the various conflicts that divided the Finns in so many ways, the class divisions, the political conflict between the constitutionalists and the collaborators, not to mention the bitter language conflict. Undoubtedly there were times when he was drawn into the wake of the latter. Heikki Klemetti, the critic of the music periodical *Säveletär*, was an aggressive champion of the Finnish language: 'Why don't composers set poems in Finnish?' he thundered and did his best to fan feeling between the Swedish gentry and the Finnish majority. Sibelius did not remain insensitive to Klemetti's attack, though he continued to perform a balancing act between the claims of the two languages, writing incidental music alternately for the Swedish and Finnish theatres, composing a cantata for the centenary celebrations of J. V. Snellman, which was marked by a campaign to reinstate Finnish proper names in place of their commonly used Swedish equivalents. At the same time, Sibelius set poems by Gripenberg, one of the spokesmen of the Swedish-speaking upper classes.

In Helsinki itself Sibelius was worshipped and adored: every foreign newspaper review, favourable or unfavourable, unfailingly appeared in the Helsinki press, and his stature was constantly measured against the leading figures of the day. It was rumoured that the Swedes were busily championing their young Hugo Alfvén: what is Sibelius in comparison to Alfvén? And the result was that when the latter came to Helsinki to conduct his Second Symphony, the event became a contest of prestige.

1 From V. Smirnov, *Gorky in Finland*, 1968.

Oskar Merikanto, writing in *Säveletär*, firmly put Alfvén in his place: 'The Swedish rhapsody, *Midsummer Vigil*, which includes every kind of popular Swedish tune, is altogether too coarse to be played at one of our symphony concerts.' Wounded national pride shone through his review but on the other hand, Evert Katila, writing in *Uusi Suometar*, reacted quite differently: for him, Alfvén's Second was one of the most remarkable of modern symphonies, and its composer a serious artist who did not take refuge in idle experiment. One can wonder whether this response was wholly genuine or whether he was merely using Alfvén as a stick with which to beat Sibelius. The following autumn he wrote unfavourably about some of the songs though it must be conceded that he was not the only Finnish critic to write in these terms. Even Sibelius's former pupil and biographer-to-be, Erik Furuhjelm, discerned a decline in the quality of invention in such pieces as *Kyllikki*, a development that he compared to the recent falling off in Strindberg's output. A composer undergoing a stylistic metamorphosis can often be regarded as *passé* even by his most zealous supporters. Sibelius became somewhat withdrawn and quick to take offence: indeed, at Ida and Karl Ekman's Sibelius recital in October, he even left before the last work so as to avoid taking a bow.

Taste in Helsinki, as in other cities, was volatile: in the spring of 1906, Georg Schnéevoigt had given Bruckner's Fourth Symphony to the great satisfaction of both the public and the critics, but when he took up the Seventh the following year, it was greeted by cries of 'always only Bruckner and Strauss'. Debussy and Mahler were yet to come. Kajanus's programmes were confined to the less controversial contemporary repertoire: Grieg and Sinding, Lalo and Saint-Saëns, Dvořák and Dohnányi, Goldmark and d'Albert, Rimsky-Korsakov, Arensky and above all, Glazunov. But among Finnish composers, however, Sibelius dominated the scene. During the spring he was represented at no fewer than thirty concerts in Helsinki among them by the revised version of the Violin Concerto, which received its Finnish première on 12 March 1906, while six weeks later it was given again by the young Russian violinist, Lev Zeitlin. In later years he became leader of the celebrated Persinfans, the conductorless symphony orchestra that flourished in Moscow during the 1920s.

On 1 March Sibelius wrote to Carpelan announcing the imminent completion of a new symphony, though his news proved to be somewhat premature: yet another year was to pass before he put the finishing touches to the score. In the meantime, the orchestral tone poem *Luonnotar* dominated his thoughts along with a number of occasional pieces such as *Pan and Echo*. This was first performed at a benefit concert in Helsinki in aid of a new concert hall, a project that did not materialize until some sixty years later! It bears the subtitle 'Dance-Intermezzo' and is a delightful bagatelle whose opening almost conveys the intoxication and fragrance of the Mediterranean spring:

48

Ex 12

In the final *commodo* passage the clarinet has a lively, chirpy idea that is echoed by the flute, but the atmosphere of enchantment that pervades the opening has vanished.

Two days earlier, on 22 March, Sibelius's old mentor and teacher, Martin Wegelius died. Only a week before, he had written to his 'dear Master Erik', as he called his favourite pupil, Erkki Melartin, and his very last evening was spent in going through Erik Furuhjelm's Piano Quintet. His relations with Sibelius had remained unresolved and in some way puzzling. After 1892 they had not corresponded more than very occasionally and then on official matters. Even when he was at Bayreuth in the summer of 1894, Sibelius forbore to send an account of the Festival or the other Wagner performances he attended to this arch-Wagnerite. In Finland itself they hardly ever met, and there is no evidence to suggest that, even during his last illness, Sibelius ever visited his old master's sick-bed, though he did conduct his *Elegy* at his funeral.

The rift between Wegelius and Kajanus had been healed when they met at the Basle Festival in 1903. Wegelius and Sibelius, on the other hand, did not need to be brought together since they had never openly quarrelled but merely drifted apart. Their encounter at Wegelius's summer house in 1902 had passed off amicably enough but they never really spoke frankly or intimately to each other. Wegelius's magnum opus, *The History of Western Music* came out in a Finnish edition in 1904, some eleven years after the appearance of the Swedish edition. The expanded final chapter, 'Newer Musical Developments', would have undoubtedly enjoyed Sibelius's special attention. Mahler was paraded as the bearer of Bruckner's mantle, a symphonist of ethical and spiritual dimension; he and Richard Strauss were allotted two pages each. Little more, perhaps, could have been expected of so committed a Wagnerite. For Wegelius, Mahler and Strauss bestrode the contemporary musical scene like two colossi and 'in their company none of their contemporaries is worthy of a place. Even if one or two composers show signs of greater originality of thought, no living composer has yet attained the universality and mastery that Mahler and Strauss possess.'

Sibelius did not need to read any further to draw his own conclusions. His symphonies did not match those of Mahler in 'ethical and spiritual'

49

power of a kind that made them the equal of Beethoven; nor did his tone poems with their Finnish accents 'achieve the same transcendental heights as *Also sprach Zarathustra*'. He who had at one time been acclaimed for his princely gifts was no longer admitted to the elect, and it must have been adding insult to injury to find himself merely mentioned after Fredrik Pacius, 'and the new Finnish music can already include one name that is already famous in Europe, namely Jean Sibelius'. True, Wegelius excuses himself from discussing new Finnish music on the grounds that it is invidious to evaluate present-day composers, but there was really no reason why he should not have dealt with them in much the same way as he had their Scandinavian contemporaries, choosing, say, five or six leading names and ending with a paragraph about his former pupil. Instead he chose to repeat, almost contemptuously, what he had written in the Swedish original, published only a year after the *Kullervo* Symphony first saw the light of day, 'In Finland we must first have a music before its history can be written.'

In any event, it is some comfort that the gradual drifting apart of the two men was a natural process, prompted by artistic rather than personal considerations. No signs of affection or gratitude on Sibelius's side and no common memories of his student years drew the two men closer. As a pupil, Wegelius had wanted to mould Sibelius very much in his own Wagnerian image; his was a dominant personality and Sibelius had, of course, to resist such influence that was not in harmony with his own artistic ideals. Hanna Wegelius had on one occasion described Sibelius as 'a man swimming against the tide, whose cries in his struggle against the waves would resound round the world'. It was this fight against the tide and Sibelius's insistence on going his own way that forced him to free himself even from Wegelius. When Sibelius conducted his *Elegy*, no doubt the cello cantilena bore his thoughts back through the labyrinth of his youth to the years of his B flat Quartet, which Wegelius had praised so eloquently.

These weeks did not find Sibelius in the best of spirits. Carpelan announced that he proposed to visit him but Sibelius wrote to put him off:

> You know full well that you are always welcome here when you come. But at present you will have no pleasure from my company since my time is eaten up by social duties, business matters, a new commission and so on. And now that I have two week free, I must spend it struggling with my present headache.[1]

The 'present headache' to which he refers was the tone poem *Luonnotar* about which he wrote to Lienau a little later. '*Luonnotar*, the new symphonic poem, is ready. It only remains to make a fair copy, which I have not yet been able to do because of illness.' Lienau insisted on having the score by

1 Written on 26 March 1906.

June at the latest so that he could inform concert promoters. 'Let me have it quickly, as much of it as you can. We must have something to show as a counter-attraction to all the old Breitkopf und Härtel repertoire.' Lienau's promptings were hardly designed to put Sibelius in a better frame of mind.

On the centenary of Snellman's birth on 12 May, Sibelius conducted a fiery performance (the adjective is his own) of his jubilee cantata, *The Captive Queen* to words of Paavo Cajander, though for political reasons it went under the title 'There sings the Queen'. The introduction describes how the Queen is held captive in a castle on a mountain top:

Ex 13 'A castle frowns o'er the valley. Its turrets are grim and tall.'

The allegory is altogether transparent. Mother Finland is held in Russian captivity; Runeberg arouses the people with his poems, Snellman pleads for Finnish as the national language and proclaims the idea of a Finnish state. The public, and probably both Cajander and Sibelius, saw in the cantata a vision of a future independent Finland. Whether or not it was intended to kindle great nationalist fervour, it is unfortunately not a particularly good piece. Even in Helsinki, it did not arouse undivided admiration though, surprisingly enough, Olin Downes wrote of it with enthusiasm: 'The artistic and expressive means used in *The Captive Queen* are many-sided and the whole layout is done with a surer hand than in *Finlandia*.' Sibelius himself seems to have made no great claims for the piece when he wrote to Lienau in May 1906, speaking of it as no more than an occasional piece.

More than a year had now elapsed since Sibelius had signed the contract with Lienau. So far he had delivered only two pieces, *Pelléas et Mélisande* and the Violin Concerto, instead of the four he had agreed. He was not anxious for *Pan and Echo* or *The Captive Queen* to be performed in Germany; indeed they were later included in the publisher's lists rather against his will. Lienau sent him the balance outstanding for the first six months of 1906 with a mild warning not to lend it all, as he had done in Paris. Sibelius responded by saying that it would be a matter of honour to send him something both new and good.

What actually happened to *Luonnotar* is not quite clear. As early as May it was in its finishing stages, while in June he wrote to his brother Christian that he was working hard to complete it. Thus, it comes as a surprise to find him writing to Lienau only thirteen days later about 'a symphonic fantasia' with a completely different programme, namely the episode from the *Kalevala* about Väinämöinen and Pohjola's daughter. This new work was evidently ready since the composer was busy with the composition of some German-language songs, and had the Third Symphony in the forefront of his mind. In the same letter (26 June 1906) he told Lienau that he had not altogether given up the idea of *Luonnotar* but the tone of the letter very much suggests that he has. To what extent the new tone poem sprang from the ashes of the old (or whether it was simply rechristened) is difficult to establish. Sibelius wanted to call the new work simply 'Väinämöinen' but Lienau expressed doubts as to the attractions of such a title, and it is to him that we owe the work's final title, *Pohjola's Daughter*. At first Sibelius resisted this suggestion – Oskar Merikanto had written an opera with a similar title – and offered a counter-suggestion obviously inspired by *Ein Heldenleben*: namely, 'L'aventure d'un héros'. But Lienau held firm and *Pohjola's Daughter* it became.

In June an event occured that Sibelius and his brother had always feared: their sister Linda succumbed to insanity. The composer hurried to the hospital but was not allowed to see her. He seems to have reacted sensibly to the situation: instead of worrying (and perhaps producing similar symptoms of his own), he simply tried to put the whole situation out of his mind. His letters to Aino and Christian report her condition briefly and go on to other matters. At the height of the summer the Sibelius family took the sea air at Virolahti, where the composer fished and hunted, at least to judge from what he told Lienau. He spent some days together with Arvid Järnefelt at Ainola where he finished the Six Songs, Op. 50. With them the first year of his contract ended.

That autumn Sibelius turned again to his symphonic toils though he broke off in order to write incidental music to *Belshazzar's Feast*, a play by his friend Hjalmar Procopé. By all accounts the play itself is a kind of pale Salome with a mixture of cardboard characters and stock situations, jealousy, passion, murder and suicide in a quasi-oriental setting. The heroine is a Jewish girl called Leschanah who is chosen to save her people from servitude, and who finally kills Belshazzar and then herself. The play had its first night in Helsinki on 4 November and there was no doubt that it was saved from disaster by the music. A caricature of the day depicts Procopé being borne aloft in the arms of Sibelius and the press generally found little in its favour.

In 1906 Breitkopf und Härtel sent Sibelius a copy of their newly published book, *Die Musik Skandinaviens* by Walter Niemann. Out of the 146 pages Sibelius was allotted 6, while Grieg had to content himself with 5. No doubt Niemann's observation that 'Sibelius' Musik ist reine Heimatkunst' must have prompted prayers from the composer to preserve him from his friends. Nor was the news that his music was 'deeply serious, dark, grey and sunless' likely to win his art many friends. All the same, Niemann's admiration is genuine enough: he speaks of Sibelius's 'brilliant scoring' and the mastery with which his poetic ideas are integrated into a formal scheme. 'Here is a master of purposeful orchestration, sonority and counterpoint; in all truth, a great artist with perfect taste,' he writes. He goes on to shower great praises on *The Swan of Tuonela* and *En Saga* but in the same breath underrates the two symphonies, which he finds 'more rhapsodic than epic' and lacking monumentality. In other words, though he concedes that they are important in the development of the Finnish symphony, he suggests that they are 'provincial', an adjective to which Sibelius's later critics, among them Virgil Thomson, were to return.

In St Petersburg Sibelius had a loyal advocate in Alexander Siloti. Like Busoni, Siloti was not merely content with his career as a pianist but also promoted concerts with a bent towards new music. When he read in the latest issue of *Die Signale*, the organ of the German publishers, that Sibelius had just finished a new symphonic fantasy, he invited him to conduct the work in St Petersburg. Sibelius accepted with alacrity. Before the score was even in print, he had dreamt of having it played by Prince Scheremetyev's large symphony orchestra in Pavlovsk. In St Petersburg he had the Marinsky Theatre Orchestra at his disposal with its large string section (sixteen first violins, fourteen seconds, and so on). News of his impending visit to Russia produced the usual anxiety symptoms in Carpelan who worried about the treacherous Neva air, the 'Black Guards', and Sibelius's reception by the Russians. Carpelan was well informed about the political scene in Russia where right-wing elements were growing daily stronger. Opposition was effectively crushed by Stolypin, and groups of the so-called 'Black Guards' terrorized the leftists. These developments boded ill for the Finns, as the Tsarist government looked with displeasure on the sanctuary that the Finns gave to Russian revolutionaries. Neither the Tsar nor his closest advisers had forgotten the fate of Bobrikov. As far as they were concerned, the Finns had merely been given breathing space in the last year or so.

The Russian intelligentsia on the other hand was as friendly to the Finns as ever, so that Carpelan's dismal prognosis was confounded. Before going to Russia, Sibelius conducted two concerts in Viipuri, two in Vaasa, and one in Uleåborg. Altogether he made 1,000 Finnish marks and gained further conducting experience to boot. Afterwards he boarded the train for St Petersburg – there were no passport formalities in these days and one travelled undisturbed. The Siloti concerts performed a valuable role in Russian musical life, for their programmes included a far higher ratio of novelties than the more conservative Imperial Russian Music Society as well as the concerts put on by Mitrofan Belyayev. Stravinsky wrote that he could not remember ever seeing a work of Franck, d'Indy, Chabrier, Fauré, Dukas or Debussy in their programmes. For the modern chamber music repertory there was an outlet in the 'Evening Circle for Contemporary

Music', where the public for Reger, Strauss, Schoenberg and new French music was drawn. Even if Siloti's concerts were not quite as up to date as these, they were eminently lively. Siloti himself was a pupil of Liszt, a cousin of Rachmaninov and the son-in-law of Tretiakov, a patron of the arts, so that he was well placed to engage famous composers and conductors.

At the concert on 29 December (16 December, Old Style), Ysaÿe played Mozart, Beethoven and Bach, while Sibelius conducted *Pohjola's Daughter* and *Lemminkäinen's Homeward Journey* to the great satisfaction of the public who called him back to the podium several times. The orchestra itself appeared to be enthusiastic about the new work and even the critics were favourably disposed. *Russ* thought that Sibelius had been responsive to the influence of Wagner without in any sense becoming epigonic; indeed, he went out of his way to stress Sibelius's individuality and national character. 'Sibelius is a particularly gifted and imaginative composer on whom one can place the highest hopes,' he wrote – according to the Helsinki press (4 January 1907). The *Russian Musical Gazette* compared him to the young Russian composers and also to Strauss, finding

> the same national feeling, spontaneity and freedom, the same attraction for orchestral colour, interest in myth and, above all, something that is a particular characteristic, an imaginative and bold use of orchestral sonority. As far as form is concerned, the young Sibelius has greater range and is more modern in approach. Most Russian composers working with programme music . . . model themselves on Liszt's forms. Sibelius is much closer to Strauss. [. . .] This music has something of the nomad's earthiness, primeval boldness and sense of joy.

The critic ends by saying how much Stasov would have liked this music had he lived to hear it.[1]

Pohjola's Daughter was equally well received when Armas Järnefelt conducted it for the first time in Stockholm the following February. Wilhelm Peterson-Berger went into raptures about this tone poem 'of a radiant and new beauty, a music that opens up clairvoyant vistas into a future world'. Sibelius, he went on, owes this both to us and himself after 'the thin, bloodless, unatmospheric and artificial music he wrote for *Pelléas et Mélisande*'.[2]

In fact *Pohjola's Daughter* does find Sibelius at a crucial turning point of his stylistic evolution. It is also his very first major orchestral work written directly for a German publisher, and one can well imagine that, having heard *Ein Heldenleben*, Sibelius would be anxious to compose a work that in its handling of the orchestra could hold its own with Strauss's masterpiece. Undoubtedly, Sibelius achieved his purpose in this respect. In the context of

1 The great Russian critic and scholar, who had been Director of the Department of Fine Arts at the Imperial Public Library at St Petersburg, champion and friend of Mussorgsky, died only shortly before in October 1906. Tr.
2 *Dagens Nyheter*, 21 February 1907.

the period *Pohjola's Daughter* can be thought of as a Nordic cousin of the Strauss tone poems, conceived in the sound world of the *Kalevala* myths that Sibelius had made so much his own, with some impressionistic touches and even on occasion a hint of the colours of Rimsky-Korsakov. Without going to the same lengths as Mahler or Strauss, Sibelius does permit himself to draw on somewhat larger orchestral forces than is his wont. To the woodwind he adds cor anglais, bass clarinet and double-bassoon as well as piccolo; there are two additional B flat trumpets and the harp makes its return to the Sibelian orchestra. However, as far as the percussion is concerned, he remains austere and allows himself timpani only.

The poetic inspiration for *Pohjola's Daughter* comes from the same part of the *Kalevala* from which the libretto of *The Building of the Boat* was drawn. Väinämöinen is on his way home from the Northland in his sleigh when he meets and falls in love with Pohjola's daughter, the moon daughter of the opera. He declares his love for her and to rid herself of his attentions, she sets him a series of impossible tasks, such as making a boat from the fragments of her spindle and tying an egg into invisible knots. These tasks prove beyond even his magic powers and in desperation he mounts his sleigh and finishes his journey alone. Sibelius himself wrote a prose note to explain the story, which Lienau rewrote in verse and whose last stanza Sibelius found a little sentimental. The full score reproduces Lienau's verses.

Nimmer kann der Held verzagen,	[The hero never can lose heart.
Alles Leid wird überwunden.	All sorrow will be overcome.
Der Erinn'rung sanfte Klänge	The memory of gentle sounds
Lindern Schmerz und bringen Hoffnung.	Eases pain and offers hope.]

The free sonata form of the tone poem ideally matches the programme itself. The chief protagonists of the drama, Väinämöinen and Pohjola's daughter, can be thought of as the first and second subjects respectively, and it is not too fanciful to suspect that the tension between the two themes reflects something of Sibelius's own predicament musically. The massive, firmly hewn contours of Väinämöinen stands for the rhetoric of late romanticism while the ethereal world of the daughter of the heavens looks forward to the horizons of impressionism. The opening melody grows out of the mythical, primeval gloom:

Ex 14

The aged Väinämöinen meditates. The intervals of the fifth, second and fourth all figure prominently in his musings, which are bound by the limited compass of a fifth and the dark G minor colouring. A more rhythmic idea with a dactylic character lends the music kinetic energy:

Ex 15

From these darker exchanges between cor anglais and clarinet the mood gradually lightens as the oboe introduces a new idea. Now the theme begins to expand, moving outside the normal minor scale to the flattened seventh. All this takes place over a B flat pedal point while the main idea hovers ambiguously between G minor and B flat:

Ex 16

B flat now strengthens its grip and acquires a Lydian inflection by the introduction of E natural instead of E flat. The brass intone 'Väinämöinen's fanfare' with its gradual crescendo effects:

Ex 17

A sudden modulation from B flat to E major, the distance of a tritone, brings us face to face with the second group. Its first idea derives from the introductory cello invocation (example 14), while the second is a free expansion both in its melodic and rhythmic outline of the dactylic figure of example 15:

Ex 18

The actual contrast in terms of sheer sonority is so striking in its impact that the effect is almost visual. It is as if we are suddenly confronted with a completely new world: the horizon is bathed in altogether brilliant colours as the daughter of the heavens makes her first appearance.

Incidentally, it is worth noting that up to this point *Pohjola's Daughter* anticipates the Fourth Symphony in its tonal layout. It has moved from G minor through B flat to E major just as the exposition of the first movement of the Symphony moves from A minor to C major and then F sharp. So we can see Sibelius replacing the classical tonic–dominant key relationships with a contrast based on the tritone. But the parallel between the tone poem and the Symphony goes even further. In the final group there appears a sequential motive into which the tritone is woven. These four notes exactly anticipate the opening idea of the Fourth Symphony:

Ex 19

The texture suddenly dissolves into an impressionistic mist of string tremolos, harp glissandi, distant timpani rolls, fleeting wind figures and muted horn cries:

Ex 20

The sequential figure (example 19) that opens the development brings us back to earth. The ethereal colours of the Maiden seated on her rainbow at the spinning-wheel vanish; the light of impressionism gives way to the weight of late-romantic sonorities. The earthly Väinämöinen acquires almost an expressionistic rhetoric. The tritone interval is much in evidence while the sequential figure undergoes a gradual metamorphosis:

Ex 21

The outcome of all this is a rising figure of demonic power which looms dramatically into sight. This is composed of a semitone and tritone, a contour that again looks forward to the development section of the Fourth Symphony:

Ex 22

The frenetic woodwind cries had earlier served as an accompanying figure in the second group, when Väinämöinen is first confronted with the vision of the Maid of Pohjola, but have now acquired a scornful, mocking intensity. Generally speaking, this development section includes some of the boldest and most imaginative orchestral writing in all Sibelius: the sequences of example 19 storm on violins and violas against surging whole-tone figures on other instruments. After Väinämöinen's fanfare has been heard with even greater power and intensity over a massive ground swell derived from the first four notes of example 16, the second subject reappears and shows how musical and narrative purposes blend in Sibelius's hands. The demonic figure of example 22 serves as a mere pendant: the heart has gone out of Väinämöinen's desperate efforts to satisfy the Maid's wishes.

Ex 23

This selfsame figure, much subdued, dominates the coda, climbing higher and higher on the strings before it disappears altogether. Tonally it seems poised between a Dorian B flat minor and a Lydian D flat. Finally the cellos and double-basses return one to the area of G minor–B flat from which the music set out. The vision of the Maid recedes and fades into nothingness leaving Väinämöinen to peruse his solitary fate:

Ex 24

In a sense *Pohjola's Daughter* is drawn towards two magnetic poles: Strauss in the west, and Rimsky-Korsakov in the east. The sense of impetus kindled by the opening melody, the feeling of forward thrust, remind one of *Don Juan* and *Ein Heldenleben*, but there is none of Strauss's sensuality. Väinämöinen hovers between the ecstasy of a seer and the fury of impotence, while the Maid of Pohjola herself radiates the same icy charms as Volkova, the daughter of the ocean god, who in *Sadko* is turned into a swan and swims away into the twilight. But at a deeper level, it is the remarkable inventiveness in his handling of thematic metamorphosis and his mastery of the poetic as well as the symphonic that makes *Pohjola's Daughter* so impressive an achievement.

Two other works of the period, the Op. 50 Songs and the incidental music to Procopé's play, *Belshazzar's Feast*, call for less detailed comment. The Six Songs, Op. 50, are all settings of contemporary German poets, among them Richard Dehmel and Margaretha Sussman. No doubt Lienau had a hand in the choice of poets, for he would have been anxious to advance Sibelius's reputation as a *Lieder* composer in Germany. Only three of the songs really stand out, two of which are Dehmel settings. Here Sibelius achieves a genuinely close relationship between the vocal line and the accompanying piano part. In 'Aus banger Brust' the vocal line goes to the heart of Dehmel's sensual symbolism and the keyboard writing reflects every shifting nuance in the poem. One can see that Sibelius's fascination with the tritone was not confined to *Pohjola's Daughter*, for he modulates during the course of the song from D minor to G sharp minor. The atmosphere is full of despair and longing.

Sibelius is no less successful in matching the poet's mood in 'Die stille Stadt' which reflects Dehmel's feeling for the world of legend and innocence. Again the tritone is in evidence and a powerful sense of atmosphere is generated. The broken chords of the accompaniment seem to evoke the vision of a silent town nestling in the valley and enveloped in the night mist. The vocal line itself has a ballad-like quality:

Ex 25 'A town lies in the valley, a pallid day slips by'

In '*Im Feld ein Mädchen*' to a text by Margaretha Sussman, in which a young girl laments her lover's death, we also find a folk-like simplicity of line:

Ex 26 'A girl sings in the meadow . . . all too quickly her lover is dead'

The heroine's grief is gradually softened by the soft evening atmosphere and the gentleness of nature:

Das Abendrot verglüht,   [The reddening evening fades,
Die Weiden stehn und schweigen   The willows stand silent]

These two themes, the presence of death and the sense of nature, struck a particularly sympathetic chord and this song has distinctly Finnish overtones in character. The remaining songs, 'Lenzegesang' (Arthur Fitger), 'Sehnsucht' (Emil Rudolf Weiss), and 'Rosenlied' (Anna Ritter), do not show the same responsiveness to the words of the poems; nor for that matter are the poems the equal of Dehmel's and Sussman's.

Belshazzar's Feast was no literary masterpiece either. From the incidental music he composed for the production, Sibelius compiled a suite for small orchestra comprising four movements. In the first, 'Oriental March', he creates a surprisingly authentic oriental atmosphere, making use of a normal major scale with a sharpened fourth and flattened seventh. A drone bass, repeated ostinato figures and a variety of colouristic devices contribute to the effectiveness of the piece. But it is the second movement, *Solitude* for strings alone, that is the most subtle of his atmospheric pieces. In the play Leschanah sings her incantation, 'Jerusalem, how can I forget thee', and Sibelius's music conveys a magical sense of longing and nostalgia:

Ex 27

Like the *Nocturne* that follows, it builds on the simplest of musical means. The *Nocturne* itself seems to grow out of the preceding music and is every bit as atmospheric. The flute cantilena is marvellously evocative, though its Arab feel is undoubtedly Europeanized by the absence of microtones. It moves from the modal to the minor but has a genuine sense of intoxication with nature:

Ex 28

'Khadra's Dance', the last movement, is in the simplest ABA form, the A representing life's dance and the B standing for the dance of death. The opening Lydian flute theme is answered on the oboe with a descending melodic figure with its Phrygian second that has an affecting pathos:

Ex 29

CHAPTER THREE

The Third Symphony

After the first performance of *Pohjola's Daughter*, work on the Third Symphony brooked no further delay. Sibelius had accepted the Royal Philharmonic Society's invitation to conduct the new symphony in the spring of 1907. 'The London letter did me great honour. It will be strange to stand on the same podium where everyone from Haydn to Tchaikovsky has conducted their own music,' he told Carpelan. Already by the middle of December Robert Lienau had asked if he could have some new songs or a chamber work for an all-Sibelius concert but met with a refusal. 'All my energies are being devoted to the Third Symphony at the moment – my whole being is consumed by it.'

Sibelius's cause was being actively promoted in Berlin: the *Pelléas et Mélisande* suite was well received, but the Violin Concerto, with Max Lewinger as the soloist, left the public unmoved. The First Symphony was taken up by Weingartner and the Royal Opera Orchestra, and Adolf Paul could report that 'Weingartner generally conducts Sibelius well, with fire and panache, and sensitive phrasing.'[1] According to Lienau, the Symphony made a greater impression on the small band of professionals that attended the rehearsal than it did on the fashionable audience that went to the concert itself on 11 January. The selfsame day Ida Ekman included no fewer than eighteen Sibelius songs in her recital, four of which were encored. This success not unnaturally prompted yet another plea from Lienau for some more songs.

By agreeing a deadline for the first performance of the new symphony, Sibelius was putting himself to some additional nervous strain. Even though he worked throughout the spring of 1907 with great zeal and enthusiasm, determined 'to show the critics what for', the new symphony was not ready in time and his London appearance had to be postponed.

In a letter to Mikko Slöör, Gallén's brother-in-law, he complained that time was simply running through his fingers.

---

1 In a letter to Sibelius himself the day before the concert, 10 January 1907.

When we last met you said a couple of things that troubled me. First and foremost: that Kajanus is finished. And afterwards that someone had said that I must be saved before it is too late. Both these remarks made a great impression on me. As far as Kajanus is concerned, I don't think that things have gone so far as you think. But in my case something has to be done. I am now in my prime and on the threshold of big things, but the years could easily melt away with nothing to show for them, unless I am taken in hand – above all, by me. This drinking – not that I don't enjoy it – has gone too far. They say that the path to damnation is paved with good intentions – but I haven't paved too much of the path yet, but I must try to turn the tide – and avoid damnation. In any event my intention in writing these lines is to thank you from the heart for your friendship in speaking so frankly. No one else does! There need be no real fear of 'bankruptcy' since my income is rather better now; it's rather my ability to manage money. Aino is quite at the end of her tether. I really must have it out with her.

I know full well that you have your hands full with many people's problems so that I turn to you with reluctance, but it's not just the boozer Sibb who is at stake but the composer in whose music I believe, and which can still develop into something much bigger. I have ideas in plenty and both the capacity – and, indeed, appetite for hard work! But time – time! That simply runs away. All this is not easy for me to admit to myself, as I am spoilt, superior and weak-willed.

Sibelius's allusion to bankruptcy must have been prompted by something Slöör had said, for the skeleton in his childhood cupboard haunted him. True, his standing in Finland was such that his name alone commanded credit; yet his debts were steadily mounting and the cost in terms of nervous strain was scarcely appreciated by others. Strangely enough, Sibelius writes more openly to Slöör than he does to Carpelan who was much closer to him, or perhaps it would be truer to say that he reveals yet another of his many sides! Slöör had charm and was good-hearted, and in fact was all too easy-going and sympathetic to be a really successful businessman. In his company Sibelius assumed a more relaxed and human mantle, laying aside some of the mask that made him appear 'spoilt and superior'. The relationship with Carpelan was different: here we have the world-famous composer writing to his Eckermann about future symphonic plans, his triumphs on foreign shores, the dreams and struggles of genius. Even when he describes a common cold, he assumes an heroic mien. Had he done otherwise and descended from Parnassus, Carpelan would have doubtless been disappointed. But to Slöör he wrote simply as one man to another.

Lienau began to apply more pressure during the spring of 1907. He showed lively disappointment at the postponement of the first performance of the Third Symphony as he had wanted to use the London reviews in his publicity. But by July, Sibelius could send him reassuring news: the Sym-

1. Ainola

Komponisten H. Jean Sibelius.

~~Helsingfors~~

Wårkby väret Finland

Hangö banan

Troldhaugen p. Bergen
26/6/03

Hjærtelig Tak til Dem og de
andre medundertegnede af Tele-
grammet til min 60 års dag.
Jeg er rørt og glad over denne
Hilsen, som jeg endnu håber, per-
sonligt at kunne få takke for.
Tak samtidig for deres skjønne
Sange, som jeg meget beundrer
og elsker!   Højagtelsesfuld
                 Edvard Grieg.

2. Card from Grieg thanking Sibelius for his greetings
telegram on his sixtieth birthday.

3. Aino Sibelius, by Venny
Soldan-Brofeldt.

4. The cousins, Sergei Rachmaninov and
Alexander Siloti.

5. Sibelius at the coffee table.

6. Sibelius in the drawing-room at Ainola. The composer sent this, together
with the photograph above, to his publisher sometime between 1905 and 1909

7. Mahler in Helsinki, 1907, painted at Hvitträsk
by A. Gallén-Kallela.

12. The actress Harriet Bosse.

13. Busoni conducting in Berlin in 1909.

14. Sibelius and Aino picnicking in Kuhmo, 1912.

phony was 'almost finished', even if there was still a lot of work to be done on the finale. Although he conceded that he was behindhand with deliveries, Sibelius nevertheless asked for money. During the second stage of the contract, Sibelius had so far sent him *The Captive Queen* and *Pan and Echo*, which Lienau counted as the equivalent of one work – and the music to *Belshazzar's Feast*: the Third Symphony had yet to be delivered. Lienau wanted yet another work, preferably something popular and therefore lucrative, along the lines of Brahms's *Hungarian Dances* – perhaps a set of Nordic or Finnish Dances for piano or piano duet, or a chamber work for a not-too-large group, such as a trio, or why not eight or ten good piano pieces? This otherwise perceptive publisher was continually fostering expectations of 'greater commercial success'. Lienau told Sibelius how well his music was faring in the shops: the Violin Concerto was doing rather well, and the *Pelléas et Mélisande* music had at times gone very well, but everything else, including the songs, had so far not done well enough. However, the overall situation was evidently good enough for Lienau to agree to send him the advance for which Sibelius had asked according to the contract.

In May Sibelius wrote telling him that he proposed coming to Germany the following month to run through the new symphony with Kapellmeister Neisser's orchestra in Eisleben. Neisser had been for a time in Vaasa where Sibelius presumably came into contact with him. Lienau offered to attend the rehearsals but in actual fact Sibelius did not get away until August, and even then the Symphony remained unfinished. Besides, it is unlikely that the orchestra would have been available at that time of the year when normally German provincial orchestras would have been on holiday. In any event Sibelius's German trip is shrouded in some mystery: it is not even established whether he ever got as far as Eisleben or whether he remained in Berlin to go through his future work plan with Lienau. There is not a single letter from him to Aino from the summer of 1907 and indeed the only line so far to have come to light is a greeting to Gallén-Kallela appended to a postcard sent by the painter Aki Sandlund. The card itself reproduces a detail from Max Klinger's painting, *Noahs Weinprobe* [Noah's wine-tasting]: a woman is lying on her back and balancing on her forehead a bowl of blood-red wine from which a black panther is eagerly drinking. One wonders whether perhaps Sibelius's 'run-through' was less of symphonic than other bars!

In Helsinki itself the shops were full of Sibelius's picture. A 'Sibelius cigar' of foreign manufacture had recently appeared on the market, and the boxes were adorned with 'a good likeness of our celebrated composer'.[1] On 10 September, Lienau wrote asking for the finale, the first two movements having already been engraved. Presumably it arrived at the very last

---

1 *Hufvudstadsbladet*, 1 August 1907.

moment. The first performance took place at the end of the month when Sibelius conducted it alongside two other recent works, *Pohjola's Daughter* and the incidental music to *Belshazzar's Feast*. In actual fact the public took *Pohjola's Daughter* to its heart much more readily than it did the new symphony and even the critics of both *Hufvudstadsbladet* and *Helsingin Sanomat* thought the tone poem had the more immediate appeal. Flodin, however, hailed the composer's new style unreservedly.

> Sibelius is a classical master. Never have I so fully realized that Jean Sibelius belongs to all five continents as when I had the good fortune to make the acquaintance of his Third Symphony. It can – and indeed, will – be understood in every part of the globe where people have a feeling for music in its newest and most sublime form. The new work meets all the requirements of a modern symphony, but at the same time it is, at a deeper level, revolutionary, new and truly Sibelian. I believe that our Finnish master should not go beyond these stylistic frontiers.

In a sense, Flodin went to the heart of the matter: the Third Symphony launched a kind of radical new classicism. However, his prediction proved wide of the mark. Of all Sibelius's symphonies, the Third was to be the least successful with audiences abroad, and in the Fourth Sibelius was to leave its stylistic boundaries far behind.

Sibelius once characterized the finale of the Third Symphony as 'the crystallization of ideas from chaos'. Indeed, one could go as far as to describe the whole work as the crystallization of a classical symphony from the relative chaos of late romanticism. The work is more concentrated than its predecessors: the number of movements is reduced from four to three by telescoping the scherzo and finale. The first movement retains a sonata-form outline but each of the component sections is denser. The duration reflects this greater density: the whole symphony lasts a mere thirty minutes as opposed to the forty-five minutes of its predecessor. The big romantic gestures, the passionate violin cantilenas, the massive brass writing have been replaced by lighter, more athletic string writing and altogether much lighter textures in the wind. Many of the ideas are borne along by ostinato rhythms but whereas in Prokofiev and Stravinsky the ostinati are in themselves the focus of attention, in this symphony they are still subordinate to the melodic interest. Moreover, the orchestral forces are reduced: in the Second Symphony he managed without harp, bass drum and cymbals; here he scaled down his resources even further by omitting the third trumpet and tuba. The contrast in the respective sound worlds of the Third Symphony and *Pohjola's Daughter* is even greater. This is hardly surprising, perhaps, since the symphonic poems and the symphonies follow a different evolutionary process even in their use of the orchestra. Generally speaking, Sibelius shows restraint in his use of the wind in the symphonies: the main exceptions are the piccolo in the finale of the First Symphony and the bass clarinet in the Sixth. Perhaps he thought their highly evocative and strong personalities more appropriate in the context of the tone poem, as, for example, the cor anglais in *The Swan of Tuonela*, than in the sound world of the symphony. But even if Sibelius lightened the orchestral forces involved, he did not evisage too pale a colouring. In a letter to Lienau he recommended that the strings should comprise twelve firsts, ten seconds, eight violas but eight cellos and as many double-basses. 'As you see, my dark strains reappear.'

Of course, the Third Symphony was totally out of step with the times. Its Viennese classical orchestration could hardly be at greater variance with the ethos of Mahler and Strauss. Think of the orchestral forces involved in *Elektra*, or the eight horns, five trumpets and vast array of percussion in Skryabin's *Poem of Ecstasy*, not to mention such a gargantuan enterprise as Mahler's Eighth Symphony. The more 'normal' classical-romantic orchestra employed in Glazunov's Eighth or Rachmaninov's Second Symphonies are very much the exception and, in its very different way, Schoenberg's *Kammersymphonie*, Op. 9, was equally prompted by a reaction against the inflated orchestral palette of the times. But in the Third Symphony, Sibelius was doing more than merely just reacting against the opulent sound world of *Ein Heldenleben* or Mahler's Fifth; he was following a logical path that left him free to explore more exotic colours in the tone poems while reducing his orchestra to Beethovenian size for the symphonies. Yet it would not be correct to think of the Third as 'neo-classical' in the true sense of the term. Neo-classicism concerns externals: the structure is not reshaped but used as a mould into which fresh musical ideas and harmonies are poured.

Sibelius's Third does not bear the same relationship to Beethoven that, say, Stravinsky's *Capriccio* does to Bach or Prokofiev's *Classical Symphony* does to Haydn, since Sibelius takes the classical form as a point of departure not as a model. In fact, with its classical sense of thematic metamorphosis, it almost approaches what Busoni would call *junge Klassizität*.

But, in moving away from late romanticism, Sibelius also turned his back on his 'nationalist' past. In contrast with the earlier symphonies, there is scarcely any specifically Finnish flavouring as far as thematic substance is concerned. Such national feeling as there is lies at another level where it is more difficult to disentangle what is Finnish and what is Sibelius. It is perhaps best summed up by saying that in this work Sibelius is Finnish in the same sense that Beethoven or Brahms are German: indeed, from this time onwards one can say that he becomes more international. One can sensibly speak of 'European classicism' as opposed to 'national romanticism'. There is scarcely any precedent for this, save perhaps in the year immediately before *Kullervo*, in the String Quartet in B flat, Op. 4, where one has some foretaste of the light pastel colours, the pastoral feeling and the gentle melancholy of the Symphony.

The first movement possesses remarkable formal clarity: Gerald

Abraham speaks of it as fully worthy of comparison with a Haydn or Mozart first movement. It derives its special quality from the unconventional key relationships, which rest largely on the tension between modal and major-minor scales. The athletic, keen-edged first theme is heard in unison cellos and double-basses without any harmonies whatsoever.

Ex 30

In the course of the argument a Lydian F sharp soon stands out in the C major context, forming a tritone with the pedal C on the basses:

Ex 31

A concluding figure acquires its bucolic character by means of the interval of a fourth: generally speaking, this plays an important role in the movement:

Ex 32

All this unleashes a flow of semiquavers, which give the impression of continuous movement and inexhaustible energy, while a wind motive derived from the first group anticipates the second subject – one example among many of the constant process of metamorphosis and thematic

renewal that characterizes not only this movement but the whole symphony. The first group culminates in a stepwise figure encompassing the
tritone C–D–E–F sharp. Now, we see the way in which Sibelius makes
structural use of the modal element he has introduced thematically. The
tension is released when the pivotal function of the F sharp becomes
evident. It serves as the dominant of B minor, and thus obviates the need for
a modulatory bridge passage. Moreover, the modal flavour would have
already weakened the impact of G major. The elegiac second group, highly
characteristic of Sibelius with its long-held initial note is heard on the cellos:

Ex 33

The final idea of the second group is also related to – or rather grows
naturally out of – this theme and moves on to G major:

Ex 34

The inherent dynamism of the music finds further expression in the last
group, which takes the form of tranquil string chords followed by scale
passages in contrary motion:

Ex 35

Sibelius had never before written in so completely linear a fashion. After a tentative start, the *perpetuum mobile* of the development gets under way. The texture has the transparency of chamber music with semiquaver movement alternating between wind and strings over sustained horns. The relationship between the second group and the main idea of the first is emphasized at this point:

Ex 36

The pedal point B functions first as the dominant of E minor and afterwards as the leading note of C major in preparation for the reprise, which surges irresistibly onwards. Apart from the second subject, which is restated in E minor with greater emphasis and in fuller colours, the last idea is the most transformed in character, being full of vitality and power. The coda, by contrast, is distinguished by great tranquillity of spirit, the *cantabile* theme being derived from the third section.

The meditative, inward slow movement shows just how skilled Sibelius has now become in the art of dramatic contrast. Its key alone (G sharp minor) lends it a feeling of remoteness, almost mystery; and there is a magical effect of light at figure 6, when the music moves into A flat major enharmonically. The form is so transparently straightforward and simple that it scarcely calls for analysis, wrote Cecil Gray; but it is not so straightforward that it has not given rise to a wide variety of interpretations. Eino Roiha, Ilmari Krohn, Nils-Eric Ringbom and Leo Normet all call it a species of variations; Marc Vignal finds it 'proche du rondo', and this view is not contested by Simon Vestdijk, while Simon Parmet sees some parallel with sonata procedure. Even so what we are concerned with is hardly a complex new structure, like the Seventh Symphony or the finale of the Third. The impression made on the listener is of a main theme, **A**, which appears four times in changing guise with two interludes, **B** and **C**, plus a short coda. Thus:

A – **A₁** – **B** – **A₂** – **C** – **A₃** – Coda

Behind these bald symbols there is a more subtle reality. Does Sibelius really vary the theme or not? In actual fact the theme itself undergoes few significant changes, nor does the harmonic background. But it does appear in a new orchestral garb with added contrapuntal interest and in different keys. In both the slow movements of the Quartet in B flat and the Piano Sonata has Sibelius previously treated a theme in this fashion: in the *Andante* of the former and the *Andantino* of the latter. Much depends, of course, on how much importance one attaches to the **B** and **C** episodes. Judgements inevitably differ in this respect: Parmet goes as far as to say that they include thematic matter of a symphonic nature while, at the other extreme, Gray speaks of them as 'of no structural importance'. For my own part they seem to me sufficiently characterized and independent to function as episodes in a rondo movement.

Trumpets and trombones are silent throughout the movement and the strongest dynamic marking is *forte*. The main theme, **A**, appears fragmentarily on the flutes and is interleaved with a ritornello-like motive on clarinets:

Ex 37

It soon appears in a more fully fleshed form on the strings:

Ex 38

The bass parts are no longer locked in sustaining a pedal point but develop a gentle wave-like motion. At this point the *Andantino* acquires as a result a new sense of grace. The first episode, **B**, on the cellos could be described as Sibelius's *Alleingefühl*; it has a withdrawn quality that almost points the way to *Voces intimae*:

Ex 39

When the main theme, coloured by the strings' anxious pizzicati, suddenly modulates up a minor third to B minor, one is plunged into a dreamlike state: everything is familiar and yet somehow strange. In the second episode one is drawn even deeper into this atmosphere of unreality. The familiar Sibelian thirds with some unusually dissonant counterpoints glide away while the horns with an open fifth and the introductory three-note motive signal the return of the main theme for the last time. The third movement appears to be the result of a fusion between scherzo and finale. Its structure could be roughly summarized thus:

I. Scherzo $\frac{6}{8}$
1. An exposition with two groups of themes, **A**, **B**.
2. A restatement, **A₁**, **B₁**, with different tonal relationships.
3. A development-like transition in which material from **A** and **B** is reworked leading to
II. Finale $\frac{4}{4}$
composed of one sole theme with a strong rhythmic profile.

One could describe the 'scherzo' as a kind of sonata-form structure where the development comes after the restatement. In the first group the composer starts off with this oboe idea,

Ex 40

which almost immediately changes in character:

Ex 41

The Lydian sharpened fourth links the idea to the first movement. Another important ingredient in the movement is the following:

Ex 42

The contrasting thematic group is in A minor and is both more homogeneous and stronger in profile. The *staccato* of the strings gives way to a *legato* movement from which the main theme emerges thus:

Ex 43

Usually Sibelius allows his thematic material to disappear into the background to form a fund of new melodic substance. But here the procedure is reversed: from this fund he takes an idea, which is subtly transformed and emerges into the foreground.

In the free restatement that follows, with C major and F minor as the two tonal centres, the undulating movement on the strings assumes the upper hand and gradually changes to an even quaver movement. All this builds up into an imposing, almost terrifying climax. Throughout the bulk of the exposition and the restatement Sibelius sustains a pedal point on C, serving first as a tonic, then as the mediant in A flat or dominant in F minor. In the development, however, he lifts anchor and embarks on a passage where the tonality shifts so frequently that it is difficult to keep one's bearings:

Ex 44

So far we have not touched on perhaps the most important feature of the movement: the growth and emergence of the final theme. Already, at the end of the first group, one notices a small idea that attracts attention by its alien, insistent character.

Ex 45

It vanishes only to reappear again at the transition from the second group, **B**, to the restatement, **A₁**:

Ex 46

The duplet rhythm stands out against the triplets of the remaining texture, and the clarinet's tritone (C–G flat = F sharp enharmonically) calls to mind the Lydian tensions of the first movement. But the time is not yet ripe for the cells of the new theme to form. Suddenly, in the restatement between A_1 and B_1, we see its first flowering:

Ex 47

And at this point we see the descending duplet third as the motivating factor in the rhythmic shape of the theme. After the development section is played out, the hymn-like main theme begins to emerge into the foreground:

Ex 48

The remainder of the movement calls for little detailed exegesis: its processes are eminently straightforward and self-evident. But Sibelius's achievement in this movement is a considerable one. Because of the relationship between the scherzo's exposition and the main theme of the finale, one experiences the whole movement as a unified entity, and the slow growth of the main theme during the course of the whole scherzo lends the piece an even stronger sense of organic cohesion.

At the end of October, between two conducting engagements in St Petersburg, Mahler paid a brief visit to Helsinki. He was to conduct the Philharmonic Orchestra in a Beethoven–Wagner programme; and arriving on the 29th attended a popular concert that selfsame evening. He went in the company of Axel Gallén whose acquaintance he had made in Vienna three years earlier, and heard a programme conducted by Kajanus that included Sibelius's *Spring Song* and, as an encore, *Valse triste*. Given the fact that this was the first occasion that Mahler had heard any Sibelius, the choice of programme could scarcely have been more unfortunate. Kajanus should have seen to it that *Spring Song* was replaced by, say, *The Swan of Tuonela* or the *Lemminkäinen's Homeward Journey*, which often appeared in the context of these concerts. From the point of view of their future relationship, the choice of programme was to prove disastrous.

After his first day in Helsinki, Mahler wrote of his Finnish impressions in a letter to his wife:

[The orchestra] is surprisingly good and well-disciplined, which says a great deal for their permanent conductor, Kajanus, who is of good repute in the musical world. In the afternoon he came to see me and keep me company. A singularly sympathetic, serious and unpretentious person. [. . .] After the concert we [Mahler, Gallén and his wife] sat a while talking to Kajanus, his wife and a pianist from Brussels, [Arthur de Greef]. Gallén was in very good spirits and made a great impression on me. I made my excuses at eleven o'clock, however, and went to bed, something that caused quite a stir, since people here seem to sit up half the night and even to the crack of dawn.

At the concert I also heard some pieces by Sibelius, the Finnish national composer who they make a great fuss about, not only here but elsewhere in the musical world. One of the pieces was just ordinary 'Kitsch', spiced with certain 'Nordic' orchestral touches like a kind of national sauce.

They are the same everywhere, these national geniuses. You find them in Russia and Sweden —.and in Italy the country is overrun by these whores and their ponces. Axel is made of altogether different stuff with his twelve schnapps before the soup, and one feels that there is something genuine and robust about him and his kind.[1]

The day of the concert Sibelius went to see Mahler at his hotel, and their encounter seems to have passed off pleasantly enough. 'Sibelius came to see me this morning. He, too, like all Finns, seems a particularly sympathetic person.' Unfortunately it was a quarter of a century later, before Sibelius recorded his impressions of their meeting:

Mahler and I were together a great deal. His long-established heart complaint forced him to lead an ascetic existence, and he was not fond of ceremonial dinners and banquets. We came on good terms during a number of walks together, where we discussed all of music's problems in deadly earnest. When our conversation touched on the symphony, I said

1 Alma Mahler, *Gustav Mahler*, Vienna, 1949, pp. 396–97. English edition: Alma Mahler, *Memories and Letters*, third edition, edited by Donald Mitchell with Knud Martner, London, 1973, pp. 297–98.

that I admired its style and severity of form, and the profound logic that created an inner connection between all the motives. This was my experience in the course of my creative work. Mahler's opinion was just the opposite. 'No!' he said, 'The symphony must be like the world. It must be all-embracing.'

Mahler's way of life was wholly unpretentious. He was a highly interesting person: I respected him as a human being and an artist, for his high ethical principles, even though his opinions about artistic matters differed from mine. I did not want him to think that I had come to see him merely to interest him in my compositions. When he said in his abrupt way, 'What would you like me to conduct of yours?' I merely answered, 'Nothing.' The orchestra, on the other hand, did not particularly warm to him, which may have been due to the fact that during his Helsinki visit, Mahler was not in the best of health. The long-experienced Anton Sitt, its leader for a quarter of a century, said with a note of wonder, 'And he was supposed to have been the new Hans von Bülow!'

Sibelius would appear to have given an accurate picture of the relationship between Mahler and the orchestra. The conductor's initial favourable impressions soon faded, and in the main item of the concert, Beethoven's Fifth Symphony, a false entry with some resulting bars of dissonance brought a dark cloud to the composer's mien, according to the critic Flodin.

It is obvious from his account of their meeting that Sibelius was anxious to approach Mahler as one composer to another, rather than appear to be begging favours from an internationally celebrated conductor. There was no personal rivalry between them at this stage: others were taking care of that! Had not Sibelius's own teacher, Martin Wegelius, played off Mahler against him? And had not Busoni in all innocence spoken of the relative enthusiasm of the applause at a Berlin concert where works by Mahler and Sibelius shared the same programme? As yet Sibelius had not been used as a stick with which to beat Mahler, but that was to come only a few weeks later in St Petersburg. In terms of international standing both composers were relatively evenly matched. Mahler was better known in central Europe in spite of the hostility that his career as a virtuoso conductor and his Jewish origins aroused. Sibelius was handicapped by his own provincial background with its lack of musical traditions. This naturally evoked prejudice, and this was compounded by the fact that Sibelius's musical ideas were alien to the Central European mentality. Paris responded to neither. In Russia, Mahler had a persuasive advocate in Oscar Fried, who was a frequent guest conductor in the larger Russian cities, while Sibelius was championed in his turn by Siloti and also by Kajanus. Here they enjoyed equal prestige. In the Anglo-Saxon world and the Scandinavian countries, it was Sibelius who had the stronger foothold.

It would have been quite natural for Sibelius to have shown some of his most recent scores to Mahler, if for no other reason than to correct the impression that he knew must have been made by the two bagatelles that Mahler had heard. Sibelius's actual words – 'I did not want him to think that I had come to see him merely to interest him in my compositions' – prompt the thought that the very reverse was his intention, and that it was pride rather than modesty and sensitivity that caused him to answer Mahler's question with 'Nothing.'

Of course, Sibelius should have seen to it that Mahler was given the opportunity of getting to know his work. Both *En Saga* and the Second Symphony were works that Carpelan had wanted him to send to the great conductor. Moreover, the 'Nichts' with which he had answered Mahler's question undoubtedly sounded less modest and sensitive than he himself imagined. One could argue from the premiss that Mahler's question was a mere courtesy rather than a genuine enquiry. But the great conductor was always fascinated to hear from other composers, their views on the interpretation of their own work, and no doubt he looked forward to a serious and detailed discussion. In any event Sibelius's response must have seemed distinctly chilly.

It goes without saying that their famous exchange about the nature of the symphony could hardly have come at more extreme points in their careers. Nothing could be more 'all-embracing' than Mahler's newly completed Eighth Symphony, while Sibelius's words obviously sum up his thinking as a result of the Third. Both words and deed could well have been in part a reaction against Mahler's Fifth, the score of which he had studied in Berlin. There was no further contact between the two men.

Sibelius lacked some of the qualities that distinguished both Mahler and Busoni: the pervasive, speculative intellectuality as well as the combination of creative and interpretative genius. However, they had one thing in common: a highly developed awareness of nature, even if they reacted differently to it. After having been to the Niagara Falls, Mahler conducted a performance of Beethoven's Pastoral Symphony and summed up his reactions thus: 'Now I realize that a finished work of art is always the superior of mere natural beauty.'[1] Sibelius, on the other hand, responded differently to the same phenomenon. After his visit to Niagara, 'Of all that I have ever seen, this comes nearest to being a religious experience, nearer in fact than music.'[2] This perspective is of course mirrored in their music: Mahler's is centred on man even though his relationship with nature is an important ingredient in his make-up, whereas Sibelius's reflects an almost mystic sense of identification with nature.

With their different temperaments and outlook on life, they should have enjoyed a lively exchange of ideas. But while he was in Helsinki, much of

1 Alma Mahler, *Gustav Mahler*, p. 230.
2 Carl Stoeckel, 'Some Recollections of the Visit of Sibelius to America in 1914' MS. Yale University Library.

Mahler's time was taken up by Axel Gallén. The day after the concert, and in spite of the cold weather, Gallén took him by motor boat to Eliel Saarinen's villa at Hvitträsk to the west of Helsinki, where he painted his portrait, but Sibelius was not included in the party. Mahler never actually conducted any Sibelius, though he came near to doing so. His concert for the New York Philharmonic Society on 13 March 1911 was to have been devoted exclusively to 'national geniuses': Svendsen, Tchaikovsky, Dvořák and Sibelius, the latter being represented by the Violin Concerto. The *New York Times* thought this the most interesting of the works on the programme, but unfortunately Mahler was not well enough to appear and his place was taken by Theodore Spiering, a friend of Sibelius from the Berlin period, and now leader of the New York orchestra. Within a few months of this, Mahler had died.

On or about 10 November, Sibelius went to St Petersburg to conduct his new symphony at a Siloti concert. He stayed at the Hôtel d'Angleterre, from which he wrote home to Aino:

Have just come back from the rehearsal. The wind are really not very good. The rest are so-so. They have played far too many operatic pot-pourris. Still, I think my symphony will be all right. I have four hours' rehearsal time each day. My calm manner and hm! hm! have made an impression. There are a lot of mistakes in the score and parts, and I will have to spend the whole day going over them. Look after yourself. I will write again soon. Siloti has the critics against him. I will tell you later what I have noticed.

As the rehearsals progressed it became obvious that the finale was going to be a hard nut for the orchestra and the critics to crack. His next letter to Aino was by no means as optimistic about the way the rehearsals were going.

Siloti shows a great deal of interest in me. He has fully grasped the first two movements but is not entirely at home in the finale. It is strange just how difficult it is for artists to throw off the 'good deeds' of their forefathers. They don't realize that so rich and self-renewing an art as music performs other functions than merely beguiling the ear. In my view merely to divert would be demeaning for my art. Today I was invited to lunch by the Silotis. They are terribly kind and friendly. The wife is extremely talkative; it is a trifle exhausting but what can you do? I should have asked you to come here had I been doing a complete concert. Naturally, there is a large part of the audience that has made up its mind beforehand that the symphony is a necessary evil. I have fourteen violas! Twenty first violins and so on! I am learning a lot about conducting again. In my opinion it is easier to learn to conduct than rehearse – the latter is very difficult.[1]

1 Letter dated 13 November 1907.

Aino came to St Petersburg for the concert itself. She sat in one of the Marinsky Theatre boxes together with Siloti's wife. First, Siloti conducted an overture by Alexander Taneyev, after which it was Sibelius's turn to mount the rostrum. The Third Symphony was not a real success with the public. Hardly had the applause died down than the door of their box opened to admit a well-known doctor, Botkin, who swore profusely about the new work. Mrs Siloti, who knew that Aino spoke Russian, did her best to stem the flow of oaths but in vain![1]

The young Prokofiev was in the audience on this occasion. The following day he submitted an orchestration exercise to his teacher, Rimsky-Korsakov, in which he had allotted one part to a single cello. If it was his purpose to annoy Rimsky, he succeeded.

'Why do you use a solo cello here?' he asked.

'Because at this point I do not want the effect of all the cellos playing,' Prokofiev replied.

'Oh really! Have you ever heard solo cellos?'

'Yesterday, in the Sibelius symphony.'

Rimsky was furious. 'God in heaven! Sibelius! Why listen to Sibelius? Isn't the second subject of the *Ruslan* overture good enough for you?'

Sibelius met with a hostile press. 'When he does something new,' wrote Koptiaiev in *Birzhevya Viedomosti*,

he gives us bizarre combinations which offer contrasts – in horror. He is a frequent visitor to Berlin, London and Paris, where it is all too easy to be infected by the decadence of Debussy, Elgar and Strauss. We have obviously said goodbye to the earlier Sibelius, who has interpreted his country's legends so fascinatingly.

Another critic thought its brevity the only thing in its favour. Even the German-speaking press was unfavourable: 'The new symphony has none of the character of this previously much respected and admired composer . . . Is it really possible that he has already written himself out?' asked the *St Petersburg Herald*. The *St Petersburger Zeitung* accused him of either misunderstanding the demands of the symphonic form or loss of his powers of self-criticism. Only one voice, the *Novoye Vremya*, was raised in his favour.

In terms of clarity of motivic development, Sibelius comes nearer Mendelssohn and his school rather than Wagner and his followers. The orchestration is modern without striving for originality at all costs; if Herr Sibelius thinks that a new combination of sonorities is appropriate to the musical material, he uses it, but if not, he refrains. In this respect he is very different indeed from a composer like Mahler, whose whole aim is to astonish us with everything he can think of. Herr Sibelius is a serious and sincere artist, without the newest Jewish composer's offensive circus

1 Aino Sibelius in conversation with the author.

tricks and the pretentiousness that one finds with Strauss [!] and Mahler.

This was the first but not the last occasion on which a newspaper used Sibelius as part of its anti-Semitic armoury.

But on one point all the St Petersburg papers were agreed: that Sibelius had made use of Finnish folk melodies. 'The orchestra and the audience may have been pleased with me, but I can't say that I was with them,' wrote Sibelius to Lienau after the concert.

After his concert Sibelius went back to Järvenpää for a few weeks, then the time came for a second Russian trip; this time to Moscow. On his way there, he met a promising young conductor, Oscar Fried who belonged to Lienau's circle and who was scheduled to give the Third Symphony in Berlin. While in St Petersburg, they spent some time at the Hermitage. In point of fact, although he was later to conduct the Fourth, Fried never actually gave a performance of the Third. In Moscow itself the orchestral rehearsals with the Symphonic Society's orchestra appear to have started more auspiciously than in St Petersburg.

I have just come from a rehearsal. Have formed a good relationship with the orchestra. They are, as far as I can tell, better than the one in St Petersburg. My only worry is the soloist, who is a young violinist. He will rehearse tomorrow. The orchestra, by the way, applauded me. I have spent a lot of time together with an Italian oratorio composer, Bossi. [. . .] Just now there was a lady here, a Russian, who will play my pieces at a concert. She played *Pelléas et Mélisande*, the Romance in D flat, 'Minun kultani' (my arrangement of a Finnish folk song) and the third movement of *Kyllikki* excellently. Now I believe that my music will live – and for a long time, because it is absolutely real. Moscow is an extraordinary and interesting place. It has a strange atmosphere, that one seldom ever experiences anywhere else. And the people are sympathetic. Admittedly I haven't yet learned to know any of them. There has been a string of celebrities here, one after the other, Nikisch and so on. I haven't yet properly seen the town yet: the weather is dismal – with snow turning to slush.[1]

He did, however, stay at the typically Russian Slavyanski Bazar.

At the rehearsal the next morning, the young soloist did not manage well enough, and the Violin Concerto was hastily removed from the programme. Sibelius had to replace it with some popular pieces, *Karelia, Pan and Echo, Valse triste*, the 'Oriental March' and 'Khadra's Dance' from *Belshazzar's Feast*, but the main items on the programme were *Pohjola's Daughter* and the Third Symphony. In general he had a much better reception than in St Petersburg.

On the day of the concert *Russkiye Vyedomosti* published a leading article

1 An undated letter written to Aino some time in November 1907.

about Sibelius and Finnish music, saying that he had given expression to the very soul of the Finnish people as well as to the country and the calm beauty of the mythology. When reviewing the concert, the same critic singled out the Third Symphony as typical of the mastery of Finnish folk melody that Sibelius had so effectively captured. A more critical voice was raised in *Russkoye Slovo* where the well-known critic N. Kashkin made much the same points as Niemann and some other German critics were to do. 'We are almost prepared to say straight away that he does not sufficiently command all the complexities of symphonic form: in the Third Symphony ideas are not developed in so logical and unified a way that we have come to insist upon.' But *Pohjolas's Daughter*, he thought, must be numbered among Sibelius's most important works to date, and in general admired most 'those compositions that reflect the colours of the *Kalevala* whose characters for the most part inhabit the gloom of the long Polar nights'.

The Moscow and St Petersburg critics seem to have been at odds about Sibelius as conductor. In St Petersburg one critic had written that he was not an outstanding conductor, though he managed to present the symphony as well as any other competent conductor would have done. Kashkin, on the other hand, was much more impressed and thought particularly well of him on this count: 'a fine conductor, which is by no means always the case with gifted composers'.

Sibelius did not conquer either Russian city with the Third Symphony. After *Pohjola's Daughter*, critics no doubt expected a brilliant virtuoso piece for a large orchestra or alternatively something dissonant or in some way shocking. They were certainly not prepared for this transparently harmless Mendelssohniad, as they thought it, where the evolution of ideas was cleverly concealed beneath the surface. Nor did the new symphony meet with much greater success in Stockholm when Armas Järnefelt presented it there. *Svenska Dagbladet*[1] spoke of it 'going its own national way at the risk of at times being incomprehensible to non-Finnish audiences'. These critical commentaries about its going its own national way and its use of folk music must have irritated Sibelius. Two years earlier he had written in a letter to Rosa Newmarch:

> I would be pleased, Madame, if you would correct a general misconception. I often find in newspapers abroad that my melodies are spoken of as folk tunes; up to this point I have never used any themes other than those that are entirely my own.[2]

1 18 November 1907.
2 8 February 1906.

CHAPTER FOUR

Night Ride and Sunrise

The year 1908 was a critical turning point in Sibelius's life. His personal problems had come to a head; he often felt unwell and he was drinking as heavily as ever before. Nor did his constantly mounting debts improve his spirits. On the other hand, his stylistic evolution was at a stage where new expressive possibilities were open to him. After his initial successes abroad, his international career was at a crucial stage. As he entered the new year he must have inevitably pondered about his fortunes on the international stage, whether his star would rise or decline, and whether he would be able to hold in check the destructive forces within himself.

In one respect the situation almost foreshadows his position in Germany and Austria in the 1960s. His works were performed by the great conductors of the day but were regularly denigrated by the critics. The First Symphony was becoming more widely played: Nikisch gave it at a Gewandhaus concert in Leipzig in November 1907 but he did not succeed in winning over the public to Sibelius's cause. The two middle movements were greeted by applause but the silence after the two outer movements was deafening. The critics, with Walter Niemann at their head, advanced the thesis that Sibelius was not really a symphonist, and had Nikisch thought of Leipzig as the springboard for a Sibelius campaign, then he was well and truly disappointed. Things were a little better in Vienna when Weingartner conducted it. The critic of the *Neue Freie Presse* made the stock comparison with Grieg and Tchaikovsky but eventually put the inevitable question that arose in this part of the world: would Sibelius ever be admitted into the great European symphonic tradition? 'The music he now composes seems to us like a foreign national dish: one samples it with curiosity but feels no inclination to put it on one's own table.' When the symphony had been performed in Boston earlier in 1907 under no less a conductor than Karl Muck, its reception had been far more positive. 'Seldom does modern music speak so direct and immediate a language,' wrote Philip Hale in the *New York Herald Tribune*. According to Olin Downes, the First Symphony was sufficiently close to the musical climate of 1906–7 to be overrated, just

83

as in subsequent decades it was to be overshadowed by the Second and its successors.

Of Sibelius's more recent work, the Third Symphony had not proved to be the strong card for which he had hoped in Russia and Sweden, but in *Pohjola's Daughter* Sibelius knew that he possessed a trump, and one that should not be idly thrown away. And so it was with mixed feelings that he learned that Busoni was intending to conduct it at one of his New Music concerts on 3 January 1908 in Berlin. 'I am a little anxious about Busoni,' he wrote to Lienau. 'He is no great conductor and *Pohjola's Daughter* in particular calls for a really good one. May God prevent it from being placed at the beginning of the programme.' But Sibelius's prayer went unheard and *Pohjola's Daughter* acted as a warming-up piece before the Busoni Violin Concerto. Writing in the *Allgemeine Musik-Zeitung*, Paul Schwers expressed fears that things would go the same way for Sibelius as they had done for Grieg. 'I believe that it will be difficult for him to free himself from his native country soil . . . and if this proves to be the case, his art will lose its interest for the non-Finnish listener.' Under Busoni's baton, *Pohjola's Daughter* went virtually unnoticed in Berlin, almost as had Debussy's *Prélude à l'après-midi d'un faune* some years previously. Willy Burmester had been pressing Sibelius to mount a concert of his own in Berlin and with good reason. As things were, 1908 had begun with a fiasco, which was the first signal of a general decline in his prestige in the German-speaking world that was shortly to gather force.

Another source of anxiety and unpleasantness was his contract with Lienau. In November 1907, Sibelius had written to him, 'I am unhappy not to have sent you anything new. I am all the time in your debt for something from the previous year.' It became more obvious by the beginning of the new year that some change in the contract would have to be made sooner or later. Adolf Paul stepped in as an intermediary, as he had done with Breitkopf ten years before. Lienau wanted to reduce the amount of his advances, while Sibelius on his side wanted to bring down the number of works he had to deliver annually from four to two. There is no real reason why these two positions could not be reconciled. But Lienau went further: he demanded all rights in the works in question or alternatively Sibelius should receive a royalty only on the first and second editions. Having sold *Valse triste* on such poor terms, it is hardly surprising that Sibelius refused to countenance this suggestion, so the contract remained unchanged. But Lienau had gone to the brink of tolerance: Sibelius's words to Aino in February 1908 show the extent of his feelings: 'Above all, the condition about four works per year must be removed. Otherwise the only result will be hasty and shabby work.'

In going through Sibelius's papers for 1907, one finds remarkably few letters of a personal nature. All his correspondence seems exclusively centred on business matters, and there is no doubt that his relationship with

Lienau preoccupied him a good deal and consumed much of his psychic energies. It is unlike him to neglect writing home to Aino, but he wrote neither from Germany nor when he was on a visit to Turku at the beginning of November. As for Axel Carpelan, he received no word from Sibelius throughout the whole year, even though he remained on his side a prolific and faithful correspondent. He had given his reactions to *Pohjola's Daughter* ('much too short in design') and the Third Symphony, whose second movement

> sounded wonderful, like a child's prayer. The movement seems to me fully worthy of comparison with the *Allegretto* of Beethoven's Seventh. I want to live long enough to hear many more symphonies from Sib. The next will surely be visionary (the *Adagio* from Pavillon Henri IV)? Yet I have already heard so much wonderful music from you that all my dreams seem to have come true.

One cannot fail to be impressed by Carpelan's intuitive feeling for Sibelius the composer, for what is the next symphony (the Fourth) if it is not visionary!

Sibelius remembered to send Carpelan scores and complimentary tickets for his concerts. In 1906 the newly published *Pohjola's Daughter* was Carpelan's sole Christmas present but as the year wore on, he doubtless grew tired of the one-way dialogue and Sibelius's sloth in responding to his letters. He must have felt hurt and the autumn found him falling deeper and deeper into depression. In November while Jean was in St Petersburg, and some eleven years before his actual death, he wrote a farewell letter to Aino whose tone of self-pity and melodrama would strike one as absurd were it not for the appalling sense of loneliness and desolation it reveals.

> Please receive my warmest thanks for the score of the Third Symphony. It is probably the last I shall read, for soon, very soon, I will be gone to that bourn from which no traveller returns. My strength has been rapidly ebbing and day by day my tiredness increases so that I can scarcely hold myself upright. There is a great deal that I want to say but I do not have enough strength to write at length. I want to make my last farewell and to send you my infinite thanks for all the goodness and friendship which you have both given me, a friendship that has, if I may say so, brought light and joy to my last difficult years. I would like to do so infinitely more, but my powers and my capacity have been so small. I thank you for all the understanding and patience you have shown me. When I am no longer here, show Janne these lines. It is my wish that there should be no announcement of my passing in the papers, but you will have word by letter when the struggle is over. How life seems mysterious and dream-like and death so totally unfathomable; an unveiling of that reality that is limiting and illusory.

Carpelan lived for Sibelius and his moods were undoubtedly affected by him. They had met during the autumn concert season and one wonders whether Carpelan had suspected that something quite serious was wrong with Sibelius's health, and that this further intensified the death wish that seemed to dominate his psyche at this time.

At about the same time as Carpelan's letter arrived, Aino received two from her husband in St Petersburg, parts of which have already been quoted. In them he touches on his throat condition:

> I treated it twice yesterday, and today once. I spoke altogether without difficulty today. My voice is now altogether restored, and I am sure I have that treatment to thank for it. (I must confess that just at this moment I am smoking a cigar – and a good one at that! It is the first for a very long time, including the time I was in Turku – and I shall wait a long time before having another.)

Sibelius was suffering from hoarseness at the rehearsals but the treatment to which he refers makes it clear that this was no new phenomenon. The symptoms may well have appeared during a concert tour he made in Finland a year previously, since he mentions hoarseness in a letter home to Aino. In any event his health was quite a problem for him while he was in St Petersburg, and rumours about his condition soon spread rapidly, and as far as America.

After his return from St Petersburg he fell ill. In February 1908 we find him writing to Carpelan for the first time for over a year:

> You will be surprised to receive a letter from me. I have been ill with a severe bout of influenza, which took its toll on the nerves. Insomnia (!) etc. At last I have now had a glimpse of the hell that has plagued you all your life. Since we were last in touch – it was your last sad, tragic letter – I have gone through a lot. I dare say you have difficulty in making out my spidery hand. So I shall close my letter. Why should life be so difficult for those who love it so much. I shall go to London, if I am well enough, on the 20th. I am now working on incidental music to *Swanwhite* of Strindberg, and have many other plans, you will see. It will all be all right in the end: my finances are in a bad way, and my health too!

Sibelius was forced to call off concerts in Rome, Warsaw and Berlin. He presumably waited until the very last minute before putting off his visit to London for the second time and, as good fortune had it, he was sufficiently restored to make the journey and the score for *Swanwhite* had to wait. He stopped briefly in Stockholm where he met Armas Järnefelt who, after his experience with the Third Symphony, thought he would be better advised to play the Second in London. Sibelius on his part suspected that the Third's failure in Stockholm depended on Järnefelt who, he thought, had probably taken the second and third movements too fast. 'I shall play the new work: I believe in it.'

He reached London some hours earlier than he was expected, and Bantock waited in vain to meet him at Victoria station; he found him at a restaurant in Oxford Circus and while they lunched the band suddenly started to play. With a small smile Sibelius put his hand on Bantock's arm: 'They are playing my *Valse triste*. Isn't it strange that the very first music I should hear on reaching England is that?' His London début passed off smoothly enough, even if the Third Symphony. which was dedicated to Bantock, did not arouse great enthusiasm. Many newspapers wrote in the course of their reviews that Sibelius's themes derived from Finnish folk music but the press was full of good will. The *Musical Times* much admired its concise quality; *The Times* found the first movement a little contourless but thought the *Allegretto* and the finale had a more individual profile. As a conductor, Sibelius won great praise: the performance was described as brilliant, particularly the complex and demanding finale. Rosa Newmarch mentions that a string passage, apparently three bars for the first violins *divisi* and *con sordino*, on page 47 of the score and the corresponding passage on the following page, presented difficulties at the rehearsal and, according to her recollection, the passage was cut at the concert itself.

To Aino, he wrote:

Now it is all over. I had a great success here. I will tell you all about it when I come home. I have spent a few extra days in London to hear a big concert, which Wood has conducted. The programme was Bach (*Magnificat*), Debussy (*La damoiselle élue*) and Beethoven's Ninth. The choir numbered 1,200! I have been to dinner with Rosa Newmarch and to the Woods, and after the concert I was the guest of the Royal Philharmonic Society. I have been treated with much respect. The orchestra applauded me after the concert and the public was in ecstasies. It is strange that I have managed to get through everything . . .

And in a postscript, he adds that his hand is weak from conducting. An earlier letter from London finds him in equally good spirits:

My old passion for oysters returned today. That is a good sign and makes me feel young. I had begun to doubt whether my taste for them would ever return. I don't dare to bathe though. It might not turn out well.

For all the optimism of this letter, it is clear that something was weighing heavily on his mind and had taken the edge off his appetite for life. Mrs Newmarch noted.

The more often I met him, the greater store I set by his friendship, the greater respect I had for his independence as an artist and admiration for his courage as a person. At this time he was suffering from a painful throat condition.

Sibelius left London immediately after Henry Wood's concert. On the way home he stopped in Berlin; the intention was to try and arrive at an agreement with Lienau. But he never got as far as doing that, for he met there Axel Gallén and other 'dangerous countrymen' whose company he would have found too congenial! He left quickly for Stockholm, where he was interviewed by the *Svenska Dagbladet*'s columnist at the Metropol restaurant.

> The flowing artist's hair of former days has gone and the moustache is clipped in the American fashion. As a result his features appear more prominent, giving the impression that he is older. He is nervous and impatient, and bores a small pair of sharp eyes into anyone who dares look at him. There is a strange irregularity about the face, and it is difficult to determine how this arises, whether it is the mouth or the nose that is the cause. Perhaps it is just his nervous mouth, which he pinches together on the right-hand side, just as he speaks with only half of his mouth and then reveals only a half of his thoughts. And when he looks intently at the person he is talking to, five deep wrinkles appear between the eyebrows. There is something passionate about him and beside that a nervousness that it is impossible not to be influenced by. This in short is the outer face the great Finnish composer presents to the world.

Inevitably the restaurant band played *Valse triste* and afterwards everyone applauded, save for Sibelius.

On his return from England, work on the incidental music to *Swanwhite* took pride of place. The idea of writing this score arose as early as the spring of 1906. Harriet Bosse, August Strindberg's third wife, was then the Mélisande in the Helsinki production of Maeterlinck's play and was much taken with Sibelius's incidental music. So enthusiastic was she that she wrote to Strindberg asking if he would agree to Sibelius writing the music for the forthcoming première of *Swanwhite*. Harriet Bosse passed on Strindberg's reply at a dinner party and later confirmed 'the author's and my desire and hope that it will be agreeable to you to compose music for *Swanwhite*'. In the same letter she told the composer that Albert Ranft, the Swedish director, was proposing to mount a production in Stockholm the following season. Needless to say, Sibelius accepted the invitation with enthusiasm and subsequently wrote to Strindberg himself. The latter's reply ran as follows:

> In answer to your esteemed letter, I can inform you that I would most certainly like to have your music for *Swanwhite*, for you are the only one; but everything with Ranft is total uncertainty, so that I must ask you not to regard the commission as firm, before I have asked him to write to the publisher – Happy to have made your acquaintance, and in the hope that I shall one day see and hear you, I have the honour to send my greetings and warmest wishes. [1]

1 Dated 26 May 1906.

Sibelius was later to give two different versions of his reaction to this letter. He told his biographer, Ekman, in the 1930s that Strindberg had originally planned to compose the incidental music himself, but withdrew when he learned that Sibelius was working on the project. 'Strindberg informed me of this in a friendly letter, which I still have in my possession.' It would indeed appear that, as in many other instances in his conversations with Ekman, he relies exclusively on his memory. Possibly Harriet Bosse had told him that Strindberg was intending *to choose* the music for the play, as in fact he was to do for a production two years later. But twenty years later he told Hans Schmidt-Isserstedt quite a different story:

> Strindberg's play and his unusual personality fascinated me so deeply that I anxiously awaited an opportunity of getting in touch with him to connect my own composition to his play. I wanted to start an inspiring, all-consuming correspondence with the great poet. But from Strindberg there came an icy reply, almost an official letter, in which he at first touched on the practical limitations and the question of copyright – matters that I had given no thought to – and made no mention whatsoever of the purely artistic questions involved. I wrote the music; it was performed; but the poet never thought it worth mentioning.[1]

It is clear that Sibelius was disappointed (and hurt) that *Swanwhite* did not bring him in closer contact with Strindberg, and his confession to Schmidt-Isserstedt rings a good deal truer than his earlier utterance. But whatever his feelings may have been, it is wrong to shift the whole blame on to Strindberg's shoulders. Strindberg's letter was by no means a rebuff but left the way open for further contact. As early as the 1890s Strindberg was made aware of Sibelius, thanks to the efforts of Adolf Paul. Although by this time he was not on good terms with Paul, this did not appear to have swayed his feelings towards Sibelius, any more than the fact that he could speak of Finland as 'terrible' and 'dreary'. In any event Sibelius made no attempt to contact Strindberg for the next two years, and when he was in Stockholm made no effort to meet him.

Swanwhite was not produced during the 1906–7 Stockholm season. But the Swedish Theatre in Helsinki decided to mount it, and so its director, Wetzer, approached Sibelius during the summer of 1907 with a commission for incidental music. Strindberg was kept informed and during July wrote in haste to Harriet Bosse, 'Sibelius is now composing the music to *Swanwhite* and is overjoyed.' In actual fact Sibelius did not begin work on the score in earnest until the following year. During the spring of 1908, *Swanwhite* was at last put into rehearsal in Stockholm with Harriet Bosse in the leading role. The theatre wrote to Lienau for permission to perform the

1 Hans Schmidt-Isserstedt, 'Weite, Lieblichkeit, Trauer. Besuch bei Jean Sibelius', *Die Welt*, 8 December 1950.

Sibelius score, but in case this was not forthcoming or other difficulties came in the way, Strindberg himself gave directions for alternative incidental music for 'only horn and harp', recommending a harp piece by Adolphe Hasselmans.

But the rehearsals were abandoned and the play was not produced in Stockholm until much later. It was the Swedish Theatre in Helsinki that gave the première on 8 April 1908 with Sibelius's incidental music conducted by the composer. Afterwards Strindberg sent him a postcard with a portrait of himself, with the words: 'Master Sibelius, Thank you for your beautiful music you have written for my most beautiful poem. Soon I shall hear it!'

In fact Strindberg was never to do so. Sibelius replied by letter:

Thank you for your kind words about my music for the wonderful *Swanwhite*. I have always looked up to you. I pray that the music will succeed in coming close to your expectations, and – above all – will be reasonably well performed. In this respect I have painful memories of Stockholm. I would be willing to come over to Sweden, rehearse and conduct the music at the first performance if only I knew when it was to be. With grateful admiration,

Your Jean Sibelius.

Sibelius was obviously still eager to meet Strindberg but his letter could hardly have come at a more inauspicious time. After much suffering Strindberg was in the throes of ending his relationship with Harriet Bosse, who only a few days before the première had told him that she was leaving him for another. With this to preoccupy him, all he was prepared to do was to send a handshake, as it were, 'from the other side of the great waters that separate us' – the words he had written on his visiting card. Sibelius's admiration for Strindberg did not fail. After the concert version of *Swanwhite* was sent to Lienau, he wrote in answer to a query: 'If *Swanwhite* is to be dedicated to anyone, it is to Strindberg not Wood.' And it is evident from his diary that Strindberg's death in May 1912 greatly shook him.

Sibelius's score for the play comprises fourteen numbers for small orchestra, among them some short horn calls. For concert purposes he arranged a suite consisting of seven pieces, scored for a symphony orchestra, but with no brass other than four horns. The play itself is a symbolic fairy story of good triumphing over evil. The Princess Swanwhite breaks the spell of her stepmother, changes her into a force for good, and eventually succeeds in waking her prince from his long sleep!

There is an important harp part, hardly surprising given the fact that the instrument plays an important role in the fairy drama itself. The very opening number, *The Peacock* begins with a sustained triad that grows louder and then fades away, a musical symbol for the passing swan, who in reality is Swanwhite's dead mother. There is no want of poetic musical imagery with the oboes, clarinets and harp insistently repeating the peacock's cry on the note E. In the play Swanwhite's mother and Swanwhite herself are linked by the image of the self-playing harp. The movement called *The Harp* opens with a little prelude; the strings play a balletic *pizzicato* figure and the winds make soloistic entries almost in the manner we have come to associate with Prokofiev. One passage is incorporated from another section of the incidental music. Having dismissed her unprepossessing official suitor, the young King, Swanwhite awaits with her two faithful young maidens the arrival of the Prince, who must fly over the sea and face Death. The harp gives out a stately, subdued and melancholy theme to which the winds respond with an idea in parallel thirds whose rhythm anticipates the slow movement of the Fifth Symphony:

Ex 49

The harp spins its arpeggios around the *pizzicato* motive. This is one of Sibelius's most enchanting miniatures.

Best known is *The Maidens with roses*, a slow and melancholy waltz, which accompanies a ceremony in which the wicked stepmother tries to entice the prince with a false bride:

Ex 50

There is a charming scherzo, *Listen! The robin sings*, which describes the Princess's dreams about her Prince. The first idea is held together by a rising sequence, E flat–F–C, which later becomes a symbol of Swanwhite's and the Prince's love for each other, and is related to the rescue motive.

After *The Prince alone*, a dramatic monologue from the strings, comes *Swanwhite and the Prince*, which both thematically and harmonically offers a reminder of Rimsky-Korsakov. As so often is the case, when Sibelius allows the harmony to shift between major and minor over a pedal point that serves as tonic in the major and mediant in the minor, one feels an affinity with the young Russian school. The play ends with Swanwhite awakening the Prince from the dead by the power of love, and there is a *Song of Praise*, the final movement in the suite, which brings everything to a happy ending in the key of C major.

Although the influenza had taken its toll, Sibelius continued at his old hectic pace. Lienau suddenly telegraphed to tell him that unless he agreed to come to Berlin in April, to prepare and conduct the Third Symphony, the performance would not take place. Oscar Fried was proving difficult and did not really want to go ahead with it, and at this stage it would be impossible to find a substitute. Sibelius was so totally absorbed in *Swanwhite* at this time that he could not possibly make the journey. Indeed the Third Symphony was not to be played until two years later. Throughout April he was largely occupied with the performances of *Swanwhite*, many of which he conducted.

But on 10 May he wrote to Carpelan giving him his bad news. 'I have gone through a great deal. Tomorrow I am to have a throat operation.' A Helsinki specialist had confirmed that Sibelius had an incipient tumour in the throat, and on the 12th he underwent an operation. Presumably it was exploratory and a sample of the tumour was taken. Once the results of the operation were known, Sibelius was advised to go to a Berlin specialist, Fränkel, whose reputation at the time was second to none. The Finnish specialist's diagnosis was given to a German colleague by Christian Sibelius in case Fränkel was not available to deal with him personally.

> My brother, Jean Sibelius, has a tumour in his larynx. Part of the tumour in question has been removed by a colleague here. From what we can see, it would appear that the tumour is not malignant, even though it cannot be denied that there is a marked possibility of recidivity.[1]

Sibelius had no money for the journey. While still in London, he had written to Aino asking her to borrow against the security of his state pension, and his position had in no measure improved in the succeeding months. Lienau's 8,000 marks would have been eminently welcome, but he had not been able to maintain the agreed number of scores mentioned in the

1 Letter dated 21 May 1908 from Christian Sibelius to Dr Rosenbach.

contract. Three years had now passed since it had been signed and he should have delivered twelve works, but had now reached only the eighth, *Swanwhite*, and this was not yet ready to be sent off for printing. His usual sources of funds had learned of his ill-health and the rumours that he was doomed were rife. For them it was no longer worthwhile to lend him money and many of them turned their backs on him.

Together with Aino, he went to Helsinki and made a pilgrimage round the capital's banks, going from one to another with no result and ever lower spirits. At the end of their trek Aino sank on to a park bench at Henriksgatan, now Mannerheimvägen, which at that time was a tree-lined boulevard. But this time their fortunes at last changed. After hearing him out, the director of an insurance company had emptied the day's takings in his pocket without saying a word.

Sibelius arrived in Berlin at the end of May, and after his first consultation with his specialist, he wrote to his brother:

I have just returned from seeing Fränkel. He has examined my throat and the sample. He said very little except that a tumour was still there but, on account of the swelling in the throat, there was no alternative but to wait a little. In the morning I shall have to go back. He asked if I had written an opera. Thus has Elmgren (the Helsinki specialist) painted me. We had a good journey here.

He wrote again five days later on 1 June:

If only I could be sure that Fränkel is taking this seriously. But why should he not? But today he again postponed any decision until Wednesday. He said, 'I'll wait, for it sems to be getting better – but it could also worsen, or not.'[1] As far as my voice is concerned, he said that it will get better. Every time (five in all) he has looked thoroughly at my throat and on the last occasions also mentioned an operation. It is oppressively hot here and we long for home. Fränkel has forbidden me alcohol for the remainder of my days. As far as tobacco was concerned, he was not against 'very little', but it seems that I really have to give that up too. I have done so now for a month. Life is something totally different without these stimulants. I never imagined it could have come to this.

A letter to Axel Carpelan is dated the 10 June:

I don't know why my thoughts have turned to you almost every minute of the day, except that you could possibly be interested in news of my illness. It is not cancer as the doctors at home thought. They sent me to Europe's leading specialist, Dr Fränkel. I have been to see him nine times but so far he has not succeeded in getting to the bottom of the trouble.

1 'Es ist bedeutend besser wieder, ich will warten – es kann zurückgehen aber auch nicht.'

This throat business is a serious affair. Still, I suppose one has to die of something.

It is more likely that rather than having incipient cancer, he had a benign tumour in the vocal chords, which could possibly have presented hazards for the future in the sense that it might recur and assume a malignant form. In the 1930s he told Ekman that Fränkel had 'examined me thoroughly and diagnosed that it was not cancer but a difficult tumour that could easily be operated on'. Perhaps Fränkel's diagnosis, if Sibelius's recollection is accurate, was deliberately contradictory, since what is a 'difficult tumour' (and here one assumes the term to mean malignant rather than benign) if it is not the kind that in everyday parlance would be called a cancer? According to Sibelius's memoirs, Fränkel, who was a very old man, made no fewer than thirteen abortive attempts to remove it. Finally he sent for a young assistant, who in his turn continued the attempts until finally there was a triumphant cry and the offending growth was cut out. No doctor could have made a 100 per cent prognosis for his future progress, and for the next few years Sibelius lived in a danger zone.

As is so often the case, when confronted by a condition of this gravity, the patient rallies and pursues life with increased rather than diminished intensity, whereas minor ailments could reduce him to a total standstill. Without doubt, faced with the possibility of an early death, Sibelius redoubled his activity. At least in one respect the operation had a decisive effect on his way of life: for the next seven years he neither smoked nor drank. What Christian's and Carpelan's entreaties had failed to accomplish, his own fears for the recurrence of a throat cancer did. It transpired, moreover, that he was very well able to compose without the stimulus of wine and cigars. Many of his masterpieces, *Voces intimae*, the Fourth Symphony and the first draft of the Fifth, *The Bard*, *Luonnotar* and *The Oceanides* were all produced during his dry and smokeless period from 1908–15.

To make up for his failure to send new works to Lienau, Sibelius tried to tempt him with older pieces: *The Origin of Fire*; *Malinconia* (the fantasy for cello and piano) and the Romance in C, for string orchestra. But Lienau did not rise to the bait, and Sibelius asked him to return the scores. Something of his wounded self-confidence emerges from the lines that he sent Lienau on 9 July:

> My commitments concerning the delivery of new works will be fulfilled as well as I possibly can. But you must have a little patience with me. I shan't make any more promises for the rest of my life, but I shall willingly show you new works in the future. Naturally, you first.

He was still scarcely able to speak in the middle of July as a result of the operation. He writes to Christian with various news; two elks had passed barely a couple of metres from their steps at home, and rather more importantly, he mentions that he has just set Gripenberg's 'Teodora', which Aino Ackté was to sing that autumn. In actual fact, she did not include it in the programme but sang instead another work, 'Jubal' to words of Ernst Josephson. But after *Swanwhite*, he had a more important project in hand, the symphonic poem, *Night Ride and Sunrise*. It was virtually ready by November in spite of the fact that Sibelius was battling with financial worries that were becoming even more acute. Carpelan advised him to turn to the well-known tobacco magnate in Turku, Rettig. Sibelius replied:

Thanks for your kindness in thinking of me and the worst in me, my financial ruin. I have for a long time thought about the possibility of approaching Rettig – but I have lacked courage and my feelings of shame have not, as they have on many former occasions, been quelled. However, I had intended to follow your advice (not through the good offices of my friend Walter [von Konow] since the whole of Turku would know about it immediately) as it has always proved so good. [. . .] I am composing prolifically. I think that only now – since having given up alcohol and nicotine – have I been able to think and feel with proper intensity. My big symphonic poem is nearly ready, only a few pages are left to do. After this I shall turn with joy to something fresh. I have lots of plans.

The letter goes on to ask whether Carpelan indulges in betting, for he is bombarded with catalogues for raffles, lotteries, etc. 'A sure sign of coming doom.'

Earlier in the autumn, in September, Aino gave birth to another daughter, Margaretha. In spite of his financial problems, the family still maintained a certain style. They had a cook, a housekeeper, nurses, a gardener and part-time help, though Aino contributed towards keeping down their expenses by acting as their daughters' governess or teacher. The nursery served as a classroom and everyone was to be in their appointed place when she made her entrance at nine o'clock dressed in an austere dark frock: 'Now you must think of me not as your mother but as a teacher; you are my pupils.' In fact she saw to the education of all five daughters, in the case of Katarina right up to grammar-school level. Later on they were sent to schools in Helsinki, where they all did well, three of them completing their *studenten*; Ruth left school without taking it so as to make a career on the stage, while Heidi devoted her career to handicraft.

If Aino's time was taken up with teaching the children and occupying herself with the garden, she saw her main role in life as giving Sibelius all the help and support that she could. Alma Mahler once wrote of her husband, 'We were all slaves to his work' and to some extent the same holds true of the Sibelius household. Aino did her best to make the right working conditions for him, and if, for example, it was obvious that his thoughts were on some musical idea over his breakfast coffee, she refrained from

95

engaging him in conversation. As he was highly sensitive to the slightest sound, no one was allowed to play an instrument in the house without his consent. A note in his diary makes this clear, 'I let Kaj [Katarina] play a couple of hours for Martha's [her piano teacher] sake.' The daughters did have an instrument for a time but for the most part they had to practise at neighbours' houses. Aino would help with correcting proofs of the piano music and would occasionally play duets with him but whatever store he set by her intelligence, he did not like her to draw too much attention to herself when they were in company. On those occasions he liked to dominate the centre of the stage and became distinctly put out if the focus of attention shifted in her direction. On the whole she willingly remained in the background, particularly as he had always behaved in a considerate and loving way towards her. One of the memories that haunted her last years, for she lived to her late nineties, was the way in which he always approached her with open arms.

As was the case in the Järnefelt household, family disputes were always carried out behind closed doors, and none of the servants could ever recall any instance of raised voices. This would be wholly in keeping with Aino's character since hers was a more introspective, pessimistic nature. Sibelius on the other hand could flare up but his temper quickly subsided. Once, when his daughter Ruth had been having what he thought was far too long a telephone conversation with an admirer, he suddenly had a bout of temper and tore the phone from the wall and stamped on it. But this was very much the exception rather than the rule; on the whole he was a charming despot. If he heard voices from the nursery when he was composing during the night, he would tiptoe there, not to remonstrate but to take sandwiches which he made in the kitchen.

By the end of November 1908, Sibelius sent the manuscript of *Night Ride and Sunrise* to Siloti in St Petersburg, and immediately afterwards started work on the string quartet that was to be called *Voces intimae*. Perhaps the thought that life hung by a thread prompted his introspective direction, which found a more appropriate outlet in a chamber-music form. He possibly remembered Lienau's suggestion that he compose a chamber piece for a not-too-large combination. On his birthday on 8 December, he wrote to Carpelan telling him that he hoped to have the quartet ready within a month,

Otherwise everything will go to the devil. My debts are frightening. And if I don't soon make any money, I don't know how I shall manage. (I always swear when I work myself up in letters.) We will see how things go with my throat. If it stays as it is, or the terrible process starts all over again. I have keen hypochondriac twinges, but that is hardly to be wondered at.

A week or so later, he wrote again to Carpelan sketching the beginning of the quartet in his letter.

You can imagine my feelings now that I have worked out what my debts are likely to be in three or four weeks' time! Think of the peace of mind it gives you when you are trying to work! I have just been to see my two smallest, Kaj and Margaretha. They were asleep. Life is before them. This wonderful life that one loves and yet that is so difficult to live. Astronomy is the best solution for worries about money: 2,000 light years!! 2,000 in a private bank! What the devil does it all matter!

On Christmas Eve, he wrote to Lienau promising him imminent delivery of the new quartet, adding that by 'imminent, I don't mean six months.' In point of fact, however, it was to be a further three months before he put the final touches to the work. Meanwhile, at the beginning of the new year, *Night Ride and Sunrise* was due for its première in St Petersburg. Sibelius did not go there himself and entrusted Siloti with the performance. The whole episode started off on the wrong foot. Earlier in the autumn Sibelius had written to ask if he might dedicate the tone poem to Madame Siloti but at the same time added that perhaps it was not a sufficiently luminous score to harmonize with her personality. She answered that she was most honoured and happy, but would be perfectly happy to wait until he wrote another piece which suited her personality better, and therefore she would think it quite reasonable if he were to dedicate *Night Ride and Sunrise* to some other person. After this inauspicious start, Sibelius waited for news of its reception, but the congratulatory telegram never came. Instead a few days after the performance Siloti sent him a letter, somewhat apologetic and defensive in tone, announcing that he had made cuts in the score.

I knew that you would never forgive me for doing this. But in any event I did it – and after the performance – I am of the opinion that as a musician I did the right thing in principle, even if I can question whether I made the cuts in the right way. The tempo marking *allegro commodo* I changed to *allegro vivace*. Even Glazunov liked the piece (he told me at the rehearsal) and said it was 'a very beautiful composition'. César Cui did not like it (which is almost a compliment in itself).

Even though Siloti maintained that he liked the piece himself, it is clear that he does not seem to have grasped it but gave, according to one source, 'a slack and monotonous' reading.

In any event the St Petersburg press, with the exception of *Novy Russ*, was uniformly hostile. Between the fiascos of St Petersburg and Busoni's performance of *Pohjola's Daughter* in Berlin came yet another in New York. The Third Symphony was given by the Russian Symphony Orchestra conducted by Modest Altschuler and was coolly received. Henry Krehbiel in the *New York Herald Tribune* thought that Sibelius would go down in history as a composer of only one really characteristic work, namely the First Symphony, and complained of the poverty of invention and thinness that characterized the new work. He went so far as to say that there was not one theme of real power or beauty, not one single episode where one could discern a musical truth worth committing to paper. Krehbiel wondered whether Sibelius's ill-health could have had this adverse effect on his creative powers. It was small comfort that Max Fiedler who had succeeded Karl Muck in Boston had a success with a performance of *Spring Song* and *Finlandia*, which he billed 'Song of Finland'!

Generally speaking, Niemann's thesis that Sibelius was not basically a symphonist held wide currency at the time in Germany but one dissenting voice was raised, and this from the conductor and writer on music, Göhler, who hailed from Munich. He carefully analysed the difficulties that faced a Sibelius interpreter, the complex form, the difficult recitative-like and episodic passages, the special sonority of the scoring and the colour of northern folk influences and so on. He argued that Sibelius's highly personal music 'makes us feel that the eleventh hour has not yet struck for that art whose greatest master was Beethoven'. But his plea for more German performances of the symphonies fell on deaf ears.

'Jubal' and 'Teodora' share the same opus number, – 35 – for reasons that will be gone into later, and form a contrasting pair. The former is spacious in texture and predominantly diatonic while the later is more complex in its musical means: indeed 'Teodora' approaches a kind of expressionistic *Sprechgesang*, and its poem has a Wildean decadence. Both must be numbered among the very finest of Sibelius's songs.

The poet of 'Jubal' was Ernst Josephson, who was not only a fine poet but one of the greatest painters of his day. The youthful Jubal has slain a swan with his arrow as the sun is setting, and with his dying song –

> . . . what beautiful tone,
> youth, from thy bow intoned
> when you cruelly felled me

– initiates Jubal into the mysteries of music. He puts string after string on his lyre and returns each evening to sing of the swan's death. During the period of his mental breakdown and slow recovery Josephson made a large number of line drawings that have great classical purity, and it is even said that Picasso was at one stage influenced by him. One of these drawings is on this same theme of Jubal playing his lyre at sunset. It is possible though not very likely that Sibelius also knew the picture when he wrote his song in 1908.

Contrary to what one would expect, it is not the suffering of the swan that preoccupies Sibelius but rather the hapless youth's glorious initiation into music's mysteries. The opening recitative describes the swan's flight in expressive arches, the sparse harmonic support giving a sense of space:

Ex 51 'Jubal saw a swan flying over the waters high into the sky'

With next section in B flat major, marked *tempo giusto*, we come to the narrative element. The innocent Jubal allows his cheek to be caressed by a gentle melodic breeze in the setting sun. The vibrations of his bow string or perhaps the reflected rays of the sun, of which the poem speaks, shimmer in the accompaniment:

Ex 52

The recitative and *tempo giusto* alternate until the ecstatic climax at Jubal's cry, 'Swan, white swan, every sunset I shall return.' The final section in B flat minor mingles the joy of his initiation into the mysteries of music with his melancholy at the swan's fate.

Gripenberg's 'Teodora' had its origins some five years earlier when the Norwegian actress Johanne Dybwad recited Gripenberg's poem to an improvised accompaniment by Sibelius. When he came to set the poem later, he undoubtedly had in mind this improvised melodrama. The melodic line is based on the scale of D sharp minor, which is chromatically undermined to such an extent that the listener could easily lose his sense of a tonal anchorage if there wasn't a persistent reminder in the bass:

Ex 53 'There is a rustling of silks, a shining of rubies'

The insistent B, the submediant, almost has the force of the dominant. Next time the strophe quoted above is varied with an almost oriental melisma:

Ex 54 'She is coming, the Empress, she approaches in the shimmering, trembling light of the full moon.'

The decadence of 'Teodora' is conveyed by the simplest of means: an ostinato formula and wind-like figuration on the piano, while two ideas are contrasted and varied in the solo voice part.

Sibelius discussed the background to *Night Ride and Sunrise* on a number of occasions. Rosa Newmarch[1] recalled that he had asked her as early as 1909 whether she thought the title wisely chosen; he feared that it might lead people to expect the kind of pale programme piece that had gained

1 Rosa Newmarch, *Jean Sibelius: a Short History of a Long Friendship*, Boston, 1939, p. 47.

currency in Joseph Raff's day whereas his real intentions had been to conjure up the inner feelings of an ordinary man riding along through the darkness of the forests. He is glad to be close to nature; he is awed by the moment of stillness at dawn; he is full of gratitude and joy at the sight of the sunrise.

It is perhaps not too fanciful to imagine that joy at the prospect of the arrival of each new day was highly congenial given the psychic shock of his operation. Some years before his death Sibelius discussed *Night Ride and Sunrise* with his secretary, Santeri Levas, and told him how he had once taken a horse-driven sledge from Helsinki to Kervo at some time around the turn of the century, and experienced an unforgettable sunrise: 'The whole heavens were a sea of colours that shifted and flowed producing the most inspiring sight until it all ended in a growing light.'[1] Earlier he had told Ekman that the main idea of the work had come to him in Rome in the spring of 1901, when first he set eyes on the Colosseum, and although there is no specific evidence in the sketches to this effect, there is no reason to doubt it. Sibelius's ideas often matured slowly over a long period of time: among the sketches written in Italy that spring was a theme later used in *Pohjola's Daughter*. In any event what he told Levas and Ekman need not be contradictory; the one could have given an unconscious impulse to the other. After a sledge journey in central Finland from Kuhmois to Orivesi, Sibelius noted in his diary, 'Strange that on my Night Ride on the 25th, only insignificant scraps of melody played in my mind' (July 1912), a clear indication perhaps that his earlier trip was different in this respect.

Night Ride and Sunrise is perhaps less immediately appealing than any of its predecessors. It is less designed to beguile the ear with beauty of incident and, specially in the ride itself, the orchestration is more directed at making rhythmic points rather than expressive sonority. Of course, there are many characteristic touches; violin cantilenas of the kind we encounter in the symphonies, however, are absent but the brass is rich and sonorous. The percussion is numerous for Sibelius: side-drum, tambourines, bass drum and timpani, give the work an unusual dimension, but by excluding the harp Sibelius deprives himself of many possibilities of impressionistic detail.

The tone poem falls into the two sections implied by the title. The 'Ride' is a rondo-like *allegro* (A–B–A,–B,) linked by an inspired transition episode to the 'Sunrise', a *largo* dominated by two themes. After a dissonant, abrupt opening we are instantly plunged into the trochaic rhythm of the ride, first on violas and cellos, and then on other strings:

1 Santeri Levas, *Nuori Sibelius* Volume II, pp. 55–6.

Ex 55

The basic rhythm remains unchanged but the musical landscape is varied both harmonically and melodically. At first the horses' hooves sound remote, *dolcissimo*; then they emerge into the foreground, only to disappear again *sul ponticello*, when the side-drum marks the basic rhythm *ppp*. In the *moderato assai* section Sibelius makes a magical shift in the aural perspective: the trochaic movement recedes into the background and a second subject, related to the riding figure of the *allegro*, assumes the centre of the stage:

Ex 56

The *allegro* can be thought to present an objective picture of the rider and his inner thoughts. But in the *moderato assai* section subjective fears and menacing nocturnal voices pursue him. The idea is heard in the wind two octaves apart before the listener's interest is focused again on the trochaic rhythm, which slowly changes to semiquavers.

The second subject returns on the strings and blends with the woodwind semiquavers, the spiritualized 'ride' motive, to magical effect. The whole texture comes to life, glowing in a great pantheistic outburst:

Ex 57

But as the transition episode begins, this second theme is heard on the strings alone in a richly eloquent form:

Ex 58

It is as if this is Man's plea to the powers of Nature or alternatively their final assertion of their majesty. But now the fears of the night begin to lose their hold of the rider, and the Nordic dawn breaks. The woodwind twitterings could be thought of as the first bird calls of the day while the high string note and the accompanying tremolo is the first light on the dawn horizon. On the woodwind there is a theme distinguished by a graceful triplet idea, which again derives from the second subject of the ride itself:

Ex 59

Gradually the heavens begin to glow and the horns intone a hymnlike figure that looks forward both in terms of character and tonality, E flat, to the Fifth Symphony.

Ex 60

In some ways it could be thought of as a kind of *heiliger Dankgesang*. But equally its descriptive eloquence points to the slowly rising sun flooding the landscape with its rays. The awakening of nature is reflected by the more richly coloured orchestration with the brass occupying the centre of the spectrum. Finally, the sun rises above the horizon and fills the landscape with cascades of light.

Ex 61

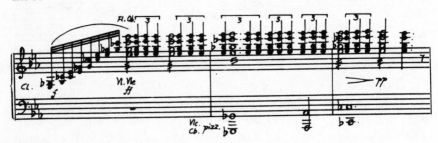

This sunrise does not possess the rich vibrant colours of Central Europe but rather the pale northern light, poorer in overtones yet stronger in definition and transition from one colour to another. This is a kind of natural, primitive impressionism but it is far from that of Debussy – a reflection perhaps of the Scandinavian worship of light.

CHAPTER FIVE

Voces intimae

Before Sibelius could put the finishing touches to *Voces intimae*, the time had come for another guest appearance in London. On 13 February 1909 he conducted performances of *En Saga* and *Finlandia* at a Queen's Hall concert. As he stepped down from the rostrum he heard Henry Wood exclaim 'Splendid!' and his letter home to Aino radiates his success.

It is all over now. Everything went well. The concert was at three o'clock, and I had to appear in morning dress with light-striped trousers. They are the fashion now; last autumn it was dark stripes! Everyone has been very complimentary. After the *Saga* I was called back to the podium seven times, and after *Finlandia* many more times. The orchestra is altogether perfect. They all stood up as I made my entrance, which is the greatest honour I have ever been paid! The hall was sold out. Tomorrow I am going to Rosa Newmarch for lunch and the day after to Wood. On the 16th there is to be a soirée in my honour and Bantock will be there. He now has an important position here. University professor. Everyone else gets positions; only I compose and live in my moods and dreams. It was so pleasant to be sober for once when I conducted. All my nervousness has gone. I conducted really well, people said. The *Saga* even prompted tears here and there among my admirers. I am thinking of staying here to work. This London is something magnificent. I have explored the city, the British Museum and so on.

Sibelius's friends organized receptions, which set off a chain reaction. Rosa Newmarch was feverishly introducing him to influential members of the aristocracy, but he was thoroughly enjoying it all. 'I was invited to dinner with Lady Wakefield, Lady Burton (formerly Princess of Anhalt) together with Rosa N., all in full gala dress studded with jewellery. Rosa N., who is an aristocrat of the purest water, was similarly clad and bore a large diamond on her breast.' Mary Wakefield was now approaching her sixties and had known both John Ruskin and Grieg and, as Rosa Newmarch recorded in her memoir of the singer, Sibelius's songs struck a particularly responsive chord in her: 'How she would have sung them twenty years earlier.'

Among others, Sibelius met Alexander Siloti, who tried to lure him to Edinburgh. Sibelius later regretted not having gone, but he did however make a trip to Cheltenham, a thriving musical centre at the time. A measure of the recognition that was becoming his due was the fact that Ernest Newman included Sibelius among the leading modern composers on whom he was lecturing at Birmingham University: Grieg, Hugo Wolf, Debussy, Richard Strauss and, on 27 March, Sibelius.

Less happy was Sibelius's appearance at the Music Club, whose membership comprised largely well-off elderly gentlemen with double chins and asthmatic coughs, together with their expensively bejewelled and fur-clad wives. However, many influential people in the musical world were members, Arnold Bax, Eugene Goossens and Edwin Evans, while the Chairman was the critic Alfred Kalisch. It was their custom to invite various celebrities, and in 1909 their guests of honour included Sibelius, Debussy, d'Indy and Schoenberg. The ritual was unvaried. First the composer of the evening was seated in the middle of the stage where he was harangued by the Chairman. After this he took his place among the audience to listen to some of his own chamber and instrumental music, after which the proceedings were concluded by a dinner in his honour. In his letters home Sibelius did not dwell on the occasion, which does not appear to have been a success. 'Ellen Beck sang some of my songs – really well' was all he reported to Aino. Beck was a Danish singer who had given *The Ferryman's Brides* in Helsinki, and whose repertoire included such songs as 'The Tryst' and 'Black roses', which she would have presumably included on this occasion. But this was not the kind of music that the Music Club would have expected, and the whole event seems to have been casually planned. Arnold Bax described the occasion in his memoirs:[1]

> The massive, bald-headed titan of the later years, suggesting an embodiment of one of the primeval forces that pervade the *Kalevala*, can at whim transform himself into a purveyor of farcical fun and Rabelaisian joviality. But the earlier Sibelius gave one the notion that he had never laughed in his life, and never could. That strong taut frame, those cold steel-blue eyes and hard-lipped mouth, were those of a Viking raider, insensible to scruple, tenderness or humour of any sort. An arresting, formidable-looking fellow, born of dark rock and northern forest, yet somehow only half the size of the capricious old Colossus of today.
>
> Such was his outward semblance, but can it be that on that evening of his London reception he was hag-ridden by an artistic conscience? As they had pledged themselves to an evening of Sibelius's smaller works, and since there was nothing better to be performed, they may be charged

1 *Farewell, My Youth!*, London, 1943, pp. 61–2.

with carelessly taking a chance with a growing reputation in that they did not first find out whether there was any chamber music of the composer's worth listening to. I believe that this lamentable affair was a serious setback to the acceptance in England of Sibelius's best work, and delayed the recognition of the grandeur of the later symphonies for several years.

Fortunately for Sibelius, he had a success with a soirée given in his honour by Lady Bective, who forty years earlier had been one of the most sought after beauties in London and, so he was given to understand, a friend of the Emperor Napoleon III. During the evening Henry Wood's wife sang some of the songs, including 'Jubal', which Sibelius dedicated to her. 'I had a marvellous time. There were two tenors who also sang some of my songs. We left her Ladyship at three in the morning in the highest good spirits, and all this without my having had any alcohol or smoked.'

Debussy's and Sibelius's paths had almost crossed in 1908 when they had both visited London to conduct their own works. Debussy had conducted his *Prélude à l'après-midi d'un faune* and *La Mer* on 1 February while Sibelius gave his Third Symphony later the same month, though it was Debussy who was given greater attention by the press. The *Musical Times* devoted a leading article to him and published his portrait. But a year later they actually did meet at a Queen's Hall concert on 27 February when Debussy was conducting the inevitable *Faune* and his three *Nocturnes*.

Sibelius was in the audience, presumably as the guest of Henry Wood, and should have been able to see that as a conductor he more than held his own with his French colleague. Henry Wood recalled that at one tempo change in *Fêtes*, Debussy lost his beat and his nerve, and tapped the desk with his baton as a signal to start again but the orchestra took no notice and went on playing. At the end the audience, having observed Debussy's difficulties, applauded so enthusiastically that *Fêtes* had to be repeated. Sibelius went and paid his respects to Debussy in the artists' room after the concert and, judging from one of his letters, it would seem highly probable that he was present also at the Music Club's Debussy evening. He would have witnessed the great French composer's discomfort as he endured what Sibelius himself had suffered, sitting on the stage, the victim of the public gaze and of Kalisch's mumblings in barely comprehensible French. Debussy declared himself ready to write a symphony rather than go through that ordeal again.

As Sibelius's French was fairly limited, their conversation would not have gone beyond the usual pleasantries. According to one of Sibelius's diary entries, they exchanged compliments and he told Aino in a subsequent letter that he felt an immediate contact with him. Debussy's compliments appear to have given him pleasure: presumably the French master could not have avoided hearing *Valse triste* and it is possible that he heard Chevillard conduct *The Swan of Tuonela* in Paris during the autumn of 1905, just before the première of *La Mer*. He ought to have found them temperamentally more congenial than Strauss's tone poems, even if he had gone so far as to declare *Ein Heldenleben* a work of near genius. He had not found Strauss himself congenial company when they had met three years earlier in Paris; he had only discussed royalties and other business matters and Debussy, who was wrestling with an ever-mounting burden of debt, relapsed into deep silence. Sibelius, on the other hand, had none of the self-confidence and the dominant personality that wealth can bring in its train, and his sensitivity and bearing ought to have appealed to Debussy.

On his side Sibelius clearly responded to the man himself: the searching soulful expression, the beguiling voice with its viola-like timbre, the powerful, almost Egyptian cranium and the olive complexion, which was said to have a Moorish quality. In a letter to Aino he had spoken of Debussy having a peasant-like appearance thanks to his woollen cuffs but *quel paysan!* One wonders whether in fact he had any idea of Debussy's problems and circumstances. In spite of his own debts Sibelius enjoyed a much more privileged position in his own country where class differences were less marked than in France with its aristocracy and rich bourgeoisie. Sibelius, like Grieg in Norway, enjoyed a special social status and when he conducted abroad, be it in Berlin, London or St Petersburg, he appeared not only as an artist in his own right but as a national figure. Hence, when he encountered Debussy, who did not enjoy these advantages and yet had greater renown than he, his reactions were complex and added fuel to his self-doubts.

What impression did Debussy's music make on him? Four years earlier he had recommended Kajanus to take up the *Nocturnes*; now, it would seem that his reactions were a little more reserved. But perhaps, as in so many other instances, he was merely hiding his innermost feelings, even from himself. Two days later we find him writing again to Aino,

I have something altogether new to say in my music. You will see. Have been cut off for too long and came away from Finland in the nick of time. It is absolutely vital for me to be abroad now. My artistic development necessitates it.

Obviously Sibelius is justifying living in relative luxury in London, while Aino is doing her best to make ends meet in Järvenpää. But the kernel of his argument was that London was bringing him into contact with new stimuli. To Carpelan he writes:

I have seen and heard much here. It has done me a great deal of good – things that weren't clear to me before are so now. My personal meetings with Debussy and d'Indy, Bantock, [Richard] Barth and [Benjamin] Dale and other composers, together with many new works, among them Elgar's new symphony[1] which I shall tell you about when we meet – also Bantock's *Omar Khayyám*, Debussy's new songs and the orchestral

1 Symphony No. 1. *Tr*

Nocturnes, etc., have all confirmed my thoughts about the path I have taken, take and have to take.'

Unfortunately his impressions are not further documented but he returns to Debussy on a number of occasions. In August 1911 the Swedish-language Helsinki daily, *Hufvudstadsbladet* printed Debussy's article on 'Taste in Music' which, judging from a diary entry, Sibelius thought 'remarkable'. After visiting the Norwegian National Gallery in Christiania (Oslo), he noted, 'There are many good things here even if they are clearly influenced by French art (in particular Matisse). What power French art has over the senses. The same with Debussy in music.' In his diary entries he hardly ever mentions other composers, which lends special significance to the fact that Debussy is an exception., 'Studied Rachmaninov and Debussy,' reads one entry;[1] 'Heard Debussy's G minor Quartet. A small-scale composer. Refined, but in my view, small-scale.'[2] But when, in January 1914, he heard some Debussy including 'La fille aux cheveux de lin' and *L'Ile joyeuse* at a Berlin piano recital, he thought that something big and important was beginning to emerge. In the exchange recorded by Bengt von Törne in his book, *Sibelius: A Close-up*, one suspects that he put his own words into Sibelius's mouth (Debussy was 'lacking in depth and greatness') or at least put a high gloss on their conversation. More revealing are his remarks to Walter Legge, which show the reality of his admiration: 'I do not care for the piano – it is an unsatisfying, ungrateful instrument, which only one composer, Chopin, has fully succeeded in mastering, and two others, Debussy and Schumann, have come on intimate terms.'[3]

While he was in London Sibelius began keeping a diary, at first 'almost as a game'. However, two thick notebooks survive: the first covers the period from February 1909 up to the end of 1913, while the second extends over a much longer period from August 1914 through to the 1940s. During the spring of 1914 he also made some loose-leaf entries. Up until 1920 the diary entries are relatively frequent but fall off dramatically during the succeeding decade while there are only one or two jottings during the 1930s and 1940s.

A variety of factors may have prompted this impulse to turn diarist at the age of 43. The threat of cancer undoubtedly heightened his feeling of life's evanescence, and the importance of capturing ideas on paper. At times his diary became a surrogate for his cigars and burgundy. After his operation and his enforced teetotalism we find an entry: 'Don't give in to tobacco or alcohol. Better to write rubbish in your "diary". Confide your miseries to paper. In the long run it's better so! Yes – in the long run.'[4] The diary also served other functions as a kind of safety valve: 'I will soon have written

1 29 June 1910.
2 21 October 1910.
3 'Conversations with Sibelius.' *Musical Times*, March 1953, pp. 218–20
4 31 August 1911.

myself out of a heavy and depressing mood. So this diary has its uses. And what? It serves the role of a good and intimate friend.' Sibelius may have thought that keeping a diary was part of the image of an established composer. Or, of course, there need not necessarily be a rational explanation for this sudden impulse to start a diary.

Naturally, Sibelius's diary jottings are open to the charge of egocentricity. They concentrate on his own moods, his composing, his responses to nature, business matters and so on; they are relatively little concerned with his relationships with other people and even less with the world of music, books and politics. Only occasionally does he touch on the music of his contemporaries. It is not easy to decide the extent to which Sibelius kept his diary for himself or posterity. One is intrigued to note the following: 'This diary is only for my eyes and Aino's – and possibly one other person's.' With this possibility in mind he has occasionally toned down or even taken back some harsh comments, as, for example, was the case with Busoni's music about which he wrote unfavourably and to which is added in a different pen and thicker script, 'Judgement on Busoni not to be taken too seriously. Told B. something different.' Here and there, a few words have been inked over, rubbed out or even cut out with scissors. In most cases these are usually obvious absurdities or embarrassing outbursts: thoughts of suicide, depression on account of marital problems or squabbles, or – *mirabile dictu* – regrets at not having been born into the nobility, for the most part things that must have struck him as ridiculous the instant he committed them to paper. But the mere fact that he poured all this willy-nilly into his diaries shows a spontaneous and uninhibited desire to give expression to *much* that went on inside his mind, without the thought of posterity looking over his shoulder. Much, but not all, of course: 'My innermost self is something I could never confide to paper. It remains my *jardin secret.*'

One must be on one's guard too. Many of the views it expresses were formulated in the heat of the moment and do not represent a considered position that he would have been prepared to defend later. His state of mind was constantly shifting, and this volatile temperament could find him one day plunged into the depths of despair and depression, only to emerge the next in excellent spirits. But even if he had on occasion touched on his longing for death, there is no reason to believe that he ever seriously contemplated suicide. Many such entries strike a pose, not so much for the benefit of others but for his own eyes. Even in childhood he had been self-regarding.

The first notebook and the earliest part of the second give a relatively complete picture of Sibelius's state of mind in so far as there are entries on both black and bright days, so that depressions, anxieties and so on mingle freely with exultant moments. However, from about 1917 onwards, the tones of the picture darken and Sibelius concentrates more and more on the days of anguish and pessimism, while the days in which he is in high spirits are passed unnoticed. Entries about his composing grow sketchier during the earlier 1920s and virtually peter out, while their place is taken by all manner of trivia that has agitated him. Indeed some passages justify his own description of his diary as 'the mirror of a sensitive being or, if you prefer, *crachoir*'.

By way of introduction to the venture, he drew up a list of his cash commitments, over thirty in number and totalling almost 53,000 marks, no small sum. These black economic clouds hung over Sibelius throughout his stay in London. Against this darkening background and the need for money at home, all his 'high life' assumed an unreal, almost unpleasant dimension. All he could do was to exhort Aino to be of good heart and keep up her spirits.

My work is going well. I'm writing energetically. If they try and frighten you with their bills and such like, send them packing. Tell them I am not home and don't concern myself with their bagatelles. Remember that!

From this distance I have a much better perspective about everything. Above all, see what a superb wife and mother you are. There aren't many with your frail (yet at the same time tough) constitution who could manage so astonishingly well, given our up-to-the-present hardly brilliant management of money. Even if I have to fashion my own destiny, to which you in your love have bound yourself, it is still easier for me with the prospects I already have than it is for many others. Besides, 's'il ne faut pas trop espérer de la vie, il ne faut rien craindre.' There's a lot of truth in that! I've understood your courage in that way too. You have chosen to share this composer-fate with me, who has returned you a good deal of pain, but who has never loved any but you, so we are both in need of help. Wandering hand in hand along strangely lit, hazy and rugged paths. Up and up, higher to the light and wide vistas – grand contours. Ah! yes, if only one could always see the grand design in things.

Mrs Newmarch was well aware of Sibelius's precarious economy and made oblique approaches to bring Sibelius together with Sir Edgar Speyer, one of the great patrons of music in London, who had among other things financed Debussy's guest appeareance in London. 'Sir Speyer has 300 million francs!' Sibelius exclaimed a shade expectantly. But Mrs Newmarch's stratagem came to nothing.

Meanwhile Sibelius was plagued by other fears: namely, the recurrence of his throat tumours. The London fog had made him a bit hoarse and he developed, as he put it with a touch of self-irony, 'a hypochondriac cough'. 'But if only I could be sure about my throat. Specialists here charge £10 for every consultation. Admittedly I have the money – but . . .' In the event, Mrs Newmarch's son, whose medical studies were nearing completion, looked after him. Nothing, however, was allowed to get in the way of composition. In mid-February he took up the string quartet again. A diary entry for the 18th shows him resuming work on what he calls the second movement but what was in fact the third, since he repeatedly refers to the second as I½! By the 25th, work on both the second and third movements, as we know them, was well advanced. So that he could work undisturbed, he moved from his hotel to a private house in Gloucester Walk. The room itself was attractive and pleasant but he soon had an unwelcome surprise: 'In the neighbouring house there are sounds of someone practising. I can hear it faintly!!! We'll have to wait and see how long the damned Englishwoman carries on.' The 'Moonlight' Sonata, butchered by the 'witch next door', soon drove Sibelius out, and he took refuge in a new flat at Gordon Place in Kensington. In her book Mrs Newmarch records that he was working hard at this time, usually spending the whole day at his desk and relaxing with friends in the evening. He rarely seemed depressed or irritable, though there were days when he felt a little below par, and when nothing save strong coffee could replace the forbidden cigars, and no subject, apart from astronomy, could distract him from himself.

Things were beginning to move as far as his publishing problems were concerned. Breitkopf's representative in London, Mr Kling, made approaches to him and sensed that this might be the psychological moment to win him back. The head of Breitkopf, von Hase, came to London in person and gave a lunch for Sibelius and his English friends. Sibelius wrote home: 'Breitkopf seems to want me quite badly. We'll have to see what Schlesinger [Lienau] says.' In actual fact Sibelius had already made up his mind not to renew his contract with Lienau.

But he was beginning to tire of London and imagined that certain hands were raised against him. Bantock conducted the second part of his *Omar Khayyám*, and Sibelius went to wish him good luck. Yet he began to wonder whether Bantock's attitude was quite the same as it had been in the past: 'Perhaps some of my enemies have been making mischief for him. But in any event he has invited me to conduct a whole concert of my music in Birmingham,' he reports to Aino. His diary reveals those he took to be enemies at this time: 'that snake Delius' was one. 'But my heart bleeds about Bantock; I never imagined that I would lose him of all people. Destiny gradually catches up on me: alone, penniless, disgraced and miserable.'

There seem few grounds for believing that there was any substance in Sibelius's misgivings. On the contrary, Bantock had only recently conducted the Third Symphony and was to remain a firm friend and champion. It is true that Delius expressed himself both appreciatively and critically, as he did about other composers, but again there is nothing to suggest that he cherished any personal animus against his Finnish colleague. Speaking of the 1912 Birmingham Festival he was far from negative: 'There was the occasion when they did *Sea Drift* and Sibelius came specially to conduct a new work, the Fourth Symphony – fine music with a genuine feeling for nature. I like Sibelius, he is a splendid fellow. I'd often met him at Busoni's.'[1] Perhaps his encounter with Delius at the time of Busoni's somewhat unhappy Berlin concert of 1902, at which *En Saga* and *Paris* had been performed, left an unpleasant aftertaste. Besides, Sibelius was well aware of the fact that he was not the easiest person to deal with: 'I find it difficult these days to be "modest" and "humble", which is no doubt unwise. But never mind, things seem to be working out. But I must get away from this place, in case these other composers begin to get moving in earnest.'

'Why am I running away from the quartet?' Sibelius asked himself in a diary entry of 1 April – in Paris. There he was enjoying himself in the company of a Provençal composer and singer, René d'Avesac de Castera, whom he had met in London and whose grand manner had made quite an impression on him. He was also in the company of his compatriots: there was Antti Favén, a lively and exuberant portrait painter, Wentzel Hagelstam, the publisher, and, of course, Axel Gallén, now known as Gallén-Kallela, who had settled in Paris for a year with his family:

> Gallén lives in a veritable palace, which he rents for a mere 12,000 francs for the whole season. Can you imagine it? Apart from that, however, he does not seem at ease, and is going through a sterile period. His wife is nervy and full of caprices.

His letter home did not mention one thing which he told Aino later: when he first arrived Gallén did not come and greet him immediately but kept him waiting in an ante-chamber, presumably without thinking that Sibelius would regard this as an insult coming from a close companion of his symposium years. Sibelius's worries about his throat still pursued him and his unfinished quartet was preying on his mind. He had moved in to a cheap room costing 5 francs a day for the sake of economy, so did not take kindly to waiting in a luxuriously appointed room, counting the minutes go by while his erstwhile drinking companion took his time. Somewhat unimaginatively perhaps, Sibelius did not take into account Gallén's difficulties: he was at a creative impasse, in a state of crisis, and was just on the point of taking his family to Africa in search of inspiration and stimulus. The two friends were doubtless not in a position to show each other the warmth and admiration that they both felt for each other.

The sudden onset of sharp pains in his throat sent him running to his specialist in Berlin but Dr Fränkel put his fears at rest: ' "Everything is in very good order. You've not had anything dangerous," '[2] he told me. I have many years of work ahead of me,' he reported home. Encouraged by his doctor's verdict, he took himself in hand and returned to work on the quartet. On 15 April his diary notes:

1 Eric Fenby, *Delius as I knew him*, London, 1936, revised 1966 p. 123.
2 'Alles ist sehr schön in Ordnung. Sie haben auch gar nichts Gefährliches gehabt.'

The quartet is finished. Yes – my heart bleeds – why this sense of pain in life. O! O! O! That I even exist! My God! Four pairs of children's eyes and a wife's [then a word that is deleted] stare at me, virtually a pauper. What have I done to deserve it? At least I've composed well. And as a result I must pay for it.

The first sentence is underlined with green ink, the colour he reserves for such occasions; entries for income are always underlined in red. To Aino, however, he wrote in somewhat different terms:

My quartet was finished some time ago but I withheld it. Today I have sent it to Lienau. It's a wonderful feeling, the sort of thing that prompts a smile to cross the lips at the moment of death. I say no more.[1]

In the same letter Sibelius expressed indignation at Wentzel Hagelstam's newspaper report from Paris that had revealed the news that *Voces intimae* was not yet finished.

If Sibelius imagined that with the delivery of *Voces intimae*, he had fulfilled the terms of his contract with Lienau, he was mistaken. The quartet was only the second work (*Night Ride and Sunrise* had been the first) he had sent during this period: he was contractually bound to deliver two more. However, Lienau generously agreed to release him from the strict letter of the agreement and settled for one work. The composer stayed on in Berlin until late in May and composed a set of songs to poems by Ernst Josephson, who had written both 'Black roses' and 'Jubal'.

'Money matters are for me like going to the WC, a necessary evil,' wrote Sibelius from Berlin. He was now in a dreadful financial mess and was directing his appeal, not for the first time either, to his friend, the architect Eliel Saarinen.

I desperately need 500 Finnish marks = 400 Reichsmarks. Moreover I have to return home heavy in heart since my work here has been a joy. What a breath of fresh air Europe brings! Afterwards, when I get home, I must make the rounds in search of money. I blush to the depths of my being! Such humiliation! and at 9 per cent! What next!

But he knew well that the longer he delayed, the more difficult it became for Aino to keep their creditors at bay in Finland. Again Sibelius could give her no better advice than to borrow against the security of their pension. In spite of all this, his letter radiates optimism and is full of hope that he can clear up his financial muddles. He talks of plans for the future: such as

(1) putting the upstairs floor in order during the summer. (2) Look after yourself as well as you can, soon I will be back to help you. (3) If money is needed? (4) Try to amuse yourself as much as possible! Armas

1 The letter is dated 15 April 1909.

[Järnefelt], the opera, etc. (5) Look after the children. [Then he changes to Finnish] You, deepest ocean, You, my life, You, my most beautiful and wonderful darling. I kiss your beautiful eyes a thousand times, and love you so ardently – – . You, my own darling Aino.

Your own J.

In his next letter he tells her:

Your last long letter gladdened my heart. [Then in Finnish] It is so good for my art and my spirit and my peace of mind that our relationship has worked out so well and is so real. [In Swedish] You may say what you like, but it is so!

He decided against returning home immediately without having made any money abroad, and set his hopes on the Josephson settings:

The songs will be good, I'm in the middle of them, and in other respects things are going well. There are no disturbing neighbours playing the piano! I would willingly come home, even though my time would be consumed by money matters. But I'm not going on 'begging rounds' again, even if it means bankruptcy. Our spirit is something they can't take away from us, these wretched devils. From now onwards, I'm the one who is going to be a devil. What have I done? Composed well. Does that presuppose that my sacred home should be besieged with demands and my wife crucified. No – !

At this point Sibelius suddenly received a tempting financial offer. The dancer Maude Allan wrote asking him in flattering terms to write music for a ballet-pantomime. A gifted artist, whose career was to be ruined by a politically coloured scandal during the First World War, she had studied the dance culture of Ancient Egypt and Greece and studied the piano with Busoni, no less, who possibly suggested Sibelius's name to her. Her *Vision of Salomé*, with music by Marcel Rémys, received 345 performances in London in 1908, so that Sibelius saw this project as a possible gold mine.

'The scenario appeals to me a lot, it is namely music and movement, my genre (not opera!!) . . . I shall presumably take it on. We shall see. But 10 per cent of the takings. That will make me about 10,000 marks – even more! I looked at myself in the mirror just now. I'm looking very pale – but still 'handsome'.

In spite of the attractive royalties, the project soon began to lose its appeal: 'I am not going to go to England, and nor am I going to compose music for the dance for I'm no longer drawn to the Orient at present.' This reference would seem to indicate that the subject matter was *Khamma*, a dance legend on Ancient Egyptian themes by W. L. Courtney and Maude Allan. Some years later Debussy wrote a score for it, though he farmed out the orchestration to Charles Koechlin. Even if Debussy spoke contemptuously of 'la girl anglaise' and her 'rubbishy Anglo-Egyptian ballet', he did not disguise satisfaction with the finished score. Sibelius was undoubtedly right to turn this scenario down for the Orient never exercised the same fascination for him as it had for Debussy with his taste for Javanese gamelan music, Hokusai woodcuts, Moorish and Spanish folk music. Sibelius was not keen to repeat himself with another 'Khadra's Dance'.

While in Berlin, according to his letter to Aino, Sibelius had been occupying himself with other things than the Josephson songs: there was 'that funeral march idea', presumably *In memoriam*; he also started to sketch out the tone poem *La Chasse*, which promised to be a 'lively and spirited piece, light in its colours'. It is possible also that he intended to revise the early B flat Quartet. Op. 4. Besides that he had to find time for his sittings with the Finnish sculptor, John Munsterhjelm, who was doing a bust of him. In Munsterhjelm's hands there is less of the severe almost martial quality that Bax and Goossens had discerned in London but rather the contemplative side, the composer listening intently to his inner voices. Indeed, the sculpture radiates something of the atmosphere of the work Sibelius had just completed: *Voces intimae*. On 18 May Sibelius noted: 'The Eight Songs, Op. 57, are finished. The terms of Lienau's contract fulfilled. I went to bed at nine o'clock, worn out.' He had freed himself not only from his contract, which in any event he had terminated at the time of *Night Ride and Sunrise*, but also from his *junge Klassizität* period. On 21 May he wrote its epilogue: 'Now I must go home. I can't work here any longer. A change of style?'

Notable formal innovators such as Sibelius and his contemporaries, Mahler, Bartók and Shostakovich, can be said to write for a basically unchanging body of sonorities in a given series of works. When they embark on a new symphony or string quartet, their concern is more with its growth as architecture than in devising completely new sound worlds. Their priorities were, first and foremost, content and architecture. Composers primarily concerned with colour and sonority take a different view and proceed from different premises. After Debussy and Ravel had tried a certain combination of chamber composition, they moved on to something else rather than try their hand at a series of string quartets or trios with the inevitable challenge of new formal problems. Even the two Ravel concertos are strongly contrasted in terms of sonority, one being written for the left hand alone. Of course, it goes without saying in such a crude generalization that Debussy both motivically and colouristically achieved new forms, just as Sibelius created new sonorities in his symphonies. Given Sibelius's fascination with form and its challenge, it is hardly surprising that he should return to its problems consistently in the series of symphonies and tone poems that extend from the beginning through to the very end of his creative career. It is true that he composed only one violin concerto but that

116

is something of a special case: many composers with a long series of symphonies to their credit contented themselves with only one. On the other hand it is not only uncharacteristic but almost inexplicable that after his student years, he wrote no quartet other than *Voces intimae*. The string quartet was the ideal medium for him.

His mastery of its tonal possiblities and colours was impresssive, even if orchestral habits of mind were not wholly put aside. Certainly some of the doublings in the part-writing are an instance in point, and are orchestral in conception. He himself was aware that after so long an interruption in his concern with the quartet medium he had not been wholly successful in adapting himself: 'The melodic substance is good but the sonorities are another matter. The texture could be more transparent and lighter and, why not say it, more quartet-like. Take that *cum grano salis*.' He reaffirms his satisfaction with its content and evidently felt it to be his most successful work to date: 'Believe me, with the quartet I have left the training ship and gained my master's certificate. Now I shall set course for the open sea. You've achieved something!' he wrote in a diary entry of 27 July 1909. But the open seas proved to be symphonic and *Voces intimae* was to have no successor.

Why, one wonders, should this be so? *Voces intimae* is, after all, one of Sibelius's finest works and could have well been the starting point for a quartet cycle comparable in quality and range to the symphonies and tone poems. The explanation may, in part at least, be psychological, even if it is unwise to draw too close a parallel between his personal and musical development. Yet in this instance it is obvious that both *Voces intimae* and the Fourth Symphony reflect his inner life during the years immediately after the operation when he had passed through the shadows of the valley of death. There are inevitably problems when stepping back, as it were, from the edge of the abyss and returning to the rhythm of everyday life. Both are works with a mystical dimension in which he reveals himself most fully and though in the case of the symphony he returned to its challenge, the Fifth was to give him more trouble than any other: eight years were to elapse before it was to reach its definitive form. However, there was a continuity in his symphonic activity that was lacking in the field of chamber music: there was a nineteen-year gap between *Voces intimae* and the Op. 4 String Quartet.

In *Voces intimae* Sibelius continues and develops the innovatory approach that he had begun in the Third Symphony. However, the fusion between first and second movements is by no means as radical as it was to be in the definitive version of the Fifth Symphony: the first movement, a fully formed sonata structure, is followed *attacca* by a scherzo that uses the same motivic substance – a closer parallel would be the 1915 version of the Symphony. The *Vivace* itself he called 'first-and-a-half movement' in his diary, so indicating its character of an appendage. The central *Adagio* movement is thus flanked by a *Vivace* and an *Allegretto*. This has prompted Cecil Gray to draw a parallel between the Sibelius and Haydn's early quartets, an analogy that is not wholly valid since the symmetry of Haydn's minuet–slow movement–minuet design is disturbed by the intimacy with which Sibelius's *Vivace* is linked to the opening sonata movement. If anything the Sibelius is closer to the movement design in the late quartets of Beethoven. The model to which Sibelius was instinctively drawn would have been the Razumovsky quartets – and in particular, the F major, Op. 59 No. 1, one of the great musical experiences of his Berlin period during the autumn of 1889 – as well as the Schubert quartets.

The first movement (*Andante – Allegro molto moderato*) can be thought of as the discourse of the inner voices. In the introductory bars the first violin poses a question that immediately draws a response from the cello:

Ex 62

The idea is developed along normal sonata principles. The allegro movement builds up the main figure (a major second and a descending fourth, an outline similar to the principle idea of *Lemminkäinen's Homeward Journey*). The theme splits up into smaller and smaller segments until the line dissolves into a series of descending fourths. The unrelieved intensity of the movement barely slackens: the second subject is in A minor but ends with a glimmer of light in A major with the main idea woven into its contour:

Ex 63

The final idea grows organically from the preceding material and, like the whole movement, acquires its special colouring from the chord of the dominant ninth. Almost imperceptible quaver movement gently effects a transition to the development, which concerns itself with material from the first group:

Ex 64

The basic idea of a major second and descending fourth returns some eight times in its original form and even appears, albeit somewhat modified, in the background texture. The very climax of the movement sees a further trans-formation of the idea: its character is vehement and at the point at which one expects the fourth, the line ascends a minor second, thus:

Ex 65

In the emphatic dominant minor ninth the A flat falls to a G, and the tritone to which this gives rise seems to protest against fate, an effect reinforced by the dynamic marking *ffz*. However, the note of bitterness subsides and from the G flat major the music meekly returns to D minor. By the time we reach the coda there is a note of fatalism and acceptance. Everything is prepared for the music to end in the tonic, but suddenly Sibelius modulates to A minor as if he is seeking a more positive resolution. The new key is poised to become the tonic of the *Vivace* which follows *attacca*.

Everything assumes a dream-like quality. What was desolate and tragic in the first movement is transformed into a fairy-like atmosphere that serves as a reminder of his admiration for Mendelssohn, though the music itself is not reminiscent of him:

Ex 66

The viola takes up other figures from the second group of the first movement. Suddenly the argument is interrupted by a number of hesitations, sudden rests of the kind that have prompted some critics to call in question Sibelius's mastery of musical syntax, albeit without justification, for his aphoristic musical thinking has its own special rules. Afterwards, with a modulation to C major, the texture assumes a sharper focus and an almost orchestral character. Ideas now shift into the foreground rather than continue their ethereal dance. Two cadential chords *pizzicato* bring back the fairy-like opening but this time in F sharp minor before the music finally fades away in A major.

The third movement, *Adagio di molto*, is the centrepiece of the quartet as well as its centre of musical gravity. It symbolizes the tension between the physical world and the world beyond. Its main theme quietly radiates a love of life:

Ex 67

The following passage, in F minor, has a passionate lamenting intensity in the middle of which one is surprised by three E minor chords played *ppp, più adagio*:

Ex 68

The effect is striking. It is over these three chords that Sibelius wrote in a copy of a miniature score, the words 'Voces intimae'. The abrupt change in colour, texture and pace, and the eloquent, breathless pauses, seem to mirror, as the poet Bertel Gripenberg put it, 'a distant murmur from a distant world'.

The music builds up to an anguished climax in F minor and the cello occupies itself with the main theme. The second group returns in the major and forms the basis of a kind of development, the climax of which is an ecstatic eruption:

Ex 69

With the last page of the score, the inner voices resume their discourse but the F major cantilena is on this occasion interrupted by the same three hushed chords, this time in C sharp minor. The vision of the other world that they bring fades less quickly this time. It is as if in this movement we see him clinging to the world of the senses with all its beauties, while at the same time being increasingly aware of the lure of the reality behind reality. National barriers are often difficult to transcend in music but the *Adagio* of the *Voces intimae* quartet should have gone some way towards dispelling the Central European notion of the iciness and inaccessibility of Sibelius. Of course, these barriers are not just one way: the poet, Elmer Diktonius once wrote that in Debussy he found little spiritual consolation and no doubt there are many Frenchmen who would return the compliment about Sibelius. With the *Adagio* of this quartet, however, Sibelius puts much of his Nordic reticence on one side and, in revealing more of his inner feeling, the music assumes a special warmth. It goes without saying, surely, that both these great masters have depth.

For all its minuet-like character, the fourth movement, *Allegretto ma pesante*, has a bold stride; fate is neither challenged nor accepted – but if there is neither hope nor is there any fear.

Ex 70

Unlike so many minuets in the minor, the atmosphere is not relieved by a trio section in the major. In fact the first violin has a plaintive tune over triplet figuration, which is answered by the cello:

Ex 71

Nils-Eric Ringbom has pointed out the connection between these figures and those that follow on immediately after the E minor chords in the *Adagio* movement. The descending fifths and the quaver stretto of the coda suggest something of the atmosphere of the *Andante* of the Second Symphony:

Ex 72

In the final bars Sibelius rams home the main theme without any sense of victory over fate but rather a feeling of inevitability.

In the final *Allegro* many of the voices that have been discerned in the earlier movements have been silenced. The composer is now listening to more earthbound ideas: there is a desperate, even demonic quality to this finale, and as in the case of the corresponding movement of the Violin Concerto, there is a virtuosity that bursts into flame. As far as the thematic substance of the piece is concerned, we are reminded of voices from the past. Some of the rhythmic outlines of *Pohjola's Daughter* are to be found in the main idea which I shall call **A**, and which is made up of two ideas.

Ex 73

The second subject is derived from the Overture in A minor, which was first given in 1902 at the same concert as the première of the Second Symphony:

Ex 74

In the transition passage that follows, the texture is distinctly reminiscent of the development-like passages in *Lemminkäinen's Homeward Journey*:

Ex 75

Reminiscences of much earlier works are also to be found. The stormy descending semiquaver figures, a variant of the main idea, have a precedent in the Fugue he composed for Martin Wegelius, which was at one time intended for the finale of the String Quartet in A minor of 1899:

Ex 76

The second episode, C, ends with three emphatic statements of the tonic D:

Ex 77

Can this be an echo of the three *Voces intimae* chords from the *Adagio*, no longer spiritualized but frenzied and earthly? The finale is a rondo in its structure having the following layout:

A - B - A₁ - C - B₁ - A₂ - C₁ - Coda.

Its thematic homogeneity and finely proportioned structure owe some of their impact to the gradually accelerating tempo and increasing virtuosity that distinguishes the writing. *Voces intimae* has never gained wide popularity in the international repertoire; in this respect it has suffered the same fate, though to a different extent, as the two symphonies with which it has a spiritual link: the Fourth and the Sixth.

The other work from this period is the cycle of Eight Songs, Op. 57, to words of Ernst Josephson. This is only the second occasion on which he had turned to a single poet for a group of songs, the first being the seven Runeberg settings, Op. 13. But they occupied him for a longer period than the Josephson cycle, which was composed in about a month. The Op. 57 songs show the expressionistic element in his style surfacing more prominently, throwing those songs more influenced by the *junge Klassizität* into greater relief.

'The river and the snail' functions as a kind of sculptured portal:

Ex 78 'The wide river draws its blue ribbon through the bosom of the forest.'

As in earlier folk-song arrangements, the piano part has a bold, dissonant flavour that is almost reminiscent of the piano accompaniments of Bartók's folk settings. The vocal line is more declamatory than lyrical.

'The wild flower by the wayside' is a little fable that tells of the poor flower, picked by a small girl, and left by its friends, the butterfly and the bird, to die alone. Sibelius's setting is folk-like with the piano part imitating the vocal line canonically:

Ex 79 'And the girl put the butterfly with a bird in its cage.'

This forms a contrast both with the introductory song and the next setting, 'The mill wheel', in which Sibelius indulges in some naturalistic musical effects. The relentless motion of the newly tarred mill wheel is represented by appropriately liquid piano writing, while the old discarded wheel, overgrown with wild rose, moves in a heavier march rhythm; its thoughts are of its own exhaustion.

'May' falls somewhat outside the framework of the cycle. Its colouring is light, as indeed is its character, and the ending has resonances of the spring-like melancholy, the 'tristesse du printemps' of his youthful pieces. Perhaps on this count, it held a special place in Sibelius's own affections.

'The tree' is one of the most deeply felt of all Sibelius's songs. The poem about the tree, stripped in its prime by the storm, standing naked, its branches stretched towards the sky in a longing for death, perhaps gives expression to Josephson's presentiment of his coming insanity. In the same way Sibelius could well have identified his own fears of cancer with the tree's fate. The song begins with a cry of despair in a characteristically Sibelian Dorian melody.

Ex 80 'I am a tree who promised and whose future was sure'

When in the third strophe, the tree pleads for death, bold tolling chords are heard in the piano. Possibly the example of Mussorgsky was in Sibelius's mind; his music library did include copies of some of the *Sunless* songs.

'Duke Magnus' is written in the style of an old Nordic ballad. Right from the very outset Sibelius strikes the right tone; from his window the Duke looks out over the moonlit waters of Lake Vättern, and the piano accompaniment suggests the calm motion of the waves:

Ex 81 'From his window Duke Magnus . . .'

The mermaid appears and sings her seductive song, albeit in the contrasting key of G flat, but Duke Magnus emerges safely from the experience and ends up unhurt, sleeping by the shore. The whole song has something of the melancholy of the Scandinavian summer night.

'Friendship' has a sprightly rhythmic gait together with harmonies that almost foreshadow Prokofiev:

Ex 82 'O friendship, fairest flower, when I am assailed by all'

'The Watersprite' is of special interest in that we see an idea surfacing in the framework of a miniature that Sibelius was later to develop on a larger scale in the Fourth Symphony. The theme of the poem is central to Josephson's work both as a painter and a poet. A pale youth with dark, curly hair is sitting on a stone by a waterfall: he draws his bow across his violin. A watersprite appears before him and strikes up a dance on his harp; the boy follows suit and loses himself in the music, so entranced is he with this Elf-King. Naturally, Josephson identifies himself with the youth, absorbed in his own inspiration, and the poem would have special resonances for Sibelius who would wander in the open air during his own youth playing his violin. The setting is expressionistic in character, the cascading waterfalls depicted in the piano part also serve to symbolize the youth's attempts to capture his inspiration. The tritone (E flat – F – A – G), the same idea as in the symphony, is here a symbol of the youth's creativity, and perhaps it is this symbol that is a resonating force in the coming years.

CHAPTER SIX

The Fourth Symphony

In his diary entry, made before leaving Berlin and noting the completion of the Eight Songs, Op. 57, Sibelius had scribbled, 'A change of style?' and during the next two years new expressive means were to develop in his artistic armoury. In his reaction against the national romanticism of his first two symphonies, he had developed a language inspired by the ideals of the *junge Klassizität* espoused by Busoni and perfected in the Third Symphony. But at the same time his musical personality was not completely integrated. The impressionistic pictorialism of *Pohjola's Daughter* and *Night Ride and Sunrise* and the expressionism of the Songs, Opp. 35 and 57 and to some extent *Voces intimae* show him in search of a new and richer language. His voyage into new territory was made possible by the securer psychological climate he enjoyed. For whatever his periodic fears – 'Health!! Oh God!' – he was becoming basically optimistic: 'Stop worrying and get on with work! Perhaps you will still live for a long time.' His experience had left him regarding life with greater gratitude than before, and as something that one should make the most of.

Moreover he was now living the healthier life-style of a non-smoker and teetotaller. But this, of course, called for great strength of character, particularly on those occasions when he was in the company of his old drinking companions. There were always people at the Kämp restaurant who would ask him how he managed to stoke the fires of inspiration without the usual fuels. He preferred not to answer such queries but instead heaped abuse on them in his diary. He told no one, apart from his brother Christian, how much he longed to smoke and drink as he had done before. His diary reflects his craving: 'Have been in hell. It's difficult to learn to work without stimulus. It's a must.' But some days later he had broken down his resistance to working and he records progress at last. No doubt the absence of stimulus served to strengthen his constitution, for he slowly lost his vulnerability to illness and laid the foundation of his granite-like physical condition.

In May 1909 he returned home to face an avalanche of bills and had to lay his hands on ready money. He had parted from Lienau in Berlin on good terms but the annulment of their contract had terminated regular business dealings. They had dined at the Habel restaurant in Berlin and Lienau spoke of his belief in Sibelius's art and even commissioned some piano pieces from him. But even though he was exposed to so much financial pressure ('Humiliations at every turn,' he confided to his diary), Sibelius was reluctant to embark on this project: 'Writing for the piano is alien to me.' Moreover, he was anxious to make headway with his new tone poem, *La Chasse*. But eventually he resigned himself to the inevitable and set to work on the piano pieces. In July he wrote to Lienau offering all ten pieces for an outright payment of 5,000 Reichsmarks. Strangely enough, Lienau seems to have taken some offence because he responded relatively sharply saying that so high a figure was altogether out of the question. Moreover, he made no counter offer, thus driving Sibelius into the arms of Breitkopf und Härtel, who in their own time paid some 3,000 marks for the Op. 58 pieces, to which he put the finishing touches in August. No sum was too high when it came to winning over the composer from a rival house.

That same summer saw Sibelius fulfil a longstanding promise to write incidental music to the play *The Lizard (Ödlan)* by Mikael Lybeck whom he had known since the 1890s. He had fallen under the spell of its poetry the previous autumn but by the time he got round to composing the score his enthusiasm had cooled. Perhaps, when he came to reread the play, he realized that for all its literary merit, it was wanting in dramatic power. By mid-October the score was ready and even though he wrote to Carpelan that it was 'among the most sensitive pieces' he had written, an aside in his diary indicated that he attached scant importance to it. *The Lizard* was first mounted the following April and was respectfully received by the critics but promptly disappeared after a few performances.

Sibelius was also troubled by having to deal with trivial practical matters. A letter to Carpelan during the summer gives vent to his feelings:

No one who has not experienced it can realize the tension produced by money problems. And what a demoralizing effect it has. I would advise no one to be a composer unless they have private means. Any other course spells disaster. Aino has been very poorly. Her health has declined quite alarmingly and her nerves have gone to pieces. All this because of our 'disaster'. Your interest in my new work [*Night Ride and Sunrise*] has given me such joy. You are a phenomenon. When I think of these Kapellmeisters with their circus showmanship (they only want pieces to show off their particular circus acts) along with those idiots, the critics, I am lost in admiration of your profound musical understanding and unerring artistic judgement. You mention interconnections between themes and other such matters, all of which are quite subconscious on my part. Only afterwards can one discern this or that relationship but for the most part one is merely a vessel. That wonderful logic (let us call it God) which governs a work of art, that is the important thing. From time to time I read critiques, bad and overflowing with bile, most of which I send up in smoke. May I live long enough, for I am now sure of my artistic path.

The bile flowed some days later when Lev Zeitlin played the Violin Concerto in Pavlovsk. *Novoye Vremya* was dismissive, sympathizing with the poor soloist who had to try and make something out of this moribund piece! Much of its venom was inspired by the envy Sibelius was often to encounter in life: here was a composer who enjoyed special status in his home country which (it was thought) had relieved him of any material worries by granting him an annual pension. Of this he was not worthy in the eyes of *Novoye Vremya*! Others were more responsive, however, and *Novy Russ* found the Concerto full of much that was 'inspiring and appealing'. Zeitlin had one attentive listener in the violinist Efrem Zimbalist who had hated the piece at the morning rehearsal only to be swept away by it at the actual concert.

At the end of September Sibelius and his brother-in-law, Eero Järnefelt, made a trip to Koli, a then unspoilt mountain outpost by the side of Lake Pielinen in northern Karelia. Here seventeen years earlier, he and Aino had spent their honeymoon on the other side of the lake. As Järnefelt set up his easel, Sibelius wandered in the mountain forests, looking back over his life and putting his worries into perspective. He had had high expectations of the trip, so he wrote to his brother Christian, who looked after his affairs in his absence. There is no doubt as to the powerful impression it made on him, for a diary entry made on his return reads: 'Koli. One of my life's greatest experiences. Many plans. 'La montagne'!' Back in Ainola, he composed two songs for a production of *Twelfth Night* at the Swedish Theatre. But he was not particularly happy: 'What a long way all this is from *real* work of the kind that gives satisfaction and fulfilment to the composer and those around him. I ought to console myself with the thought that this sense of satisfaction is egoistic even though it brings pain . . .!'

The sureness of artistic purpose of which he spoke in his letter to Axel Carpelan did not mean that he was free from self-criticism or self-doubt. His struggles with *In Memoriam*, a funeral march for orchestra, bear witness to this. He was at work on the score during late October and a diary entry reads: 'Want it to be on the grandest scale. 'It's strange to think of it but I suppose it will be played when I am buried.' He finished it by the end of December, and it earned him an honorarium of 3,000 Reichsmarks from Breitkopf und Härtel. When he received proofs of the score some months later, however, he was plunged into gloom. 'The scoring of *In Memoriam* is quite hopeless. It needs greater plasticity but it will be good, this piece . . . I shall rescore it all, every bar! Yes, the whole lot!' He took himself in hand the following day: 'Remember! the naturalness of your instrumental writing is more important than any so-called brilliance. Remember your sense of colour tones! Shame on you! Hell! Don't ever lose contact with the orchestra for any length of time! N'oubliez pas!'

Sibelius sent off the revised version of *In Memoriam* to Breitkopf in March. His relations with them were developing smoothly: they destroyed the original plates without demur, and even went so far as to advertise Munster-hjelm's bust of him in their bulletin and wrote telling him that they had asked for two casts of it in bronze for their head offices in Leipzig and London.[1] His own difficulties with *In Memoriam* had plunged him into deep depression; everything seemed black and empty, and he himself listless and drained of energy. In this mood it seemed to him as if the sun would never shine again, and that his life was running through his fingers without his having achieved a fraction of what he wanted. His money worries compounded his gloom.

His spirits were hardly lifted by the thought of having to work on a new ballet, *The Bears' Death Ceremonies*, which Maude Allan had commissioned for the Palace Theatre, London. But suddenly the anxieties were at least partially relieved. Once again it was through the agency of Axel Carpelan, who despite his own straitened circumstances continued to concern himself with Sibelius's financial plight. He paid a visit to Ainola at the beginning of December to take stock of the situation. What he found was hardly encouraging: Sibelius's debts had now mounted to 100,000 Finnish marks. Even by the most optimistic calculations Sibelius needed 12,000 marks for his living expenses, 4,000 for mortgage repayments, 6,000 for interest payments: 22,000 marks in all. His pension had remained static at 3,000 marks for the past thirteen years in spite of inflation. He could count on something like 12,000 marks from Breitkopf und Härtel and a further 1,000 marks from other sources. The shortfall of 6,000 (in practice he needed far more) had to be made up either from freelance earnings or by further borrowing. But Sibelius had by now exceeded his credit limits many times over, so that raising further loans was not simple.

So Axel Carpelan, with the support of his cousin Tor, began a rescue operation. In a confidential letter to one of Finland's richest men, he outlined Sibelius's situation in the frankest terms: Christmas was upon them, Aino was ill and their funds barely covered such necessities as milk for the children! Carpelan's pleas did not go unanswered and on Christmas Eve itself the first tangible evidence of support arrived. Sibelius now determined to tackle serious creative ventures: 'Thanks to your generosity and that of Magnus Dahlström, I do not need to compose ballet music but can once again venture on to a symphonic course. I have long cherished ambitions to devote myself to a big venture but more of that anon.'

Carpelan replied that Sibelius had no need to thank his patrons in Turku (Dahlström and his brother):

1 'um Sie immer vor Augen zu haben.'

Your best thanks will be in new and beautiful works. When the new symphony [No. 4] is finished, I shall hasten to inform M.D. . . . Yes, I have thought a very great deal about the symphony – what you played for me from 'The Mountain' and 'Thoughts of a Wayfarer' were the most impressive things I have yet heard from your pen. I long to hear the symphony in its glowing orchestral garb.

There is little doubt from this letter that the experience of Koli was a primary source of inspiration for the Fourth Symphony. Judging from this letter, it seems likely that some or all of the ideas for 'The Mountain' and its companion piece found their way into the final version of the symphony, the former, perhaps, into the first movement and the latter into the third. It goes without saying, however, that there is no case whatsoever for attaching titles to these movements.

At the time of Carpelan's visit to Ainola, the Fourth Symphony was in its earliest throes of gestation: embryonic ideas in the composer's mind on which he would improvise at the keyboard. Diary entries would seem to indicate that he actually began committing his ideas to paper during the Christmas period. He abandoned work on a piece that had been planned for charity and concentrated his energies entirely on the new project. All was now 'lightness and power'. His work fired his spirits. 'I am intentionally burning my boats. Holding high the banner of real art. Hold on to the pathos of life.' On New Year's Eve, 'all was expectation', but by 6 January the new work was fully under way.

'I no longer feel at home in the city. My solitude begins. The important thing is to maintain one's balance and keep up one's spirit in spite of *Alleingefühl*,' he wrote in his diary. However, it was not the fault of others that he began to cultivate isolation but rather a conscious choice on his part. Obviously he was the central figure in Finnish musical life but he found difficulty in assuming the role expected of him. He was not really at his ease with his fellow composers. Their admiration and affection – and occasionally too fervent devotion – hardly helped matters. On occasion he fancied he could discern 'cold, envious glances', and at such times he withdrew more deeply into his shell. Although he was very happy to appear on terms of equality, he was at the same time fully aware of his own standing. Yet he felt threatened by the success of a rival. He was not wholly free from a streak of artistic envy but was more than aware that such sentiments were unworthy and self-destructive. When he felt overshadowed by others, he spurred himself on to even greater efforts.

Greater contact with the younger generation of composers might have helped him overcome a growing sense of isolation, but he had never collected pupils or disciples. His natural warmth and generosity of feeling was tinged with suspicion of the young: they were his 'natural enemies', he once wrote, though he had difficulty in regarding them in this light. At some stage a teacher has to come off his pedestal even at the risk of appearing foolish. Sibelius all too readily succumbed to the impulse of the moment and later regretted it. He reproached himself in a diary entry:

> Don't you understand now? By being so open, you have forfeited the respect that you feel to be your entitlement. Keep your thoughts to yourself and guard your tongue in talking to others. And then your pupils (!), stand fast by them. Otherwise the best and first will have every right to treat you in kind.

All the same, he was fully aware that his two pupils at this time, Toivo Kuula and Leevi Madetoja were highly ethical and in no sense backbiters.

As early as 1907 Sibelius had heard some of Kuula's pieces and had warmed to their dark, virile character; he had told him to take good care of the folk-like elements in his musical language and not to start 'composing in evening dress'. For a short time during the spring of 1908 Kuula left Armas Järnefelt to take lessons with Sibelius, and one of the very first works he went through with him was the Piano Trio in A major. He evidently believed in his young and complicated pupil but was careful not to encourage a dependency. That he had a high opinion of him emerges in a letter he sent him discussing the choice of pianist for this Trio: 'In this world pianists are two-a-penny but such a work as yours calls for someone very special.' Soon after he was instrumental in securing Kuula a valuable scholarship to Bologna to study with Enrico Bossi, and the following year while on a visit to London he spoke about the Trio to Alexander Siloti. 'I expect Siloti has written to you by now about the possibility of performing your Trio. He wants to put it on in St Petersburg,' he wrote to Kuula, adding, 'I am sure I can get your works performed here in England.'

Although the St Petersburg performance transpired, nothing came of his efforts in England. Sibelius evidently overestimated his powers of persuasion in this respect. Yet for all the paternal tone of Sibelius's letter, no real kinship ever developed between the two. Kuula's music derived much inspiration from the folk music of his native Ostrobothnia and he was much drawn to Leino's lyrics and sacred songs in the *Kalevala* style, and not to Swedish poetry. Moreover, Kuula was abrasive and by no means easy to deal with.

Madetoja, who began studying with him in 1909, was another matter, and their relationship was much closer. His was a more inward-looking temperament with a streak of Nordic melancholy and a keen feeling for nature that struck a responsive chord in Sibelius. Not that he always took pleasure in his company. When Madetoja and a music critic called Katila visited him in August that year, he found them both heavy going: Madetoja could often be withdrawn and moody. But generally speaking, his relationship with the younger man was not altogether free from moments of tension, though the latter was scarcely aware of them. The problem was Robert Kajanus. In his youth Sibelius had pained his own mentor, Martin

Wegelius, by his close relationship with Kajanus, and now it was his own turn to feel that he was being put to one side when Madetoja showed his eagerness for Kajanus's friendship. A diary entry from 1912 reads: 'Today Madetoja came. He is a sympathetic presence but wholly under Kajanus's thumb. Let's hope it will do him some good – I doubt it though!'

He feared that Madetoja would not remain unaffected by all the praise and flattery that was showered on him – and perhaps he also feared that the younger man would supplant him in public esteem. But he was careful never to give expression to such doubts except to the privacy of his diary, and the result was a valuable and enduring relationship. Something of Madetoja's feeling for Sibelius comes through in this letter:

> Are you coming to Paris soon? I would be very pleased if you did. I am very lonely here. And my spirits are often low, because I have not yet been able to settle down to work. But I hope to do so very soon when my appetite for composition returns; then life's sorrows will, if not be forgotten, appear in more enticing colours. I want to thank you yet again for all the kindness and goodwill you have shown me. You have inspired my work; you have given a faltering youngster courage to set out on the right path, albeit a thorny path but one that leads to the sun-clad and richly coloured heights. I shall always feel deeply grateful to you for all that you have done.

Madetoja studied with Sibelius for a longer period of time and at greater depth than did Kuula and momentary irritations apart, their relationship at a personal level was basically more harmonious. His music, too, is more overtly influenced by his teacher. Yet, as so many commentators have noted, Sibelius's musical language is so wholly personal, so deeply idiosyncratic and basically so inimitable that it is not the foundation on which musical schools can be built.

Language presented a barrier between the two. While Sibelius continued to set Swedish poetry, the sympathies of both Kuula and (perhaps to a lesser extent) Madetoja were with Finnish poetry and folk music. Such a small matter could give rise to some feeling in such circles as Eino Leino's or that of the Finnish language fanatic, Heikki Klemetti. Moreover such interest as Sibelius took in folk music was directed at the archaic runic incantations and melodies not at the kind of folk tunes and dances that exercised a hold over his pupils. Moreover, in both Helsinki and other towns, Sibelius moved predominantly in the Swedish-speaking community and their élite, whom the young Finnish activists regarded with some suspicion. Even though his Finnish sympathies were well proven, both the language factor and the company he kept could have contributed to his growing isolation.

Erkki Melartin, who was some years older than Madetoja and Kuula, never became a Sibelius pupil but he did pay him a number of visits at Ainola. After one of them Sibelius noted in his diary: 'Melartin! I admire his methodical way of working. How is it possible to keep up that *nulla dies sine linea*? And his technique!' Sibelius worked in response to the call of inspiration and was a trifle envious – and perhaps even ironic – when he was confronted by the phenomenon of an artist who kept office hours at his working desk. But in any event Melartin was never to achieve a really satisfactory symphonic technique, and Sibelius was even at this stage aware of the strange pallor, both as an artist and as a person, that was to inhibit this gifted composer.

Although Sibelius mixed easily with others, at the same time socializing presented problems for him. Outwardly he maintained an urbane enough front, but inside he had little time for the idle and mean-minded chatter that could pass for social intercourse in Järvenpää. He did not care for its middle-class society and its self-important businessmen and landowners.

We would gladly spend more time in their company but their lack of imagination and in a certain sense their self-satisfaction renders this wellnigh impossible. Otherwise, we are entirely on our own!! No doubt our own fault since we can't sink to their level. My wife is an aristocrat and, as an artist, so am I. The gentry here can't grasp that.

So their circle of friends were drawn from the artistic colony in the near neighbourhood: Eero Järnefelt, Pekka Halonen, Juhani Aho and their families.

Juhani Aho and Sibelius must have presented a bizarre spectacle as they sat with their fishing rods in a rowing boat, Aho in a sou'wester, Sibelius in a fly-collar and white cuffs – he never appeared dressed in sports clothes or in an unpressed suit. Sibelius had the highest opinion of his friend both as a man and artist; their rivalry for Aino's hand was long forgotten. He contrasted Aho's life-style with his own disorderly plight, and was wholly convinced that Aho would enjoy far greater fame in Finland when he died than he would himself. Their two families were on the best of terms as well, and their children played happily together. When Sibelius overstayed his time abroad, Aho's wife would take pity on Aino and come to see her, giving her pictures to copy and other work. She was the painter Venny Soldan-Brofeldt and was rather masculine in temperament. Aho's marital situation was not wholly straightforward: as dusk fell he could be seen from the windows of Ainola making his way for an assignation with his sister-in-law. Pekka Halonen was another artist in whose home Sibelius was a not infrequent guest. During the first years at Järvenpää, he would seat himself at the piano and improvise. 'He was no virtuoso . . . but right from the first chord, his improvisation captured the intensity of the moment and clothed the idea with those special tone colours that mark him off from other great composers.' The two wives, Aino and Maija Halonen, played duet arrangements of the classical repertoire throughout their lives while Pekka Halonen worked at his easel. Over the years Sibelius and his brother-in-law, Eero

Järnefelt, grew closer. They took long walks together and discussed all life's problems. Sibelius philosophized in a somewhat dilettante fashion in Järnefelt's company and, as likely as not, the latter would demolish his arguments and dismiss his fantasies in a single sentence. But if Sibelius returned home in somewhat subdued spirits and with his self-confidence wounded, he would telephone Eero the next day to suggest another walk. Even if his brother-in-law punctured his *naïvetés*, he could not but 'love this noble, upright friend'. As a painter Järnefelt remained true to his youthful ideals. He continued to paint portraits – there is a particularly fine drawing of Sibelius from 1908 – groups and landscapes in the style of Puvis de Chavanne with a colouring that at times calls to mind his student years in St Petersburg. He remained untouched by late impressionism and symbolism, and felt scant sympathy with the newer trends, which he viewed with some degree of cynicism. In his musical tastes, however, he was less conservative and it is no accident that Sibelius dedicated his most advanced and demanding symphony, the Fourth, to him.

The relationship between the two families was not, however, without its tensions. Saimi Järnefelt was a lady of strong personality and powerful temperament. On one occasion, for a midsummer celebration, she put together some rather self-conscious verses centred on the achievements of the Järnefelts, which did not go down at all well with the Mistress of Ainola. Sparks could indeed fly between the two ladies. Indeed, it is difficult to believe one's eyes on reading one diary entry which records that Aino sank to the floor 'in a seizure' when Saimi on one occasion entered the drawing room at Ainola unannounced! The daughters, too, often returned from a visit to their cousins at Suviranta reduced to tears by their teasing. Saimi Järnefelt was fond of dramatic gestures and in her time had been an actress, but none the less at times of sickness or during Sibelius's long visits abroad she furnished Aino with help and support, and with the passage of time, relations between the two women grew warmer and more relaxed.

There was also a Russian colony nearby centred on the wealthy Ushkov estate. Madame Ushkov was Chaliapin's sister-in-law and lived in great style at Syväranta, not far from Halosenniemi. Apart from Fyodor Chaliapin himself, Sergey Rachmaninov was a frequent visitor and so, too, was Serge Koussevitzky, who had married into the family. Koussevitzky made an abortive attempt to visit Sibelius at Ainola, though at this time he did not wholly respond to his music. He spoke of it, not wholly inaccurately, as 'dark', and many years were to elapse before he took it to his heart and became one of its greatest interpreters.

Although the Fourth Symphony occupied the period from January 1910 to April 1911, it was not his sole concern. There were new works and the revision of earlier ones, and he was also busy travelling and conducting. One of the new pieces was a tone poem, *The Dryad*, which he finished at the beginning of February with a view to presenting it at a forthcoming

Helsinki concert. However, his preoccupation with the new symphony was such that he decided to abandon the concert. His diary entries at this stage rather surprisingly offer few glimpses of his progress on the work: on the contrary, one lists eighteen pieces under a heading 'works to be revised'. The *Impromptu* for women's voices and orchestra is high on the list, and was soon despatched to Breitkopf und Härtel for publication. Another piece that he reworked during the year was the cantata *The Origin of Fire*, sometimes known as *Ukko the Firemaker*, and 1911 saw other works subjected to revision or arrangement including *Rakastava*.

His thinking was partly motivated by the fear that illness might still claim him, and that he must try to prepare these earlier works for publication, and partly as a fund-raising operation. In the latter respect Sibelius's calculations were awry, for he would undoubtedly have made more money with one new work of substance rather than a string of smaller pieces. From a purely practical point of view his thinking was blinkered in that he had two trump cards in his hand: the two unpublished *Lemminkäinen Legends*. He could well have insisted on Breitkopf publishing them and also, possibly, the *Kullervo* Symphony.

For a time it seemed as if his symphonic plans were to be blighted by yet other preoccupations. March was a nightmare, for one day after another his time was consumed by trips to Helsinki to sort out his financial problems, though he was longing to concentrate his energies on music. It was the exception rather than the rule if he managed to spend a whole day at home.

On 3 April, as he was preparing to set off for Helsinki on his usual bank rounds, the telephone rang. Axel and Tor Carpelan had at last got their rescue operation under way. In March a number of influential figures in Finnish cultural life, including Yrjö Hirn, Werner Söderhjelm and the architect Sigurd Prosterus, had circulated a petition among wealthy business circles. In their letter they stressed that while Sibelius's health was now restored after a 'grave illness, his material circumstances in its wake were such that

economic worries are now consuming a considerable amount of his time and energies. If his countrymen could contribute to the amelioration of his circumstances they would in our view be serving the interests of their own country, and at the same time fulfil their duty to the cultural life of the international community, an obligation that is both our right and privilege.

This confidential petition touched on the right patriotic nerve and its call did not go unheeded. In three months the appeal had raised so much that Sibelius's debt could be reduced from 51,000 marks to 29,000. A further 11,000 had been promised from various sources while the remaining 18,000 was to be covered by a fund for which the industrialist Arthur Borgström and others acted as guarantors. This remarkable response was motivated primarily by the knowledge that Sibelius represented a symbol of national identity at a time of increasing Russianization. 'Without your intervention, my friend, all would have been lost,' he wrote to Carpelan, and among the losses would have been the Fourth Symphony.

Naturally Sibelius viewed this relief operation with mixed feelings; his gratitude was tempered by a sense of humiliation. His diary records:

> I woke last night with violent misgivings about this warm-hearted action. I am fearful that they may have turned to people whose confidence cannot wholly be relied upon. But should I really worry about this? Isn't this better than sitting on Helsinki street benches begging loans from passing capitalists! You know very well that that was hell!

But even if this rescue operation gave him greater freedom of manoeuvre, his peace of mind was not wholly restored. He would often wake up in the middle of the night and go to his 'black book', where all his borrowings and accounts were meticulously recorded.

In February 1910 the Third Symphony received its first Berlin performance under the baton of Josef Stransky. If Adolf Paul is to be believed, his account was 'sheer butchery':

> Stransky had obviously given your symphony one run-through and played it without any sense of commitment. The tempi were all wrong and he couldn't even get the strings and wind together. [. . .] You should either conduct yourself or ask Nikisch or Strauss and a first-class orchestra.

Perhaps on this account, the symphony did not score any great success. The *Allgemeine Musik-Zeitung* saw it as an example of the now defunct nationalist symphony. But the Violin Concerto was more warmly received in Hamburg, while in Stockholm the Second Symphony was well reviewed by the press, as was *En Saga* in Boston. But Sibelius had a capacity to see the worst in even the most positive reviews.

> How much more nonsense am I expected to endure? Yet again I read of my spiritual legacy from Russia and Tchaikovsky. I haven't developed a thick enough skin yet, and remain over-sensitive. It all pains me. But all this must be fought against. The older masters have had to fight against it. There isn't a day that passes somewhere in the world without some words of denigration, some attempt to drag one down. My music always draws some kind of punitive response. In truth what an unenviable fate. But one must soldier on regardless! To hell with it! Go on composing, keep up the façade and celebrate!

By way of relaxation Sibelius attended a performance of Massenet's *Thaïs* with Maria Kuznetsova. Yet again he wondered whether he had been right to abandon his operatic ambitions. Had he taken the easy way out? Was he suited for the operatic challenge? Was he too good for opera? All these doubts and musings emerge from his diary after having seen Kuznetsova. Perhaps it would have been more pertinent to ask himself whether he was not too old, for Strauss had already *Salome* and *Elektra* behind him at this stage.

On 25 April, *Voces intimae* received its first performance at a concert in the Helsinki Conservatory. Sibelius attended the rehearsal and noted afterwards: 'Keep to the clarity, the plasticity and refinement of the symphonic in your art. Don't allow yourself to be lured away from it.' The performance was a passable but not distinguished one but it was well received, Evert Katila comparing the slow movement with late Beethoven.[1] Performances followed in Leipzig, Berlin and other German cities when the work was taken up by one of the leading quartets of the day, the Sevčik Quartet, in the early part of 1911.

At last Sibelius scored another success with one of his major works. The *Leipziger Neueste Nachrichten* thought it gave expression to all the best in modern art, while Walter Niemann, writing in *Frankfurter Zeitung* spoke of 'it's comfortless, grey colouring and deep inner feeling'. The Berlin critics were full of praise, too, for its skill as quartet writing, and the only sour note was sounded by Otto Taubmann, an otherwise sympathetic Sibelian, who was disinclined to number it among the composer's finest works.

After the initial spurt of activity at the beginning of the year, Sibelius returned to the Fourth Symphony at the end of April 1910, and his diary records its progress:

April

21. Again in the deepest depression. Working hard at the newcomer.

27. Light, expectant, hopeful thoughts. Worked in my own way. Try to concentrate. 'A must.' Now or never.

May

2. Yesterday a wonderful day. Youth, joy and warmth. Sunlight and birdsong. Dreamed the whole day long. New ideas taking form. I have taken on a massive work.

7. Took a ten-kilometre walk while composing, forged[2] the musical metalwork and fashioned sonorities of silver.

8. Let my imagination run freely without any concentration and achieved nothing worth mentioning. Windy and light.

10. Worked hard without thought. Aino's name day. My wonderful wife.

11. Everything stagnant. [. . .] Not a word from Breitkopf. The countryside is looking wonderful. In the grip of a depression these days.

13. Don't let all these 'novelties', triads without thirds and so on, take you

1 *Uusi Suometar*, 26 April 1910.
2 Sibelius uses the image of the ironsmith at many points in the diaries, I have preferred to translate in different ways depending on context. *Tr.*

away from your work. Not everyone can be an innovating genius. As a personality and 'eine Erscheinung aus den Wäldern' [an apparition from the woods] you will have your modest place. Here at home you are a past number in the eyes of the general public! Just soldier on! Nous verrons!

16. Today came a much reduced counter offer [for the *Impromptu*, Op. 19] from Breitkopf. As a result I'll have to start work on other revisions. I ought to be able to work at big and small at the same time, i.e. the symphony and some songs. What needs must be. Look at things in a wider perspective.

17. Powerful spirits and atmosphere. E minor and nightingales . . .

Work was interrupted, however, by a visit from Mrs Newmarch and her lady companion. They left St Petersburg in mid-May and spent the latter half of the month in Finland. Sibelius went to Viipuri to meet them and accompanied them to Imatra Falls. In Helsinki he took her to hear the male-voice choir. Muntra Musikanter, who sang some of his songs in her honour. He later wrote to Carpelan,

It is two years now since I have listened to a male-voice choir. I must confess that I have completely grown away from this medium. There is something unmanly about the straining of the falsetto tenors; it almost reminds one of castrati. Even so our repertoire for male voices (I have written much for them myself) is too orchestral in conception. It's easy to understand why it should have developed here, as it has been a kind of surrogate for orchestras, which did not exist then.

Mrs Newmarch stayed almost three weeks in Finland and also paid a visit to Ainola. As always her attitude to Sibelius was motherly and protective. While she was anxious that he should not try to portray little Margaretha's rompings in any *Sinfonia domestica*, she did make it clear that, in the surroundings of his own home and family, the real Sibelius emerged more fully than when he thought himself 'plus libre et plus passionné'. In a discreet and diplomatic fashion she tried to indicate that he was in danger of neglecting Aino and their charming daughters. Her mild reproaches were not without justification. After his return from his long trip to London, Paris and Berlin in 1909, he noted: 'Strange to live again in a family.' After Mrs Newmarch's departure he made a solitary trip to the archipelago to refresh himself, and get down to composing again in earnest. Before the première of the Fourth Symphony he was to make two further foreign trips and periodically he would go off to Helsinki and shut himself away in a hotel room. As a contrast to domesticity he needed periods away from Ainola when he could feel 'plus libre et plus passionné'.

Even if Sibelius set great store by Mrs Newmarch's friendship, her visit took its toll on his time and pocket. After her departure he determined to keep himself free of social obligations. There was only one way of doing so:

to master the art of saying no to all and sundry, whatever the cost. Naturally this path led to growing isolation but also some measure of satisfaction: 'I find my life rich and rewarding. The strongest and deepest feelings come to me when I am alone.' The deeper his own self-insight and self-knowledge, the greater the social sacrifice. During the period 1905–9, when the contract with Robert Lienau forced him to compose one work after another, he had practically written himself dry.

In his diary we read of plans to spread a little time each day, if only ten minutes, in studying counterpoint:

> Don't worry about your being 44. There's still time. All major composers found their way to the stars by discipline and self-study. Don't be so overawed by youth that your creativity is stifled. They won't be able to silence your art.

He also thinks aloud about his approach to the orchestra. He writes about the narrative role of the orchestra and its epic quality.

> Don't change the colouring before it is necessary. In scoring one should, as a rule, avoid leaving a paragraph without any strings. The sound can seem rough. Remember the differences in wind instruments in different countries, layout of strings and so on, keep a flexible balance that can be adjusted depending on circumstances. A satisfactory sonority still depends to a large extent on the purely musical substance, its polyphony and so on. In small orchestras the oboe, usually badly played, has to be treated with the same caution as the trumpet. In some orchestras the bassoon in its middle and high register cannot play *piano*. Only the bottom seems capable of that. In such orchestras the lower register of the flute is almost only usable in *forte*. Usually both in the wind and brass, the initial entry can be tentative and leave much to be desired in terms of intonation and ensemble. Beginnings must be carefully marked. Also there is need for great care when the main burden of the melodic line moves from one instrument to another.

All this leaves no doubt that Sibelius set great store by continuity of musical sonority. In actual practice as well as in theory, he was more than ever concerned to take steps to compensate for the absence of the sustaining pedal! From the Fourth Symphony onwards Sibelius's scoring is smoother and more seamless than before.

The Op. 61 songs left Sibelius feeling the pangs of labour:

> The most satisfying moment is when I am planning a work and I have it in my mind. The work itself is a life-and-death struggle. Is this due to too much self-criticism or too little talent?

Small irritations and imagined wrongs preyed on his mind, and he even became angry at not being invited to a choral festival at Loviisa. Volbach's new book, *Das moderne Orchester* roused his ire:

He mentions among others poor H. Pfitzner but leaves out: Bizet, Verdi, Debussy, César Franck, d'Indy, Rimsky-Korsakov and many others. I've never heard of anything more stupid. O what chauvinism! It's doubtful, too, whether Richard Strauss has been an innovator in terms of colour; he has rather developed on foundations laid by others, albeit in a very brilliant way.

The diary bears witness to a certain wounded pride: 'No one – no one at all discusses me! I'm completely out of the picture.'

At last, at the end of July, he sent the Eight Songs, Op. 61, to Breitkopf und Härtel but he was still in a highly-strung condition and tried to soothe his nerves. 'For God's sake, pull yourself together, things aren't that bad! When you are forced, as you are, to earn your bread with your pen you cannot expect life to have the savour of a 9-year-old wine!' To take himself in hand, he went off to spend a week on his own on Järvö, an island in one of the archipelagos along the southern coast of Finland. It would seem that these days unleashed the creative forces within him, for on his return he worked on the symphony for about seven weeks without any interruption or let up.

August

1–7. All these days I spent in the skerries in storms and in good spirits.

8. Torn up what I believed in on the island.

9. My judgement yesterday was not objective. The impression Järvö made was very real. The trouble is giving it the right form. Power!

12. This business of concerning yourself with practical affairs when you are a creative artist. Think of all the time and energy you waste on them every day. For you this is corrosive. But press on, in spite of all the derision and abuse. Worked well today on the development of the first movement. Don't lose the sense of life's pain and pathos!

13. Just remember this for once and all: you are a genius!! You know it yourself. Feel it. Forget about trivia. My God! 'Man lebt nur einmal!' What do you expect?!

15. A wonderful day! Have forged a little but have dreamt of even more! The atmosphere this evening was wonderful. As always when stillness speaks: there are dreadful overtones of eternal stillness – life's *Angst*. Learn to live 'avec une ivresse toujours croissante, presque en délire'. Lengthening life by getting up at six in the morning is something you are not equal to. If you could do that – and plan your work and work intensely, well! things would be different!

16. When will I get this development finished? i.e. be able to concentrate my mind and have the stamina to carry it all through. I managed when I had cigars and wine, but now I have to find new ways. I must!

17. Crossed out the whole of the development. More beauty, and more *real* music. Not just scoring or crescendos but stereotyped writing. Now I have to speed up. Now or never!

26. There must be moments when you find that you have achieved very little and you find your talent small and commonplace. All this is necessary if you are to move forward. Your struggles with form! Your concessions to tradition.

30. Inspired. The development is ready in my head. I dare say that I shall have the whole movement sketched out today.

September

2. Have hammered out the second movement and worked a little on the other two. Wonderful day, autumnal and poetic.

6. It's a matter of vital importance that you stand in front of an orchestra and the public like a great artist and press them to the uttermost limits. Mahler, Berlioz and others. In a terrible mood all day long. Calmed down later on and worked in my fashion on the second movement.

8. Life is difficult again on account of mental lassitude, inability to work and the disdain of others. Worked more on II.

12. Now it seems that III is beginning to shape in my thoughts.

13. Worked hard this evening on III. The theme is now taking shape.

14. Worked hard again on III but no miracles. The theme is still nebulous.

15. Have had a sense of my own genius. Worked on III.

17. Have doubts about the last movement of the symphony. The day 'aus'. For many reasons. Worked a little on the theme of IV.

20. Do not ever let go of the sublime in your art in favour of 'das herkömmlich meisterhafte' [*sic*: = traditional mastery].

21. In the evening a wonderful atmosphere. A direct effect – as I suppose – on IV.

At this stage work on the revision of *The Origin of Fire* interrupted his concern with the symphony. Sibelius tried to work on them both simultaneously but they pulled in wholly different directions, the radical language of the Fourth Symphony hardly harmonizing with the earlier piece. He was plunged yet again into a fit of depression.

22 September. All my youth and childhood, the former with its terrible storms and their after-effects. The corpses still rise to the surface. Help!! Du musst dich zusammenraffen. [You must pull yourself together] [. . .] If only I could rid myself of these dark shadows. Or at least put them into some new perspective. If you can't do that, put the past behind you. You mustn't go under, there's too much on the plus side. Worked on *The Origin of Fire*. The corpses float again. To hell with it. Life is becoming more and more dramatic.[1]

1 This gives the flavour of some of the more aphoristic and morbid entries in the diaries. I should add that there is little syntactical or any other kind of coherence in some of these over-dramatized jottings. *Tr*

Sibelius also spent a little time going through some poems by Arthur Borgström, the industrialist who had acted as guarantor for further bank loans, and the composer naturally wished to repay his generosity in some way. Borgström was Anglo-Swedish and is seen to best advantage in his English poems, one of which, 'Thaïs', Sibelius had set the previous summer. Now he opposed the idea that his setting should appear as an appendix to the collection of poems Borgström was proposing to publish. He suggested that Borgström should publish them himself so that they should not fall into 'unworthy hands'; the industrialist took the hint, and waited for a further decade before finally committing them to print.

This apart, Sibelius was trying to purify his style and to eliminate anything superfluous. Writing to Carpelan, he stressed the importance of living in the past and immersing oneself in childhood memories.

In reality I believe that such spiritual ablutions are vital for the soul. One becomes more deeply aware of the main threads in one's being and can better 'understand' them. Now, when I am at peace with myself, I can gain some insight into my life and work. And I find that consistent striving forward and climbing is the only thing I can do, and the only course that gives me satisfaction. The unmusical Goethe has uttered perhaps the deepest musical truths in his *Sprüche*, and these have served to stiffen my backbone during this period.

One cannot help noticing that Sibelius withdrew more and more from political awareness during this period, a phenomenon widely shared in his circle. After a period of relative tranquillity in the immediate wake of the 1905 strike, the Tsarist regime had begun tightening its stranglehold over the country. The Finnish senator J. K. Paasikivi, later to become Prime Minister and subsequently President after Independence, thought the situation far graver than in the days of Bobrikov. The Tsar's Prime Minister, Stolypin, had assumed personal responsibility for Finnish affairs and as long as his narrow and illiberal chauvinism held sway, there was no possibility for the Finnish cause to gain advancement through persuasion or negotiation. In June 1910 the Tsar introduced legislation to the effect that all important matters involving Finnish affairs were to be decided in the Duma. 'Finis Finlandiae!' was the cry of one Russian nationalist, Purishkevitch, when this was passed in the Duma. It was presumably in the light of this that Sibelius wrote to Carpelan, 'Politics can drive me to despair but have up to the present had little effect on my work. [. . .] I can't help matters or affect them in any way other than by continuing to compose "for King and Country".' His words reflect the growing despair and resignation of so many Finns.

Now that the last vestiges of Finnish autonomy were being eroded, the door was open to total Russification. Russianized Finns or pure Russians became the dominant figures in the Helsinki Senate while refractory Finns were either imprisoned or despatched to Siberia. The differences between the constitutionalists and the other nationalist opposition group were naturally rendered an irrelevance in the face of events. Unless totally unforeseen circumstances arose, there seemed no escape from the same fate that had overtaken the Baltic provinces in the Tsarist Empire. The cry 'Finis Finlandiae' brought home the realities of the situation and the twin fears of Tsarist imperialism on the one hand and revolutionary socialism on the other, producing a kind of paralysis and fatalistic apathy among the Finnish upper classes. Fear of the socialists grew even stronger now that the class hatred, which Sibelius had discerned in 1906, now gathered force. There was little left of the optimism and euphoria of the early part of the decade when the tide of Finnish nationalism appeared to be running strong. Nor did Sibelius feel any urge to compose another *Song of the Athenians* or *Finlandia*, or even another symphony in the style of the Second, which, in spite of Sibelius's words later in life, can still be seen in one sense as a kind of symbol for the surge of optimism and resistance at that period. His thoughts were now centred on his inner journey.

It was in late September that Sibelius returned to the symphony. He did some but not a great deal of work. Then a period of stagnation set in. His routine was interrupted by a visit, first to Christiania to conduct a concert of his works, and then to Berlin, where the greater part of his time was spent on a revision of *The Origin of Fire*. In a newspaper interview in Christiania he spoke of the situation in Finland and the air of fatalism. Everybody in Finland is travelling, wiring home for more funds, but the fact that we travel at all is our only deliverance. It keeps us alive and aware.' When the interviewer pressed him a little harder about conditions in Finland he replied: 'Everything is fine. We dance, drink and make merry' – a response that raised a few eyebrows both in Norway and in his own country!

He gave another interview in which he spoke highly of the Christiania Orchestra and its sense of commitment, which is

much to be preferred to the routine, which is all too often found in some of the Continental orchestras of note, who also show a certain slackness and unwillingness to concern themselves with the refinements of tempo and rhythm, which are central to the nervous system of music.

Asked whether he thought that the understanding of music was also related to one's ethnic origin, he answered affirmatively:

People maintain that music is an international language but I am not sure that the evidence bears this out. Take, for example, the misunderstanding of Wagner prevalent in the Latin countries, in spite of the fact that his operas are now fashionable in both France and Italy. But as far as inspiration is concerned, I think that nature and landscape play a greater part than national origins. Let us take the case of Grieg, whose music it is impossible to conceive in any other than a Norwegian landscape.

The rehearsals were something of a nightmare for him, however politely he may have spoken to the press. He felt that the musicians did not accord him the natural respect they would have given to a Grieg or a Svendsen. To steady himself he took potassium bromide but then became drowsy: this led to renewed laments in his diary at the absence of alcohol whose stimulus he needed. He met a number of celebrities including the explorer Fritjof Nansen, but the emptiness of this socializing did not please him and he was self-conscious about his imposed abstinence: 'I must appear to be a terrible wet blanket and a bore.' His role as a musical ambassador was not an easy one for him. A few hours before his concert he took another dose of bromkalium and his diary notes: 'In spite of nerves and such like – your will must triumph. It is a matter of will – many have been less expert in these matters than you.'

The programme was entirely new as far as the Norwegian public was concerned: it comprised the Second Symphony, *Night Ride and Sunrise*, excerpts from the *Swanwhite* music, and two new pieces receiving their very first performance: *In Memoriam* and *The Dryad*. The audience was responsive and demanded an encore (*Valse triste*), but the press was mixed except in the case of the Second Symphony, which was received with enthusiasm. One critic found some reminders of Debussy in *The Dryad* with its 'loose impressionistic form and its seeming propensity towards thin textures and sonorities without a well-defined thematic connection'. According to another reviewer, *In Memoriam* lost much of its impact on account of exaggerated striving after effect.

After Christiania, Sibelius went on to Berlin where he worked for three weeks. He finished the revision of *The Origin of Fire*, and spent a few days resting and girding his loins for a renewed assault on the symphony, which he resumed at the end of the month. Even though the atmosphere of Wilhelmine Berlin was not wholly congenial to him, he was able to hear some new music: Rachmaninov's First Piano Concerto in F sharp minor ('there is feeling for sonority and culture but a certain tameness') and Arensky's Fantasy for piano and orchestra, given at the Singakademie. From there he took a motor car to the Beethoven-Saal to hear a programme of Reger's music given by the Bohemian Quartet with the composer at the piano. In fact after the concert he went behind to pay his respects to the artists, and his description of the encounter has an unconscious frank charm: 'I like Max Reger. He is not at all successful. But he is a great artist. And he gets 15,000 Reichsmarks for a chamber work! So eventually I can hope for more too.' His diary records his opinion of Reger's music: 'National, German, a little too ornate and occasional *longueurs*, but just because of its German quality, good.'

Sibelius suffered on each occasion that he passed a window shop filled with cigar boxes and wine bottles, and began to think that now, at 45, life was passing him by: 'Anguish, dejection, everything has turned sour – ' He found human contacts presented him with greater difficulty: he thought his friend Adolf Paul was using him and was inspired either by his visit to the composer, Paul Juon, one of Lienau's protégés, who among other things had composed a violin concerto clearly modelled on the Sibelius. The only bright spot was Busoni: 'He gave me much by his admiration for my music. The orchestra. Advised me to keep writing for it and not stray into other media.' On one occasion when Sibelius and Busoni met, the latter had the young Edgard Varèse in his company. As a youth Varèse had heard *The Swan of Tuonela* in Turin, most likely in the performance conducted by Arturo Toscanini, and had been enchanted by the mystery and sense of space in that work. Even in later years he retained his admiration for the Finnish composer.

Sibelius remained sufficiently long in Berlin to hear his Violin Concerto played by Ferenc von Vecsey, according to Busoni one of the greatest virtuoso musicians of the day. But even if he were satisfied with the performance, he had no illusions about the work's reception by the press: 'A fine musician. But the Concerto itself will still have to wait. Scorn will be poured on it. Or what is worse, a passing condescending mention.'

Work on the third movement of the Fourth Symphony came to a standstill and his diary records his doubts about the whole work, and a consequent bout of depression. Yet the feeling of emptiness that he suffered was to find an expressive outlet in that very movement.

'The idea of *In Memoriam* [the Funeral March for Orchestra, Op. 59] came to me in Berlin in 1905,' Sibelius told Ekman. He denied that he had any particular person in mind when he wrote the piece, but he told his daughter Eva that the work was composed in memory of Eugen Schauman, the patriot who had assassinated Bobrikov. The discrepancy may well have a psychological explanation. Given his political involvement in 1904, he may well have intended to compose something for Schauman, whether a funeral march or a requiem. Something he heard or experienced in Berlin triggered off the first thematic ideas – possibly a performance of Mahler's Fifth Symphony with its opening funeral march. But he put it aside until 1909 when his own plight had prompted thoughts of death. It was with himself in mind that he composed *In Memoriam* – 'when I am a corpse' – but he was not unnaturally reticent about it.

In Memoriam begins in somewhat Mahleresque fashion with timpani, cellos and double-basses, quiet side-drum rolls and an insistent string figure in parallel thirds. When the main theme returns with a rising fanfare-like motive only to sink chromatically *fortissimo*, the Mahleresque flavour is further heightened:

Ex 83

In the second group the winds howl their laments over an intense and dark background of strings and brass:

Ex 84

In Memoriam is in sonata form, though the development section is short and passes almost unnoticed into the reprise. The chromatic figure is worked up into a climax with a descending tritone in the bass. Even if its substance is rooted in late romanticism with *Götterdämmerung* and Mahler as sources of inspiration, *In Memoriam* remains a personal document. A generation that can view the whole art-nouveau period in perspective may perhaps come to judge it more sympathetically than did Sibelius's contemporaries.

In *The Dryad*, Sibelius develops his sense of texture and colour in a more Debussyian and impressionistic fashion. Even the opening with its free-floating quality is liberated from the rigid sense of bar lines, and has a distinctly Debussyian feel:

Ex 85

The oboes and flutes have a theme that sounds almost like a distant (or not so distant) relative of *L'après-midi d'un faune*, while the accompaniment is full of shimmering impressionistic seconds:

Ex 86

The introduction turns into a waltz whose theme is related to the wind motive above. The very end makes reference to the mood of the introduction and quietly fades into nothingness.

The incidental music to Mikael Lybeck's *The Lizard* consists of two movements for solo violin and strings. The solo violin is heard only in the first of the two numbers. To Lybeck Sibelius wrote that the score was for nine players but could be reduced to as few as six if need be.

The play has something of the anguish of symbolism with its half-real, half-fantasy atmosphere. Some of the names have a Gothic ring that calls Maeterlinck to mind: Ottokar, Elisiv, Eyringe. The young Count, Alban, hypersensitive in temperament, muses over his violin, fighting against his fear of life and his fascination for the sensual, demonic Adla. At the other pole is his betrothed, Elisiv, tender and pure by nature. In her he dwells in the transcendent world of music: 'Music has never done harm to the living. It has a pure conscience.' In the struggle between the two for Alban's soul, it is Elisiv who is finally destroyed but Alban takes his vengeance on Adla, whom he kills.

The first number, which is heard during the encounter between Alban and Elisiv outside the family tomb of Eyringe, begins with a serenade for solo violin to Alban's words, 'Now let my spirit soar':

Ex 87

The harmonies have something of the colouring of his earlier music, but the mood darkens at the words, 'A small child weeps . . . the lands are without sun.'

Ex 88

At the very end of the scene, as ghosts emerge from the gathering shadows, the text calls for a crescendo of growing intensity and expressive power. But Sibelius took a wholly different view. 'The music should be succinct,' he told Lybeck. 'After so long a dramatic climax, you simply cannot have "narrative" music, for the effect is pleonastic.' Sibelius relies on more subtle means and uses a solo violin recitative over a G sharp minor tremolando:

Ex 89

With its soaring line and the pervasive tritone, it foreshadows something of his thinking in the Fourth Symphony.

The other piece, *Elisiv's feverish visions*, begins with a syncopated figure consisting of major thirds moving in contrary motion and a characteristic descending figure that emanates from an idea in the serenade theme:

Ex 90

Every chord is related to the tritone and reinforces the impressionistic feeling conveyed by the harmonies familiar from the Debussy of *La Mer* and which we are to encounter in the Fourth Symphony and later on in *Tapiola*. The latter is directly foreshadowed in the following crescendo, which a little later in the piece is even heard *tremolando*:

Ex 91

Thus are the tempestuous dreams of *Tapiola* conceived in the feverish visions of *The Lizard*! This movement is effectively built on material from its predecessor, and is a striking instance in Sibelius of whole-tone harmonies undermining the sense of major-minor tonality. The final ideas, which depict Elisiv's premonition of death, are less original. The score as a whole is far too intimately linked with the action of the play to survive independent concert performance, and it is obvious that rather than fashion an orchestral suite from its ideas, Sibelius preferred to let them act as a catalyst in new pieces.

'Come away, Death!' is the first of two settings from Shakespeare's *Twelfth Night* and must be numbered among Sibelius's most memorable songs. Like Shakespeare's Fool, he sees through Life's charade and builds the song on the simplest harmonic basis: the contrast between the chord of E minor and a G sharp minor triad – the D sharp of the latter is the leading note of E minor and brings a macabre colouring to the word 'Death':

Ex 92 'Come away, come away, death'

The use of the tritone formed by the relationship of voice to accompaniment serves to underline life's anguish:

Ex 93 'Fly away, fly away, breath'

One expects the song to end in the tonic E minor but it is Death, and G sharp minor, that claims the last word. Sibelius set the poem in Hagberg's Swedish translation, which presents certain problems of accentuation if it is sung in the English original. Its companion piece from *Twelfth Night*, 'When that I was and a little tiny boy' is an elegant and charming vignette in E major. Sibelius sharpens the fourth degree of the scale producing a tritone and a slightly ambiguous tonal effect.

Ex 94 'When that I was and a little tiny boy'

'Hymn to Thaïs', a setting of a poem in English by Arthur Borgström – Sibelius's only attempt at English verse – has an interesting background. Borgström suggested the theme during a telephone conversation in July 1909, 'Thaïs, she who cannot be forgotten.' The words haunted Sibelius, who set them, continuing the music for some bars before sending his sketch to Borgström. The latter responded with a poem of ten lines:

Thaïs of Egypt and Helen of Troy
. . .
Who saw Thee incarnate, shall ne'er forget Thee,
Thaïs I would that I never had met Thee.

When he read the final poem, Sibelius decided to start again from the very beginning, even though, as he told Borgström, setting an English text was no joke for him. He finished his setting and sent it off to the eager poet in October 1909. The predominantly Phrygian colouring of the melodic line is to be noted as well as the character of an incantation. The singer is supported by a colonnade of powerful chords.

Ex 95

The Eight Songs, Op. 61, show Sibelius at his most advanced stylistically. Late romantic in outlook and with a strong element of impressionism, they are far removed from the expressionistic world of the Josephson settings. Take for example, 'Slowly as the evening sun' to words of Karl August Tavaststjerna. Where has Sibelius composed a more eloquent and elegiac vocal line or wrought so intense and evocative an accompaniment?

Ex 96 'As slowly as the evening sky drains of purple'

While Sibelius has assimilated something of Rachmaninov's pathos, he has fashioned a distinctly Nordic tone colour and a sparser texture. At the same time one recalls a diary entry noting that he had been studying both Rachmaninov and Debussy. Although it may not be so obviously Debussy-ian, there are parallels in 'Romeo', another poem in sonnet form by Tavaststjerna, to his Spanish pastiches such as 'La sérénade interrompue'! The whole song derives from this phrase (a):

Ex 97 'If one night you suddenly heard strings'

Two variants, (b) and (c), alternate, though they keep the same rhythm.

'Passionately strummed beneath your balcony'

'More likely you would like me all night long'

The musical equivalent of the fourteen lines of the sonnet (4 + 4 + 3 + 3) are laid out with a refined sense of symmetry thus:

abab – ccbb – ccb – cc a (*in the piano part*) b

and with a relatively intricate tonal scheme all in the minor.

e – f–g–e – b–f sharp–e flat – a–f–e

One can see how Sibelius by inserting a C major triad in the piano balances the first and last strophes, while the third strophe is almost an abstract of the second. Sibelius unifies diverse formal principles in an inventive and original fashion.

The 'Romance', also to words of Tavaststjerna, tells of a captive Prince singing from his prison to his Princess. The very opening is reminiscent both in its melodic and harmonic layout of the 'Hymn to Thaïs':

Ex 98 'You are the princess and I the prince'

The tritone also figures prominently during the course of the song, and the similarity to the closing bars of the *Largo* of the Fourth Symphony is quite striking:

Ex 99 'On dewy mornings when the cock crows God grant my thralldom an end'

Of the two remaining Tavaststjerna settings, *När jag drömmer* 'When I dream' gave Sibelius a good deal of trouble. He has not been altogether successful in integrating the recitative-like, somewhat expressionistic introduction with the metrical and more rigid inner section. The ending with the nightingale trill is also a little problematical: in a moment of irritation Sibelius himself described it as 'feeble' or 'paltry'. The other setting. 'Dolce far niente' begins with a syncopated figure in thirds in the piano part. Sibelius was to use a similar idea in the fifth of his *Humoresques*, for violin and orchestra, Op. 89 No. 1:

Ex 100

In his setting of Runeberg's *Fåfäng önskan* 'Idle Wishes', Sibelius poured out music of which he himself could write with pride in a letter to Carpelan as 'intense and grand'. It exemplifies his genius for using conventional means in an altogether unconventional way and to powerful artistic ends. 'The countless waves' ('Otaliga vågor') of the poem resound in the arpeggios that bestride the whole compass of the piano.

Ex 101

Yet for all his satisfaction, immediately after finishing the setting, he was beset with doubts and his diary records him finding the text 'sloppy' and the music secondhand Chopin. Three days later he wrote,

Are a few broken chords and received modulations to be described as the intellectual property of anybody these days? But one can easily change and adapt such writing so that it is totally unrecognizable – particularly in so far as those Chopinesque notions are concerned. But isn't it more honest and upright to admit frankly how one's thoughts had first come and how one had felt, without afterthoughts but with inspiration?

When he looked back the following summer over his past year's work, it was 'Idle wishes' of the Op. 61 songs that made the deepest impression on him. It is without doubt one of his greatest songs, inspired as it is by much the same theme as *Autumn Evening* – Nature's indifference to Man. It succeeds in conveying a powerful sense of desolation as the poet observes the infinite, unremitting flow of the waves, 'uncaring, cold and clear'. 'Yet were I one of them I should still have my heart. O were I as heartless as they.'

In 'Lapping waters' Rydberg uses the image of a sun-tanned Venetian youth as a springboard for a theme that has become classical in the North: 'We sense Princes when our eyes dwell on children but among adults we find no Kings.' Sibelius does not greatly concern himself with this particular theme but contents himself with an impressionistic waterplay with trills, arpeggios and the like while the vocal line describes a well-moulded path:

Ex 102 'We imagine princes when we look at children'

Bertel Gripenberg's poem *Vårtagen* 'Spring spell' does not appear to have touched any real vein of inspiration, and this is by far the weakest of the Op. 61 settings.

Also from this period are the Ten Piano Pieces, Op. 58, which show diverse musical elements from the impressionistic to the *junge Klassizität*. In the *Reverie*, the harmonies in the right hand dissolve into a hazy figure while the melodic line is centred in the left:

Ex 103

Generally speaking, the Op. 58 pieces are of uneven quality. The somewhat Schumannesque *The Evening*, for example, is not particularly interesting in either content or layout. *The Shepherd* and *Tempo di menuetto* reflect the world of *junge Klassizität*; so does the *Air varié* whose fresh linear texture almost looks back to the Third Symphony.

Ex 104

No trace of impressionist fingerprints there. The *Scherzino*, according to Sibelius himself, has 'something of the character of Benvenuto Cellini about it (not Berlioz)'. The *Summer Song* offers a foretaste of the style he was to develop in the 1920s. When Sibelius noted in a diary entry that he thought the Op. 58 pieces an improvement technically on his earlier keyboard writing, his verdict must be upheld. He has eliminated much, though not all, of the 'piano reduction' layout that disfigures his previous essays in this medium.

So far Sibelius had interrupted his labours on the Fourth Symphony three times: first, at the beginning of 1910 when his material worries were at their most pressing and shorter works like *The Dryad* and the revision of the *Impromptu* claimed his energies; then in May he put it aside to welcome Rosa Newmarch and work on the Op. 61 songs, and finally in late September he set out on his trip to Christiania and Berlin. After he had put the finishing touches to *The Origin of Fire* in Berlin, he had again turned to the symphony and continued his struggles with it on his return to Järvenpää.

November
4.   Enjoyed the day to the utmost. Its peace. Time stood still. I have worked and forged. In a wonderful mood. If only I could ignore that 'world metropolis' Helsinki. Must work everything out to the bitter end. The important thing is to work intensively; or you will merely end up as just another representative composer from this corner of the world. Third movement of the symphony.

5.   Worked well. Forged onwards into the finale. Wonderful day with snow interlacing the trees and their branches – typically Finnish.
      A symphony is not just a composition in the ordinary sense of the word; it is more of an inner confession at a given stage of one's life.

6.   Another day gone without my having managed to capture the joy in writing that is absolutely necessary if my ideas are to come to any-thing. Can I not really succeed in focusing my powers? I regard this as an absolute must. But how to achieve it? But, my friend, take comfort from the fact that you work in your own way. The results would be improved tenfold were your working methods more rational. Still, who knows? This is art – you are not concerned with science. God knows, incidentally, whether they are all that much apart.

Sibelius realized that he would have to cut himself off entirely from the outside world if he was ever to make real headway on the new symphony. Glazunov paid a visit to Helsinki to conduct a performance of his Seventh Symphony and Fauré also came with the Capet Quartet but Sibelius attended neither event. Like so many public figures with a strong sense of duty, his absence caused him some twinges of guilt, but if the new symphony were to see the light of day, his concentration must be wholly unbroken.

Back at Ainola he had time to study the press, only to find that the tone of the Finnish press was turning a little sour. Foreign press comment prompted an angry outburst in his diary:

Am I nothing more than a 'nationalistic' curiosity, who must rank second to any 'international' mediocrity?

At the same time he did not mince matters himself when it came to handing out criticism, even when it concerned his old friend, Busoni.

Why does this great keyboard master bother to compose? It is always interesting to hear a great artist working things out – but this 'music' *[Fantasia contrappuntistica]*. Ugly and thin, without any sense of movement. His *Berceuse élégiaque* is another matter – as colour and musical backcloth it has its place.

Perhaps Sibelius's outspoken reaction against the *Fantasia contrappuntistica* was a subconscious reflection of his own feelings of inadequacy as a contrapuntist and an awareness of his own needs to develop his polyphonic technique. A few days later he noted in his diary, 'Forced myself after a terrific effort to do fifteen minutes' counterpoint.' And he kept it up the following day.

Suddenly, the symphonic progress suffered yet another reverse in the form of a commission, which he decided to accept. The previous summer, Aino Ackté had suggested that she and Sibelius should undertake a concert tour in Germany. Her impresario was none other than Emil Gutmann, who had arranged the historic first performance of Mahler's Eighth Symphony, and the suggestion was that the Sibelius–Ackté tour should begin in Munich in mid-February 1911 and include a number of German cities including Berlin, as well as Vienna and Prague. Part of the plan was for Sibelius to compose a new song with orchestra for Ackté. Sibelius's decision to accept may well have been affected by some words that Burmester had uttered some years before, that his cause in Germany would be won only by making a guest appearance as conductor. And so, early in November, he went to Helsinki to discuss the tour with Ackté, and for the text he chose Edgar Allan Poe's 'The Raven', which he knew in Rydberg's beautiful Swedish translation.

He set to work on 'The Raven' on 9 November, even though his ideas were still at an embryonic stage. For the next six days he occupied himself with the song until the symphony forced itself back into the foreground. 'Everything is slowly maturing; "The Raven" as well as the symphony,' he noted in his diary. At the same time, Aino's health had taken a turn for the worse. She developed rheumatoid arthritis and had to be taken to hospital where she remained for a time. Sibelius paid her frequent visits and his diary records his own pain and anxiety. During the rest of November he divided his creative energies between symphony and song.

November

24. The miracle I am waiting for will never take place. I cannot work properly. Why these empty moments? [. . .] In the evening I meditated = 'worked'.

25. Worked on the third movement which – it seems to me – is beginning to take shape and colour.

26. Have been in ecstasy. Naive as always! [. . .] 'The Raven' back again.

27. In a good mood again! Everything is rose-coloured. Worked this evening on 'The Raven'.

28. Struggle with God! 'The Raven'! Freudvoll und leidvoll! [Happiness and pain!] Will I get it finished and perfect by February?

Selim Palmgren's new opera, *Daniel Hjort* received its first performance in Helsinki on 1 December. Sibelius was far too interested to be able to stay at home and he thought the score was done with 'much *savoir-faire* but little warmth'. The opera acted as a further spur to his own endeavours; he realized that he *must* get 'The Raven' into its definitive form if only to stop the division of his energies. Meanwhile the German translation of the poem had arrived, only to cause him some embarrassment.

December

3. Doubts about the text. Words are always a burden in my composing. Looked at the *Kalevala* and it struck me – how I have grown away from this naive poetry.

Only two years were to pass before he was to compose one of his greatest works to a text drawn from the *Kalevala*! But, nevertheless, there is no doubt that more often than not, he was hampered rather than inspired by the problems of word setting.

His struggles with the new piece continued for a few more days:

December

4. Where have I got at the age of 44? What have I achieved? I'm soon 45. An 'established name'! Well, yes, that's about all. All those lovely dreams! This has happened because of my relapse into classicism. Listen to your own inner voice and go your own modest but sure way. You won't be any the worse for that. Went skiing. A wonderful day. Worked at the 9th stanza of 'The Raven'.

6. In Helsinki. Cold, malicious glances.

7. 'The Raven' has picked up speed. I've cut out much of the old which

was too 'modern meaningless'. I am in quite an excited state about this piece. Wonderful spirits. It is as if time stood still and the heavens were awesome with portents and moons. Castagnets and *triangolo*.

After this burst of activity, however, came the realization that he would never finish 'The Raven' in time for the première in February. Only two months remained and he was committed during that time to appear in Gothenburg, which he had agreed with Stenhammar long before, and in Riga to fulfil his promise to Schnéevoigt. The psychological pressure on him was increased by Gutmann's advance publicity and the fact that it was centred on Ackté did not pass unnoticed. The French news agency Havas announced that he would be giving concerts in Rome in August. Sibelius ought to have been pleased with the plans that were developing for his European tour: the Second Symphony, *Pohjola's Daughter* and such songs as *Autumn Evening,* 'Jubal, 'Duke Magnus' and 'The Raven'. But a diary entry for 10 December shows his doubts growing: 'Aino Ackté publicity – the heroine. Work on *der Rabe*! [. . .] The pity is that the Fourth Symphony is not maturing.' But would it ever? Further thought convinced him that all his powers would have to be concentrated on 'The Raven' if it were to be finished in time for its February performance, and then his time would be committed to the concert tour.

A day later Sibelius made up his mind: 'I have burned my boats and broken with the Gutmann circus and Aino Ackté. I will have to take the consequences. I am putting 'The Raven' on one side for the time being. Have wasted a month. My soul weeps.' In actual fact, of course, he put aside the song for good. Some days later and Sibelius was wondering how he could have ever agreed, at such 'an anxious and worrying juncture', to accept a commission tied to a deadline such as 'The Raven' had been. 'It never works!' But as he told Carpelan, 'The main thing now in all that I do is the Fourth Symphony. I am totally absorbed in it – have my wonderful trances.'

Aino Ackté was in London singing the title role in *Salome* under Beecham at Covent Garden when the news came. Sibelius had despatched a laconic cancellation by telegram. Needless to say, she greeted it with no mean display of temperament.

Herr Sibelius, I am not accustomed to being treated in this fashion and being made a laughing stock. It would have been more honest if you had said right at the outset that the idea of Sibelius concerts abroad do not appeal to you. You would have saved me a great deal of trouble . . . and I would have been spared this ridiculous and embarrassing position *vis-à-vis* Gutmann and others, with whom you have ruined my prospects for the future.

But after giving vent to her fury and indignation, she went on to explain with great dignity that she had acted without self-interest in trying to promote this venture and was guided by her great admiration for his talent. And that she would not allow these events to stand in the way of performing his work abroad and she would continue to sing his works whenever the opportunity presented itself. Not unreasonably she complained to Rosa Newmarch who sounded a note of reproach: 'The least you can do is to write to this wonderful singer. You have wounded her vanity – and you should know what that means.' But Sibelius justified himself only to Carpelan:

> Me. I leave the diva Ackté to drown in her publicity. 'The Raven' will improve by keeping. The Fourth Symphony is breaking through the clouds in sunlight and power. My work is of a totally different order from these concert-givers who are commercially successful. When I give a concert no diva or prima donna should be the centre of interest – it's my symphonic music that will triumph.

Undoubtedly, the Gutmann publicity did not help matters. While he was struggling with his setting, Sibelius could read that he had

> just completed a great symphonic poem for voice and orchestra, which expert opinion has declared to be technically remarkable in its handling of the orchestra as well as being an extraordinarily effective piece, displaying the same bold symbolism and enchantment as does Finnish folk poetry or Axel Gallén's painting.

Nor was he pleased to read in an interview with Ackté: 'I am taking Sibelius with me.' This did not go down well at Ainola though in examining the whole episode one cannot escape the conclusion that Sibelius was every bit as much of a prima donna as he accused Ackté of being.

Some weeks later he mentioned in a letter to Rosa Newmarch how, while in Berlin during the autumn, he had been overwhelmed by a distaste for the modern tendencies he encountered there and perhaps this was a contributory factor in his dealings with Ackté and Gutmann. With 'The Raven' no longer in flight, he could return to work on the symphony.

December

12. Aino worries me. Fear that everything is not going all that well [. . .] Worked again on the third movement of the symphony. In Helsinki. Aino happier . . . I am altogether a stranger in Helsinki nowadays. A wonderful metamorphosis.

13–15. Work and forge on the third movement. But I can't really concentrate properly.

16. Everything still uncertain concerning Aino's fate. Not working well. I dream and let life pass by.

17. Home. Life without anything to stand on . . . The only thing that is certain is that I will be able to manage with money. Money and yet again money. [. . .] The horizon with a streak of light is a long, long way away.

18. The bear who has slept a long time begins to wake now and again. Everything causes me endless suffering. When one is 45 the future begins to pale. And now everything is subjected to criticism. I might as well be nothing as a composer according to them. Woe on me. Work with appalling effort. In the evening the sun begins to shine through. Yes, yes you have genius. Wonder how the third movement will work itself out. Everything is still in chaos and I need to concentrate.

19. See no possibility of finishing the symphony before 6th February. If only I could force myself to. Perhaps! – Worked on the third movement which is beginning to take shape. But otherwise nothing else.

20. Visited Aino in Helsinki. A powerful mood. Continued to work on the third movement during the evening with 'the quake'.[1] I can see it as a whole but – since I don't feel that I have enough time – doubt whether I can get everything worked out in time. My fate.

21. Negotiations with E. Fazer (the impresario). My concerts in Helsinki on 20th and 22nd February, L'homme propose, Dieu dispose. The situation concerning the symphony, however, is not so desperate. Tranquillity is called for, and calm if it is to be all right. The day's work: Not bad.

24. Christmas – ! An elk crossed our garden three times!!

25. Christmas – ! Aino sick . . . Continue to work. Money worries begin again! Of my State Prize [1,500 marks] only 400 remains. Eight doctors' bills unpaid. Misery whever one turns.

29. Later on in the day I worked well. Third movement of the symphony. 'A Himalaya returns!' My own home in a sorry state. Everybody's ill.

30. Soon the year ends. I think how terribly little I have to show for it. How unctuous!

31. On the last day of the year I played piano duets with Eva (Schubert *Tänzer*). An *ouverture* to Aino's tragedy. The great thing that I began to sense a year ago is at last taking form [. . .] I have catarrh. Aino worries me more than I care to say.

The year 1911 got off to a bad start. So as to get away to more neutral surroundings, Sibelius moved into Helsinki for about three weeks, staying first with a fellow musician, Adolf Berlin, for a few days, and then moving into the Hotel Fennia. Even though he was disturbed by the salon music from the restaurant, he managed to reshape the third movement of the symphony. He managed to avoid making contact with his former drinking

---

1 The diary entries periodically refer to the symphony as *bäfvan*. Literally translated this means 'tremor', the image being one of an earthquake erupting. *Tr*

companions but his attempts to live a new and disciplined life came to little. He made frequent trips home to see the family but for the most part this was not a happy period; he did not enjoy his friends and relatives; indeed, quite harmless and civilized people were denounced as coarse, stupid and ignorant. When Eero Järnefelt sang the praises of his own daughter as a linguist, Sibelius was plunged into depression!

Gradually work on the symphony ground to a halt. Evidently his forthcoming trip to Gothenburg and Riga had an adverse effect on his powers of concentration. He went out to dinner quite often and attended some concerts. He heard Wilhelm Backhaus but found his somewhat remote style of interpretation uncongenial. In his diary he wrote that Backhaus played 'like a pianola – more mechanically' and told Carpelan that he 'lacked stature'. Not an altogether surprising verdict, for Sibelius had Busoni's romantic approach to the keyboard as an ideal, and Backhaus's 'objectivity' hardly harmonized with this spirit. Even Walter Niemann thought him soulless.

At the Backhaus recital, Sibelius met Willy Burmester, whose manner was very reserved and distant, judging from his diary entry. ('Burmester reserved – it's comical! But I'll show them all who they are dealing with.') It would seem that he had forgotten that Burmester had every reason to be cool! However, Burmester's playing made a great impression on him: 'A wonderful bowing arm! In the evening he was with a charming lady. Reworked the third movement of the symphony.'

Some adverse reviews of *Voces intimae* and the Violin Concerto in the German press sent his spirits plunging.

Been 'down' the last few days. I wonder whether it's on account of work – i.e. the symphony – stagnation? I must turn to it again in earnest, in spite of the fact that the *Berliner Tageblatt* maintains that my earlier works were all right but that now my imagination has deserted me! Life is not easy! If I could only empty my glass and smoke my cigar, ah! then, believe me, my youth would be recaptured again! But I'm now following a more difficult path by holding to this *vita nuova*.

The concert tour was now fast approaching but the symphony was still unfinished. Consequently, he decided to postpone his February concerts until April. Back at Ainola, he addressed himself to another commission: Arvid Järnefelt's play, *Death (Kuolema)* was to be revived in a new version at the Finnish National Theatre, and Sibelius was to compose two new pieces to add to the incidental music he had already composed. These were the *Rondino der Liebenden* and *Vals-intermezzo,* more generally known nowadays as the *Canzonetta* and *Valse romantique*. He appears to have enjoyed working on them but before he could put the finishing touches to the score, it was time to set out for Gothenburg.

Thanks to Wilhelm Stenhammar, who had been appointed chief conductor of the Gothenburg Symphony Orchestra in the autumn of 1907, the

Swedish city had become the focal point of interest in Sibelius in the Scandinavian countries. When Sibelius arrived there on 2 February, it was to a city that his music had already conquered. 'You can reckon with a good and understanding public . . . The boys in the orchestra love you as much as I do, and you have taken me by storm,' wrote Stenhammar in the spring of 1910. On the very first tour abroad, to Copenhagen in 1909, they had taken the Second Symphony of Sibelius with them. Sibelius himself was as tense as he had been eleven years earlier on his visit to Stockholm: 'It feels strange performing in Sweden, where I have so many roots – and to be conducting music on the theme of the *Kalevala*.'

His diary records some of his difficulties and his complexes in dealing with colleagues.

At the rehearsal. Which I thought went badly, but Stenhammar praised my handling of it. Was at his home in the evening. The Swedish composer, Emil Sjögren said straight out that I am a great intellect but nothing more. Also that my orchestration is what makes everything work. Stenhammar's quartet [No. 4 in A minor] good, particularly the first movement. Have put up with much 'patronizing' talk. But I get tougher for every day.

There were, of course, special difficulties in relations between Finns and Swedes at this time – far more so than at present. The Swedes had been the dominant of the two peoples and had occupied Finland for three centuries, and Swedish was still the 'official' language of the ruling classes in Finland. Hence, there were susceptibilities of a more acute kind than existed between, say, Finns and Danes. But it is perhaps fair to say that Sibelius's hypersensitivity was such that he could be made to feel equally ill at ease in Berlin, Paris or even on the train between Järvenpää and Helsinki.

Sibelius was gratified that Stenhammar had dedicated his new quartet to him. Seven years earlier the Swedish composer had toyed with the idea of dedicating his First Symphony to him but decided that the piece was simply not good enough. The quartet is a different matter: it is an aristocratic work that blends elements of late romanticism with something of the spirit of the late Beethoven quartets that Stenhammar admired so deeply. Tor Aulin, the violinist and composer, paid tribute to Sibelius in an elegant speech but the social round was serving to crowd out time for composition and the diary records that the *Canzonetta* and *Valse romantique* were making no progress.

The first concert passed off satisfactorily but no more: 'The Third Symphony went well enough . . . In *Pohjola's Daughter* I never succeeded in getting really good ensemble.' He made up his mind that in the future he would keep out pieces 'intended for popular consumption' such as *Valse triste* and *The Dryad* from his concert programmes but it goes without saying that he was persuaded by various impresarios of the impracticability of this course. At the rehearsals for his second concert he was a little disturbed by

Stenhammar's demeanour and felt that he was not entirely approving. Afterwards he took him on one side: 'Stenhammar suggested that I should stay on here and conduct whenever the fancy takes me. But I am too polite – he said – for the orchestra. One must be courteous but demanding. That is the art of rehearsing.' Stenhammar's words evidently had the desired effect for the farewell concert took fire and ranks along with his appearances in Heidelberg (1901), Berlin (1905) and London (1909) as one of his conducting triumphs. The orchestra rose to its feet to applaud him and Stenhammar hailed him as the greatest living composer.

From Gothenburg Sibelius took the train to Berlin and then on to Riga where he began rehearsals immediately. The orchestra was new, having been founded the previous year by Schnéevoigt. During the eight days he spent in Latvia, Sibelius conducted three concerts in Riga and one in Mitau. A number of people told him that he would make an admirable permanent conductor but, as he wrote to Aino, 'in the long run this would be disastrous for my composing. Its strong atmosphere is born from solitude and pain.' Two years earlier, Sibelius had been involved in a Latvian musical controversy, albeit tangentially. A tone poem, *The Solitary Pine* by the Latvian composer Emil Darsins had been denounced as a plagiarism of *The Swan of Tuonela* by his colleague, Pavel Jurjans.

The matter was taken sufficiently seriously for it to be referred to Glazunov and then the composer himself. Sibelius took the view, as he told Jurjans, that while it seemed likely that *The Swan of Tuonela* had inspired the mood of Darsins's tone poem, he would hesitate to say that it was plagiarized. Darsins was a complete dilettante in his opinion. The episode appears to have cast no shadows over Sibelius's visit, but it is possible that Sibelius would have been aware of a certain tension between the German Balts, who comprised the upper classes, and the Latvians themselves. The former still played a vital role in the musical life of the country: Wagner had spent some time at the Opera, as did Bruno Walter and Fritz Busch, but indigenous Latvian composers, schooled at St Petersburg and Moscow, were playing a more important part in affairs.

Schnéevoigt's orchestral programmes were designed to embrace both ethnic groups. Sibelius's first two concerts in Riga at the Gewerbehaus were attended by an enthusiastic but largely German-speaking audience but his reception at his third concert, given in the Latvian Concert Society House, was no less warm: the shorter pieces were encored and Sibelius was given a garland of laurels by Latvian artists. Indeed, applause and hurrahs pursued him into the street afterwards. None the less, a German-language paper somewhat tartly noted that the audience was composed of almost every nationality represented in Riga except for the Latvians who were relatively sparse while 'prominent members of the community were conspicuous by their absence'. No doubt this kind of comment must have seemed familiar in later years when both Kajanus and Schnéevoigt had their respective orchestras in Helsinki and became the spearhead of the tensions between the Finnish- and Swedish-speaking communities.

There was a romantic intermezzo that came to nothing. An anonymous admirer wrote him a passionate letter in French suggesting an assignation at the Polish Student Corporation at Schützengarten: 'Venez, venez!' 'Invitation – as usual in Russia – to a rendez-vous', he noted in his diary. Alas, he disappointed the young lady. At Mitau he saw the less glamorous side of a performer's life: 'Wretched, dirty, hall badly lit, out-of-the-way with an ignorant public. No sense of atmosphere. Unequivocally good for one!' During the trip he had even learned to forget about his nervousness: 'Just about to go on – and *ich pfeiffe darauf.*' [I haven't a care in the world.]

Sibelius returned home on 19 February worn out after his musical wanderings. For all the success he had enjoyed during his tour, he still felt 'a deeply unhappy being', kept at a distance by his colleagues. However, his sense of inner harmony soon returned.

February

20. Aino, my wife, the most understanding of all.
21. Worked at *Valse romantique*. Back again in the heights!
22. Worked on ditto and *Canzonetta*. It's howling and snowing outside. In here at home, it's warm and the atmosphere good. Don't think about Helsinki with its concerts and social obligations. Stay your ground here.

Sibelius missed Rachmaninov no less, playing the Second Piano Concerto in Helsinki on the 23rd. He finished the *Valse romantique* and the *Canzonetta* in one fell swoop. Looking back over the past few weeks he noted, 'A whole month has been taken up by travelling and these new small pieces, more's the pity.' He had to have the new symphony ready by the end of March and his diary records the fifth and final stage in its composition.

March

2. Begin working again on third movement.
5. It is noticeable that I am becoming more indolent. But – and this is certain – not spiritually lazier. Fourth movement – second subject.
6. Heard Armas [Järnefelt] conducting Mozart. An unforgettable experience. My concerts are definitely fixed for 3rd and 5th April. I pray that I shall have the powers to finish, copy out and perform the Fourth Symphony. Today the last movement – second subject. It's already becoming clearer [. . .] I often don't feel very strong; as if I were overstrained. Of what? Perhaps the symphony. Or perhaps it is just the approach of death.

The revival of *Kuolema (Death)* and its new movements brought work on the symphony to a brief standstill – 'It is as if the devil were at work.'

March

11. Took more long country walks. Worked on the very end of the symphony.

12. Went skiing. Worked?!

13. Worked again on the symphony, fourth movement, i.e. the ending. When composing is my *métier*, why must I be dragged down by attendant reverses, unpleasantness and provocation. But time – one's span here – oh, how short! Difficult to resign oneself! But it is a necessity. Oh! these usual, all too familiar exclamations. Lasst uns doch angenehmeres anstimmen! [Let's only strike up something more agreeable!]

14. Today a wonderful winter's day. With a touch of spring in the air. Have torn up the formal scheme I have for the fourth movement but I think I am nearer the goal. A slender, very slender chance that I'll have it ready in time for the concert. Have my doubts about the 'programmatic' element in music in our day.

15. Battle with the Almighty!

16. Bad reviews from Hamburg and Vienna. On top of that, financial misery . . . Very 'improving' and 'encouraging'! A further spur. What have I got to show for all my struggles and hard work? I would rather have been anything other than a composer. And *that*, Glorious Ego,[1] you dare put on paper. Shame on you!

17. Worked! Will I get this finished? And at the same time realize all my ideas concerning the orchestration? Lightness of touch.

18. Work again *freudvoll und leidvoll*. Damned by the critics as a composer, summonsed for non-payment of debts; wherever I turn, it is black – yet none the less I wouldn't change with anyone!

28. [After a ten-day silence, the diary continues.] Life-and-death struggle with the symphony. Bear your creative 'cross' with manliness!

April

2. The symphony is ready. *Iacta alea est!* [The die is cast!] It calls for much courage to look at life straight in the eyes!

The concert on 3 April began well enough. After *In Memoriam*, which began the first half, came the 'endearing' *Canzonetta* and the 'brilliantly coloured' tone poem *The Dryad*, both of which had to be encored while *Night Ride and Sunrise* was greeted by a storm of applause. Sibelius had saved the new symphony for the second half of the programme, and it

---

1 In many instances in the course of the diaries, Sibelius apostrophizes himself in a way that sounds bizarre or self-regarding to modern ears: 'Wonderful Ego' or 'Glorious Ego'. The practice derives from Runeberg's *Epic Poems* in which Sibelius was steeped, and ultimately has Homeric origins. Accordingly, in referring to one of his daughters, Sibelius could write, 'Ruth, the Glorious Maiden' or 'Katarina, the Proud Damsel'. *Tr*

undoubtedly came as something of a shock for the audience. Not that they had necessarily expected a work with the glowing optimism of the Second Symphony: the political situation in Finland was far too bleak for that. At the same time, the ascetic, uncompromising, aphoristic language of the new work completely baffled the public. After the final chords there was a puzzled silence: was the piece over or not? No one dared to applaud. Only when the customary garlands were brought on did the applause mount and the cries of bravo echo. The somewhat timid Finnish public was not in the habit of booing or whistling, and in any event where Sibelius, a national idol, was concerned, such a course was unthinkable: tantamount to treason! However, there was no doubt in Sibelius's mind that he had misjudged his audience and disappointed them. Even in old age Madame Sibelius recalled the occasion: 'People avoided our eyes, shook their heads; their smiles were embarrassed, furtive or ironic. Not many people came backstage to the artists' room to pay their respects.'

When Sibelius left the hall, he was greeted in the vestibule by the Student Choir, Ylioppilaskunnan Laulajat, who sang Pacius's 'Suomi' and his own 'To my country', and their conductor, Klemetti, made a speech of praise thanking him for all that he had done to make Finland's cause more widely known abroad. To resounding cheers from the choir, he left the hall, but at no time could the dichotomy between his role as a national hero and as a composer in his own right, have seemed greater. Perhaps it might have given him some comfort to know that the new symphony had fired at least two young music students with enthusiasm, namely Aarre Merikanto and Väinö Raitio, soon to become commanding figures in the Finnish musical avant-garde. After the concert was over, Sibelius dined with Aino and Eero and Saimi Järnefelt, perhaps underlining by this means the dedication to Eero and marking their common experiences at Koli where the seeds of the symphony had been sown.

Bewilderment was not confined to the public. Heikki Klemetti, writing in *Säveletär* noted that his earlier musical style no longer satisfied Sibelius.

Everything seems strange. Curious, transparent figures float here and there, speaking to us in a language whose meaning we cannot grasp. Posterity must decide whether the composer has overstepped the boundaries dictated by sound, natural musicianship in overstraining the functions of various intervals in a melody.

The critic of the main Swedish-language daily, *Hufvudstadsbladet*, Emil Wasenius, writing under the *nom de plume* 'Bis', did his best to explain the inexplicable by detailing a programmatic basis for the score:

The theme of the Symphony is a journey to the celebrated mountain Koli (Kolivaara) near Lake Pielinen from whose heights one has a superb view over the neighbouring countryside from the beauties of Hersjärvi in west Höytiänen while to the east there is Pielisjärvi and on the other side of the lake the Russian border. The first movement depicts Koli and the impression it makes. In the second the composer finds himself on the mountainside. Below he can see Pielisjärvi. The sun touches the lake with gold and the sparkling waves glisten in its rays.

And so on in this manner: the third movement offers 'an imposing panorama of Koli bathed in moonlight, a painting with poetry' while the finale describes the composer's return home with the sun still caressing the horizon though 'from the north-east and the White Sea, one can see the darkening shadows of an approaching snowstorm'. The conflicting moods of the menacing storm clouds that never in fact reach us and the contrasting landscape still bathed in sunlight are 'effectively portrayed' though Wasenius felt that the movement had something of a 'touristic aftertaste'. He ends by saying that 'the powerful rapport with our people and its epic poetry that Sibelius evinced in his earlier work and which made him so powerful and impressive, this bond no longer exists in the Fourth Symphony'.

Those lines show how far removed Sibelius was from the taste of his day. Neither Wasenius nor the vast majority of his listeners was able to discern that, on the contrary, Sibelius had succeeded in forging a much deeper bond and a more universal one than the earlier romantic symphonies possess. Wasenius's description of the Fourth Symphony sounds for all the world like a programme note for the *Alpine Symphony* (1915), and though it was not his normal practice to do so, Sibelius sent a letter of protest to *Hufvudstadsbladet* which was published on 8 April: 'Your correspondent's assertions about a programme for my new symphony are quite inaccurate. It seems to me that they closely resemble a topographical description along those lines that I gave certain friends on last April the First.' But Wasenius stood his ground: he had been given the programme by a close friend of the composer's who had guaranteed its authenticity. (The friend in question was apparently none other than Eero Järnefelt.)

Why, one wonders, did Sibelius react so strongly unless there was a small grain of truth in Wasenius's commentary? Had he amused his friends at dinner by retracing the whole process of gestation back to its genesis at Koli? When he saw his topographical musings turned into a simplistic programme and committed to cold print, he was horrified. The last thing he had envisaged was that the Fourth should be thought of as some kind of Mountain Symphony. In any event his experiences of Koli were far from being the only ingredient in its gestation. Even if certain ideas can be traced back to a given experience, they very rapidly acquired an independent life of their own during the course of the work's creation. The very ideas that Sibelius associated with 'La montagne' or 'Thoughts of a Wayfarer' when he was talking to Carpelan in the autumn of 1909 would have undergone a complete metamorphosis by 1911 in an abstract symphonic context, though some of the atmosphere of the original might well survive.

Evert Katila in the Finnish-language *Uusi Suometar* poured scorn on the alleged programme, which he described as an April Fool's Day jest. The symphony itself he saw as

a sharp protest against the general trend in modern music . . . One composes automobile-symphonies nowadays and operas with deafening sonorities, works that demand an apparatus comprising a thousand performers, all this without any aim other than to astonish the listener with what is new and alien.

The Fourth he saw as

the most modern of the modern, and in terms of both counterpoint and harmony, the boldest work that has yet been written.

Axel Carpelan had expressed similar views somewhat earlier in an article published in the Gothenburg daily, *Göteborgs Handels- och Sjöfartstidning:*[1]

As a whole the symphony can be regarded as a protest against prevalent musical tendencies . . . above all in Germany, its birthplace, where orchestral music is becoming a mere technical operation, a kind of musical civil-engineering, which tries to disguise its inner emptiness behind an enormous mechanical apparatus.

Was Carpelan acting here as the composer's own spokesman? Only a month later we find Sibelius himself writing in virtually identical terms to Mrs Newmarch: '[My symphony] stands as a protest against present-day music. It has nothing, absolutely nothing of the circus about it.' The most searching review of the new symphony was by Otto Andersson, a young musicologist specializing in folk music, writing in *Tidning för musik*. Taking as his theme Goethe's lines:

Der Meister kann die Form	[When the moment is ripe, the
zerbrechen/mit weiser Hand, zur	master may, with judicious hand,
rechten Zeit	shatter the mould]

he spoke of the Fourth Symphony as representing a 'synthesis of classicism, romanticism and modernism, which might well serve as the ideal for the music of the future', adding that if by its depth and originality, it presented difficulties for the listener 'much the same could be said for many works of Brahms, Beethoven and Bruckner.'

After the concerts – the programme was repeated on 5 April – Sibelius showed that he could keep a cool head:

The concerts were good. Everything is in confusion. Wasenius's idiocies.

1 The Swedish equivalent, perhaps, of the *Manchester Guardian. Tr*

Aino level-headed! I am expectant and anxious! Breitkopf & Härtel???
Axel Carplan here, full of understanding. Otto Andersson writes about
me. I long to be in the real countryside . . . Shall I publish the symphony
in this form? Yes! – ?

A little later a cool head was even more sorely needed, for his relationship
with Carpelan was suddenly strained almost to breaking point. As so often
in these cases, the incident that triggered this off was quite trivial: a mere
bagatelle. Sibelius had invited Carpelan to an afternoon recital at the Hotel
Fennia at which Aino Ackté was to sing 'Duke Magnus'. When he arrived,
however, he was not admitted as no ticket had been reserved for him. Aino
and Sibelius himself came much later 'absorbed in various musical thoughts
and delayed by an automobile that had kept them waiting'. Carpelan felt
mortally hurt, not so much by the misunderstanding over the ticket itself
but rather the fact that neither Sibelius nor Aino had made the slightest
attempt to apologize. Sibelius had in fact not given the incident a moment's
thought but noticed that Carpelan's attitude had changed: 'My relationship
to Axel Carpelan is in jeopardy! I can't discover the reason. It pains me. I
shall lose this, my only friend! "Musical", *nota bene!*' He lost no time in
putting pen to paper:

> I see clearly that I have hurt you. This is the very last thing that I would
> ever want to do. If there is any excuse, I know that I have been totally
> absorbed in myself in the last few weeks and not given thought or
> consideration to others: that I freely admit. From my heart – and as best I
> can, I want to ask your forgiveness.
>
> It is more than difficult to write this to you of all people. You, for
> whom I have so much – enormously much to thank. You know what
> your deep understanding means to me and my music. You know, too,
> that there is nothing in the whole world that could, or can, give me and
> my music as much as your wonderful, inspiring support.

Carpelan, however, was not to be appeased. Indeed, Sibelius's letter
would seem to have fuelled his inferiority complex:

> I ask myself whether one would *dare* behave to a person of social conse-
> quence or wealth with such nonchalance – and my answer is no, you
> certainly wouldn't. But this was merely me – and I, who had felt as
> humiliated as a peasant, was ashamed.

He went on to pour out earlier grievances including those instances when
Sibelius, albeit unawares, had wounded him. They had been talking, for
example, about the Philharmonic Orchestra's departure for Paris in 1900
when the members of the orchestra had all been given flowers:

> Suddenly you became absent-minded and began saying how people had
> poked fun at this gesture and had muttered, 'Why doesn't that ridiculous

173

creature go to hell with all his flowers?' (That I was the wretch in question was something you had completely forgotten!) You can imagine the demands this placed on my powers of self-control!

Sibelius understood. After the letter came, he noted in his diary: 'Affair with Axel – he has understood all – everything is clear.' Carpelan followed it up a few days later with a slightly shamefaced letter on the lines of 'to understand is to forgive' in which he pictured himself as psychotic, an object of derision:

People have always walked over me, kicked me, lacerated me with their tongues, and viewed me with contempt and ridicule. 'Look, he will be nothing except a parasite, why doesn't he put an end to himself, and stop disturbing us in our work which contributes something useful to society.' But, of course, a man like you, with your genius and powers would always have risen to the top without anything from me.

A day or two later Sibelius wrote him a note of thanks, acknowledging his article on the Fourth Symphony, and recording the arrival of spring now that the starlings were nesting outside his window.

The press controversy surrounding his symphony continued to leave an unpleasant taste in his mouth, and the diary returns to familiar musings:

Suppose that I don't gain 'recognition'? That I am passed over by others in the general view? If envy and intrigue succeed in getting their way? Is my music any the worse for that? On the contrary, it is better for me as a composer! – And – on what grounds can I claim any different fate from the other great composers who have come before me.

On 21 April Sibelius began going through the symphony yet again: 'I work in tranquillity on one or two passages in the symphony which need to be made clearer.' During the first three weeks in May he wrote out a fair copy of the score, also subjecting it to the closest critical scrutiny. He was enjoying the spring air, the sunshine and the enchantment of the lengthening summer nights, the birdsong, the huge May moon. Few pages in Sibelius's diaries reflect a greater sense of hope and enjoyment of life than these spring days. His writing brings the whole atmosphere of the Nordic spring to life: one feels the rain gently beating down on his windows, and sees the bare branches of the trees against an overcast sky, and realizes the intensity of the northern expectation of the miracle – the coming of summer. By 20 May the score was complete and he posted it off to Breitkopf und Härtel, noting in his diary: 'Certain works – such as the Fourth Symphony – must not be underestimated. Even though perfection in these matters can never be attained by any mortal, with the exception of the transcendental Mozart.'

*

On one occasion Sibelius spoke of the Fourth as 'a psychological symphony'. It calls to mind his words about composition as 'a quest in the infinite recesses of the soul', a metaphor he used much later, in 1924, when discussing his creative processes. One might indeed say that the Fourth Symphony, with its soundings of the innermost spiritual condition, is one of the most remarkable musical documents of the Freudian era. As early as the *Kullervo* Symphony, Sibelius had gazed deeply into 'the wells of the past'. Thomas Mann's image has its counterpart in the *Kalevala*, where the old, wise Väinämöinen, seer and demigod, descends into Tuonela, the realm of the dead, to discover the ancient secrets that would enable him to achieve wonders that would surpass all human exploits. The same shamanistic idea can perhaps be discerned in the Fourth Symphony: its opening bars give the same impression of entering Tuonela. The basic tritone figure, C – D – F sharp – E, resonates *fortissimo* in the bassoons' and muted cellos' and double basses' lowest register. After the *junge Klassizität* Third, the whole approach of the Fourth Symphony represents a thoroughgoing evolution. The modal colouring of the major–minor tonality that distinguishes *Kullervo* is enriched and the treatment of tonality, freer and more masterly than ever before, approaches the very borders of atonality. We even encounter a scale of the type that Messiaen was to call 'modes à transpositions limitées'. One can speak of the Fourth Symphony indeed as 'the culmination of his inner search' of his Faust-like quest for the transcendental. In a way this is symbolized by the interval of the tritone around whose tensions the whole symphony revolves.

The tritone has deep roots in his musical thinking. We encounter it as early as the *Kullervo* Symphony, where there is also an interesting parallel with the so-called Bartók scale (the major scale with a sharpened Lydian fourth and flattened Mixolydian seventh). The horn figure in the second group of the first movement seems to symbolize mysticism and the power of fate and this impression is confirmed in the finale when the same theme is intoned by the choir to a *Kalevala* text. At the same time this 'fate' theme serves to broaden the tonal horizon. Later in the cor anglais line in *The Swan of Tuonela* and the whole-tone figures in *Lemminkäinen in Tuonela,* the tritone is identified with the concept of death. The tritone is present even in the first two symphonies, though rarely in the foreground. In the wonderful song, 'On a balcony by the sea', it is associated with longing for eternity and an awareness of God. The tritone pervades both the motives and the tonal relationships in *Pohjola's Daughter,* which in some respects can be regarded as a kind of blueprint for the symphony, while in a very different way the Third Symphony, in the context of its C major classicism, uses the augmented fourth as a means of generating tension. Those selfsame notes (C–D–E–F sharp), albeit in a different order (C–D–F sharp–E), comprise the introductory and at the same time seminal motive of the Fourth Symphony. By skilful manipulation he is able to add Dorian, Lydian and

Phrygian dimensions to the tonality and, by replacing the normal tonic–dominant tensions of sonata form by key relationships a tritone apart, he is able to suggest bitonality, an unusual phenomenon in Sibelius.

The tension between the tonal and whole-tone elements in the symphony is one of its primary characteristics. If isolated passages are taken from the first movement (for example, the F sharp major passage in the exposition) and put alongside the tense and angular violin of the development section, which borders on atonality, or indeterminate tonality, one has the superficial impression that they could derive from wholly different pieces. Yet Sibelius nevertheless succeeds in integrating them into something wholly organic. This tension between tonality as a structural force and whole-tone textures was typical of the time, and part of the wider erosion of major–minor classical tonality. In the third movement of Debussy's *La Mer*, a whole-tone theme whose beginning is identical with the germ cell of the Fourth Symphony is built up to a tremendous climax whose chords oscillate chromatically between the two opposing poles a tritone apart, only to be resolved by a passage securely in D flat. Similarly in *L'Ile joyeuse* a striking effect is achieved by whole-tone cascades contrasting with a dance theme in a Lydian-inflected A major.

Although their thinking is otherwise divergent, Sibelius and Debussy are close in this respect. The modal elements to which the whole-tone scale gives emphasis were always to be found in Sibelius. Even as early as *Kullervo*, he builds up a simple motive in the second movement along the modal lines favoured in the so-called Bartók scale (one descending major second and three ascending from the tonic, thus: B flat – the tonic C–D–E–F sharp). Also, in placing the main tonal centres of activity a tritone apart, he is putting additional pressure on the traditional framework of classical tonality. There is some precedent for his use of tonal centres with whole-tone implications in the Second Symphony: D–F sharp–B flat all rise by a major third, and have obvious whole-tone resonances. But Debussy's use of the whole-tone scale can be seen as a rational stylization of gamelan music. Moreover, Sibelius never attempted the bold keyboard-based experiments of Debussy in pieces like *Brouillards*, juxtaposing the five black notes of the piano in one hand with the white notes in the other, something Stravinsky also did in *Petrushka*, where the tritonal contrasts result in bitonality. Skryabin's use of a scale of ascending fourths (two of them tritones) and the tension between its claims and traditional major–minor tonality can be seen in the Fifth Sonata and *The Poem of Ecstasy*, and in its very different way the same superimposed fourths arise in the *Kammersymphonie*, Op. 9, of Schoenberg, which Sibelius did not get to know until 1914. Even the descending tritone at the opening of *Tosca* reflects the moves to destabilize major–minor tonality.

Yet one does not come closer to the achievement of the Fourth Symphony by putting it alongside co-ordinates such as the major works of

Mahler, Debussy or Schoenberg. One should not lose sight of the fact that Sibelius, like every other major composer, has incommensurable dimensions, and areas of his experience that can be examined only on his own terms. Right from the very beginning Sibelius commentators were anxious to assign labels, to categorize and to measure. His first native biographer, Erik Furuhjelm, found 'good cause to regard the style of the Fourth Symphony as expressionist', while a year later, in 1917, Walter Niemann's monograph stresses its impressionistic character, speaking of its first movement as a 'threnody of the high seas', comparable with his later tone poem *The Oceanides*, even though he was at pains to acknowledge the Schoenbergian naturalism and expressionism of the melodic lines. Only in Sweden was this view firmly resisted by the composer-critic Moses Pergament. Some years after Furuhjelm and Niemann he was to write: 'Every informed musician realizes in his innermost self that in the Sibelian symphonic voyage the Fourth charts the change of course towards impressionism.'[1]

If one has to have recourse to crude labels, then perhaps it is more sensible and accurate to think of the work as expressionist. Unlike the impressionist movement, the expressionist was strongly bound up with the human condition, with the tormented psyche and the inner state of being. This emerges most clearly in painting such as in the pre-expressionist *The Scream (Skriet)* of Munch; in Kirchner's concern with the unremitting isolation of people in cities; in Kokoschka with Freudian hints of the subconscious. In music, perhaps the most obvious example is Schoenberg's *Erwartung*, where the composer's concern is with the world of the dream and the subconscious, and showing as Hans Heinz Stuckenschmidt put it, 'psychic realism of the most terrifying kind'.

Sibelius never went that far along the expressionist road, not even in the darkest moments of the Fourth Symphony. Although his volatility, his moments of high exaltation and days of black depression, emerges from his diaries, he never confided them to his music. Here his feelings were subjected to the classical disciplines. Sibelius portrays his inner landscape with a discretion born of discipline or, to put it another way, with the objectivity of the greatest artists. He does not force specific details on the listener; nor does he sing of his exaltation or despair; these are viewed, as it were, from the Wordsworthian standpoint, 'emotion recollected in tranquillity'. Indeed, though it may be 'a psychological symphony', it is far from being a purely autobiographical document, a record of his inner life, for once the symphony was in the process of gestation, it *became* his life. This interaction makes the Fourth particularly fascinating: the symphony itself and his inner life reflect each other. Here we have a tense yet ultimately harmonious balance between art and life.

1 *Svenska Dagbladet*, 27 March 1924.

Much the same might be said of another work being composed at this time: the Ninth Symphony of Mahler, again written in the shadow of death. To quote Alban Berg,

I see the first movement as giving expression to an intense love of this world, a yearning to live at peace with it and enjoy to the utmost the fruits of nature – until Death takes one by surprise. Then all this fades. The whole movement is permeated by the premonition of death. Again and again it makes itself felt. All the elements of terrestrial dreaming culminate in it.

But the parallel is not exact in that Sibelius's symphony does not radiate the same all-pervasive love of this world or the same intense nostalgia. Yet, however sharply they may diverge, they have one common factor: the introspective, searching quality of the musical language, which may be seen in the chamber-music-like character of some of the scoring. In the finale of Mahler's symphony one is forcibly struck by one passage, scored for strings at the extremity of their register with a bassoon lending an edge to the slowly rising melody in C sharp minor. Hans Redlich compared Mahler's

barren 'Chinese' landscape in the final *Adagio* with the middle section from the third movement of the Fourth in the same key, scored similarly for strings only and with a painfully ascending melody in the cello, suggesting – like Mahler – a weary ascent over bare mountain ridges with no view into the distance yet in sight.

The passage in question begins at figure C in the Sibelius score. 'In both cases,' Redlich says,

definite tonality is avoided by omitting the interval of the third. Both composers have here abandoned the customary 'soft underbelly' of harmony, and with it part of their romantic heritage. Both have deliberately depersonalized their idiom to the point of bleakness. Both have reached the threshold of atonality by employing fitfully the whole-tone scale, that destructive ferment and arch-enemy of tonal cohesion.[1]

Yet another contemporary parallel springs to mind: Bartók's one-act opera, *Duke Bluebeard's Castle,* which was finished the same year. Again we find the same use of tension between key centres a tritone apart. The gloom of F sharp minor is finally contrasted with the radiance of C major before the music returns to its dark F sharp minor origins. As in the symphony and in particular its first movement, the melodic lines are modally inflected and often angular so that one encounters much the same balance of expressionist and impressionist elements. Moreover, the treatment of the orchestra is chamber-like. Generally speaking, the different sections of the orchestra are

1 From a talk broadcast in the BBC Third Programme on 15 February 1968.

used independently or in refined chamber combinations, mostly strings and wind, and the brass is used sparingly. In those few *tutti* sections the composer seems less concerned with volume or power for its own sake but as a means of underlining a motive or idea to the best dramatic effect. Much the same is true of the symphony: in the two climaxes of the finale it is left to only two trumpets supported by timpani to hammer home the tritone figure.

Sibelius's chamber-like treatment of the normal classical orchestra (the glockenspiel is his only luxury) can be traced back to the very first sketches. The *cantabile* theme of the third movement was originally sketched for string quartet, and on the same page as the main theme of the *Adagio* of *Voces intimae*. It is possible to conclude that the two ideas were conceived at roughly the same point in time, perhaps at the beginning of 1909. On another page the main theme of the symphony is also worked out for string quartet. In his Sibelius biography, the American writer, Harold Johnson asked: 'Can it be that in its early stages the Fourth Symphony was conceived as a string quartet?'[1] Even if his suggestion that the whole symphony is based on material for one or two string quartets seems wildly speculative, he can, however, have sensed, without having had access to any of the sketches, the vital link. Since the *Largo* theme in its original form was for string quartet, this might well have inspired Sibelius in his initial vision of the symphony, to think more along chamber-music lines in his orchestral sonorities.

Apart from this there is nothing else in the sketches for the symphony that has its origins in the quartet medium. I have seen a sketch of the main theme of the first movement in short score with the title *Marche élégiaque*; as in the symphony the sketch also has canonic imitation, and later on in the same page there is a series of tritone sequences reminiscent of the development. In addition the first movement can well have been related to the projected composition that Sibelius names in his diary after visiting Koli, namely 'The Mountain' presumably a tone poem which by the time he came to play the symphony to Carpelan in December 1909 had a Swedish working-title 'Berget'. The finale, as we shall see, draws on elements from the unfinished song, 'The Raven' that he had intended for Ackté.

The fascination of the Fourth Symphony resides largely in the way in which the composer allows its form to be shaped by the motives. In a diary entry of 1 August 1912 Sibelius articulated his thoughts on this theme, comparing a symphony to a river. It is composed of innumerable tributaries, brooks and streams, and eventually broadens majestically before flowing into the sea. It is the movement of the water that determines the shape of the river bed, and it is this image that entrenches his view of symphonic thought: the movement of the river water is the flow of the

1 *Sibelius*, London, 1959, p. 128.

musical ideas and the river bed that they form is the symphonic structure. Yet, if the first movement is formed by the flow of the musical ideas, the basic shape of the 'river bed' is a readily discernible sonata form. It is not in its form that this movement is in any way revolutionary but in its syntax, the way in which the actual movement of the music is built up by means of a continuous process of thematic metamorphosis.

The first bars, according to Sibelius himself, should sound 'as harsh as fate'. The bassoons, cellos and double-basses adumbrate the tritone figure, the basic and seminal idea, launching it into a gravitation-less void:

Ex 105

The last two notes (F sharp–E) continue to sway freely in this vacuum until they are drawn into the gravitational field of the main theme, in A minor:

Ex 106

Already we have the building blocks of the movement: the tritone motive, the intervals of a second and a third (the four notes of the opening are themselves a pair of major thirds: C–E, D–F sharp), and a triadic theme. It is not a great deal. Its very economy enables Sibelius to attain the concentration and unity that characterizes this movement and the whole symphony. The main theme develops canonically and the harmonic tension focuses on the Dorian sixth (F sharp), which now assumes new functions as the sharpened Lydian fourth of C and a tonic in F sharp major. A struggle develops between the two keys represented by two chords with a flattened seventh:

Ex 107

(The progression, incidentally, is the same as the bells in the Coronation Scene of *Boris Godunov*.) The tension between C major with its Lydian fourth and F sharp major shows how the bitonal tendencies in Sibelius arise from his modal thinking. C major appears firmly established with the advent of a shimmering triad (bars 25–7) but is immediately undermined by a C sharp and then an F sharp and it is in F sharp major that the remainder of the exposition takes place. So one can summarize the key relationships in the exposition after the indeterminate tonality of the opening as follows: a Dorian A minor – leading to a Lydian C major – then F sharp major. Thus we see that the augmented fourth of the germinal cell is reflected in the basic tonal layout. Much the same phenomenon occurs in another contemporary work, Nielsen's *Sinfonia espansiva* (1911), but the juxtaposition is not so abrupt, and takes place only after a number of modulations.

After the sequence-like fanfare in the brass, the strings emblazon a variant of the germinal cell on the texture, which then resolves on to a chord of F sharp major:

Ex 108

Another variant of this arises immediately and leads to a relaxation of the tension into the subdominant of the new key, and distant fanfares on the far horizon from the horns:

Ex 109

A chorale-like figure on the brass with something of *Parsifal* about it, and harmonized by major triads of E, B flat and C sharp, a microcosm of the key-centres of the exposition, leads into a final idea:

Ex 110

The closing theme is a variant of the first group but in the major mode and in F sharp. Tension is for a moment relaxed, even the augmented fourth of the opening idea is normalized, becoming a perfect fourth both in its major and minor forms:

Ex 111

A new variant –

Ex 112

– casts a shadow over the tranquil, coolly smiling landscape. This unobtrusively guides us to the development where the main theme and the second group grow together in these almost tortuous lines:

Ex 113

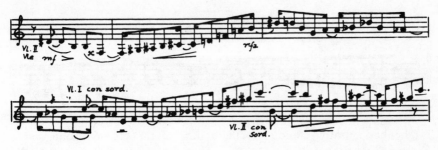

The tension is heightened immediately and from these angular lines the four notes B–D–F sharp–A sharp stand out in the texture, often emerging from lines in contrary motion. This figure – and more particularly, the seventh – play an important role in the other movements. The predominance of the tritone gives rise to textures that largely alternate between the two whole-tone poles of our system. They fade into the background as a shadowy mist of semiquavers against which a new development of the basic motive can be heard – a minor second followed by an ascending tritone – from flutes and clarinets:

Ex 114

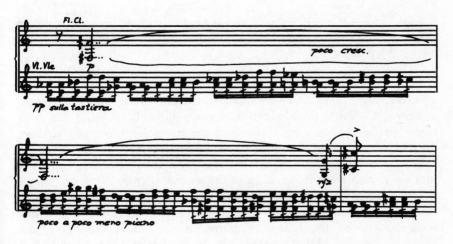

After this expressionist gesture at the beginning of the development, the texture begins to assume an almost impressionist character. The basic idea continues to lead the music from one tonal pole to the other, while a new idea (embodying the four notes that have emerged in the poignant outburst early in the development: B–D–F sharp–A sharp) in an ascending sextuplet figure appears ten times in different keys and with growing force:

Ex 115

The basic motive announces the return of the second group and a shortened reprise section in A major. The sextuplet figure appears for the last time in a Dorian C minor–Lydian E flat major, so that the modulation to the second group is also coloured by the tritone relationship (E flat–A major). The tendency to compress the reprise is even stronger than in the First and Second Symphonies. In the coda the basic four-note theme loses something of its tension, indeed it almost acquires tranquillity· the tritone becomes a diminished fifth that resolves a semitone lower on to the tonic A:

Ex 116

The concluding notes (C–D–E–F sharp–B flat–A) include many of the notes in Skryabin's 'Prometheus' chord (C–F sharp–B flat–E^{1} –A^{1} –D^{11}). Listen to those bars with C as a pedal note and the resemblance is quite striking. Otherwise the descending minor second (B flat–A) serves to prepare for the next movement, which begins in F major, the sustained tonic of the first movement becoming the mediant of the second. (For me, perhaps, one of the strongest associations that the four-note figure suggests is with *Tristan*: the moment of destiny in Act I when the two lovers-to-be first meet, which is dominated by the four-note motive in the minor. However, the orchestration, the rhythmic profile, the sense of death's proximity and of ecstasy, all remind me *mutatis mutandis* of the first movement of the Fourth Symphony, though Sibelius transforms this figure into a very different metaphysical inner search.)

The second movement *(Allegro molto vivace)* possesses something of the traditional contrast in mood between scherzo and trio, but the *doppio più lento* section at the end of the movement is produced by so complete a psychological transformation of one of the themes that it falls outside the usual framework of a classical or romantic scherzo movement, and can scarcely be categorized or labelled. Again, the tension between tonal poles a tritone apart plays an important part in the movement: there is a striking contrast between the lighter colouring and atmosphere of F major and the darker section dominated by the tritone. The overall impression is of a lighter scherzo with a sinister, dramatic *doppio più lento* epilogue, though some commentators – Abraham, Layton, Vignal – view this latter as a trio section and argue that the last six bars are a cryptic allusion to the omitted reprise.[1]

The main section of the scherzo, A is in $\frac{3}{4}$ and begins with an oboe melody with the sharpened Lydian fourth. The violins answer with a bucolic figure composed of two superimposed perfect fourths:

Ex 117

This kind of thematic thinking is familiar from the Third Symphony and returns again in the Fifth. When the oboe and the violins subsequently concern themselves with a tritone, the picture darkens momentarily but lightens soon afterwards in the playful, almost mazurka-like close of this short section. A contrasting episode, B, in $\frac{2}{4}$ and dactyllic in rhythm, starts out in F major but rapidly acquires a darker character with a tritone figuring prominently and a G flat minor triad colouring the texture:

Ex 118

1 This, incidentally, was also Tovey's view. *Tr*

185

The tritone leap downwards from the diminished fifth to the tonic becomes a familiar building brick. But this theme also appears in an ascending form with the same characteristic tritone element:

Ex 119

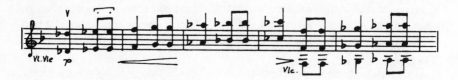

After **A** and **B** comes a number of kaleidoscopically changing episodes, among other things dramatic yet static *Tristan* chords whose resolution takes place over at times dissonant timpani rolls, and swirling tritone murmurs. From this emerges a variant of the main oboe theme on two flutes in thirds:

Ex 120

The clarinet suddenly hints at a reprise in G flat major but it proves a false lead, and the oboe introduces the reprise proper almost immediately in the tonic. The whole section fades away on a *diminuendo* trill from second violins and violas. Up to this point the scherzo has been playful, its atmosphere bathed in cool sunlight with occasional tritone shadows: Sibelius has shown us the positive side of his psyche, the lighter colours in his aura. In the succeeding *doppio più lento* section it is as if he has become the prisoner of his darkest thoughts and fears in a world where the tritone reigns. How does this sudden transformation in the musical climate come about? First and foremost, by means of a synthesis of the melodic contour of the **A** section and the tritonal element of the contrasting **B** section:

Ex 121

The A theme acquires a tormenting, demonic character as a result of this fusion. The change of tempo serves to intensify its nightmarish guise. And even the backcloth against which the drama is played is strongly atmospheric. The first two string comments (F–B and B–F) in B minor and F minor respectively resound over a double pedal point (B–F) representing the tonic and tritone dominant of their respective tonalities. In the bass there is an ascending scale with alternating tones and semitones thus: B–C sharp–D–E–F–G–A flat–B flat–C flat=B natural, the kind of scale that Messiaen was to call 'modes à transpositions limitées'. Its bitonal polarity strengthens the impression of something indeterminate and frightening.

The note of desperation increases in intensity until finally the tritone resounds on the flutes and bassoons, a strangely effective sonority that resonates in the memory: *diabolus in musica* whose hypnotic hold suddenly disappears as the violins' C sharp sinks from *ff* to *p*, and whispers a reminiscence of the opening theme of the movement.

If the scherzo proper presents us with the world of reality, the *doppio più lento* section seems to explore the subconscious. There are disturbing overtones of the psyche that make this movement difficult to analyse in established conventional terminology. If one describes the movement as a scherzo or a rondo, one can do so only by ignoring some essential features, for ideas in both the A and B sections reveal altogether new dimensions in the *doppio più lento*. In a Bruckner scherzo (and in particular the last three symphonies), it is the darker, demonic element that comes to the fore in the outer sections while the trio enshrines an idealized world of the spirit. Sibelius's procedure in the Fourth Symphony is exactly the reverse: the pastoral vision of the opening is overcast by darker voices.

The character of the third movement *(Il tempo largo)* could well be defined by reproducing a sentence from Sibelius's diary: 'I plan to allow the musical thoughts and their development in my spirit determine the form of my music.' It is as if the composer has given voice to these inner thoughts from the very first moment when the theme tries to take shape right through to its climactic flowering, and the result is a transparently free, improvisatory structure. 'A theme slowly grows, an improvisation in three phases' is how one can best define this movement rather than trying to fit it into any preconceived classical mould. Even if the three phases are in many respects different, there are important musical parallels: prelude-like beginnings from which emerges a short, searching motive, which by a process of metamorphosis reflects different aspects of a basic idea. Yet throughout this movement, with its air of improvisation, Sibelius in no way sacrifices musical continuity or formal coherence. Of course, one can identify certain unifying factors: first, the role played by the interval of a perfect fifth. In its skeletal form, the main theme consists of two superimposed fifths separated by a semitone. The tritone also plays an important part both as a contour and a harmonic element, as does the interval of a major seventh. One other important feature is the Phrygian modification of the minor scale by flattening the supertonic. As in the case of the remaining movements, the modal character is to a certain extent related to the tritone motive, which often rests on the flattened supertonic:

Ex 122

In this movement it is the Phrygian element that gives vent to the feelings of contemplation and the acceptance of fate that we encounter at various points and that contrast so markedly with the power and eloquence of the main theme. But it is what Sibelius does in C sharp minor with its flattened Phrygian supertonic rather than the mere fact that this is its tonal anchorage that concerns us.

The first phase of the movement takes us up to six bars after letter B in the score, and its point of departure are these semiquaver wisps:

Ex 123

The first can be regarded as a variant of the basic motive, and the second of the minor triad – a figure familiar from the first movement's development. The theme with two superimposed fifths (G sharp–D sharp, E–B) is already foreshadowed in the clarinet solo, which is taken up by the flute in full flight:

Ex 124

The spare texture with two widely spaced lines moving in contrary motion without supporting harmonies provides a point of contact with Mahler's Ninth Symphony and looks forward to Shostakovich. After this preamble with its other-worldly atmosphere, the basic idea begins to take shape, though in this, its tentative form, it has the glowing quality of the major mode rather than the dark power of the minor:

Ex 125

The bars immediately following concern themselves with the descending fifth and a Phrygian variant of the opening idea, which is repeated sequentially. Then, for the first time, the main theme appears in its true form on the strings:

Ex 126

The theme fades away in mid-air as if the composer does not want to relinquish it. At this point (six bars after letter B on page 31) the second phase begins and the music returns to the searching voices that opened the movement. But this time the steps seem firmer:

Ex127

The clarinet outlines the skeletal fifths but in reverse motion while the framework of the oboes' line embraces the triad and the tritone.

Elmer Diktonius's description of the symphony with its '60,000 autumn-grey lakes and in some strange way a greeting from Bach' seems to me to come closer to the spirit of this music than his more famous epithet about the 'barkbröd' symphony, an allusion to the hardship induced by the rigours of the natural environment to which the ascetic, rarefied texture is so closely attuned.

Against a string texture dominated by fifths, we now have a more complete and full-throated version of the main theme from the cellos:

Ex 128

After this more opulent texture, the music thins out and the momentum slackens. There is a static feeling: over a pedal point in the violins, the woodwinds ruminate on the basic germ cell of the symphony:

Ex 129

And from this inward-looking musing, the oboes in alternating thirds and fifths begin what sounds like a primitive folk call against which the main theme of the movement materializes in its longest and most sonorous form:

Ex 130

From the climactic G sharp the violins plunge down to A sharp and the second phase of the improvisation ebbs away. The third begins (eight bars after letter E on page 35) with renewed stirrings from the arabesque-like figures that began the movement. The movement as a whole is symmetrical in that the three sections are twenty-seven, forty-five and twenty-nine bars respectively. Although the main theme when it comes is not so extensively formulated as in the middle section, its impact is more powerful on account of its rich orchestral support from the brass and its unison statement on the strings in an unambiguous C sharp minor. After the climax, the music returns to ruminate on the basic theme of the whole work in the form to which we have become accustomed in this movement. For all its improvisatory character, it cost its composer dear, for although it retains the spontaneity of improvisation, its musical thinking is deeply organic. It posed special problems and was slow to find its definitive form: Sibelius began the movement in September 1910 and only at the end of December did he sense the shape it would finally take.

The finale is a sonata rondo. However, as was the case in the first movement, the tonic–dominant tonal relationship is superseded by keys a tritone apart, in this instance A minor and E flat. The movement poses a number of problems and in some respects resembles the scherzo in its dramatic layout. The exposition is classical and its world of feeling kept in clear focus; the development has something of the dark expressionism that surfaces in the latter part of the scherzo, and the climax gives way to a gesture of resignation. One instrument is added to the orchestra in this movement: the bells. This has proved problemmatic, for the score does not content itself by saying 'glockenspiel' but abbreviates it to 'glocken' (tubular bells). The question is not unimportant as the character of the movement is undoubtedly affected. The tubular bells are rich in overtones and more powerful in sonority, while the glockenspiel has a silvery timbre and speaks more effectively in quicker passages. In the autograph score Sibelius wrote 'stahlstäbe' which in everyday practice implies glockenspiel. Sibelius was fully aware of this as 'stahlstäbe' is to be found in the printed score of *The Oceanides* (1914), where there can be no doubt that it is synonymous with glockenspiel. How, one wonders, has the 'stahlstäbe' of the autograph become the 'glocken' of the published score? The composer's correspondence with Breitkopf und Härtel gives no clue: perhaps the publisher had confused 'stahlstäbe' and 'stahlrohre', or perhaps Sibelius himself had made this change at the proof stage. This latter possibility seems unlikely as contemporary witnesses are unanimous that Sibelius expressly wanted glockenspiel.

Nearly all Sibelius interpreters have elected to use the glockenspiel: Toscanini, Sir Thomas Beecham, Eugene Ormandy, Anthony Collins, Herbert von Karajan, Lorin Maazel, Sir John Barbirolli, Gennady Rozhdestvensky and others have all chosen this solution, but both Ernest Ansermet and Leonard Bernstein use tubular bells. No doubt Leopold Stokowski's pioneering commercial record exercised some influence for he chose to use both: in the exposition he uses the glockenspiel but in the development section, when the theme appears in augmented note values, he opts for the tubular bells, which better hold their own against the trumpets and timpani *fff*. Stokowski also resorts to the tubular bells in the corresponding passage in the reprise. Sibelius himself thought that these passages sounded 'too oriental' in character, if use was made of the bells. Stokowski's example was followed by Georg Szell and Sir Colin Davis.

The glockenspiel (and let us settle for this without closing our minds to the possibility of the alternative solutions we have already noted) provides more than just an element of colour. It also plays a motivic part in the proceedings; its four notes A, B, C sharp and B serve to counterbalance the

Lydian figure that performs so dominant a role in the movement. The glockenspiel is more important in the luminous classical world of the exposition while in the darker, expressionist sections its voice is subdued.

Whether consciously or not, the finale takes as its immediate point of departure the rising figure on clarinets and bassoons heard in the wake of the final statement of the main theme of the *Il tempo largo* (fourteen bars from the end of the movement). It is playful in character and the texture almost suggests the string quartet:

Ex 131

From the first two bars, a number of related figures are spawned. The first merely adds a turn at the end:

Ex 132

A further metamorphosis produces one of the movement's most pregnant ideas, comprising the tritone and the fifth:

Ex 133

This is related to the basic four-note cell of the first movement and the figure of a semitone followed by a tritone that develops from it. The tritone-plus-fifth is accompanied by a satellite – the glockenspiel theme to which allusion has already been made, which in its turn is answered by a leaping figure from the flutes –

Ex 134

– and a Mixolydian flourish from the strings:

Ex 135

The turn attached to the opening two bars is now extended:

Ex136

Another motive drawn from the opening theme (bar 9) assumes an impetuous solo, rather like a cellist in an imaginary string quartet, and his urgent pleadings prompt the other strings to join him:

Ex 137

The energetic cadential figures, regularly turning to A major, give way to cross-hatch string murmurings, with a sense of expectant mystery about them. Their thematic substance is drawn from the preceding *affetuoso* passage and the glockenspiel figure. Over this rustling string texture, which is at times reminiscent of the *Vivace* movement of *Voces intimae,* the second group emerges from the wind in the 'tritone dominant' of E flat major. The A major of the strings gives this passage a bitonal character:

Ex 138

The descending seventh comes to assume a powerful role later on in the movement. The tension between A and E flat subsides for the time being and we remain in A, even though it seems darker in character. The ideas of the A section become terser and more urgent as E flat continues to exert its magnetic force until it finally triumphs. So far, then, we can observe within the exposition an ABA₁ structure. The development concerns itself with two new ideas that flank another A section. It is in these that Sibelius turns to material he had originally intended for his orchestral song, 'The Raven'. Only the sketch to the ninth strophe of the setting survives:

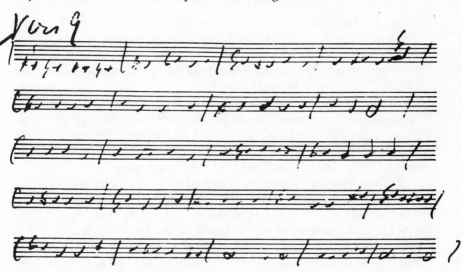

The C section begins with an expressive chorale-like figure clearly derived from bars 9 – 12 of the Poe sketch:

Ex 139

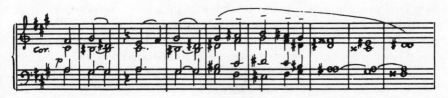

At one stroke the atmosphere is transformed. The gently rocking ostinato figure itself derives from 'The Raven (bar 14 in the sketch) and has a hypnotic quality, and even the syncopated chromatic section that follows in its train has its origins in the song (bars 16–19).

Ex 140

It is as if the composer is searching for the innermost secrets of the soul, only to find in this theme a mimosa-like contour. In these bars we feel we hear the young Sibelius's voice, poetic, vulnerable and melancholy. Nostalgic, *Tristan*esque harmonies return us from the introspective musings to the real world as embodied by the material of section A and the key of C major, albeit with an augmented fourth. Here we find ourselves in the kernel of the development, the tritone-plus-fifth sears through the texture *fff* against the glockenspiel motive. Other derivatives of the opening theme are heard before we re-enter the darker world from which we have just emerged. 'The Raven' takes wing over pulsating string *pizzicato* chords.

To what extent the development section embraces the musical substance of his Poe setting and reflects its atmosphere must inevitably remain a matter for conjecture. Yet it is obvious that it plays some part: Sibelius would not have embarked on the setting in the first place had he not felt drawn towards Poe's imagery and felt its relevance to his own closeness to death. (Indeed, there is an earlier precedent in the slow movement of the Second Symphony, whose main theme was identified with another Messenger of Death, The Stone Guest.) But as he worked on the song, there is no doubt that what he recognized was the spiritual link between its world and that of the symphony.

In the reprise the main theme, A3, now winds up in E flat major, which one could construe as a kind of subdominant with a sharpened D. The cross-hatch string writing of the second group, B1, continues in the same key while the woodwind cry is heard in A major, thus reversing the earlier tonal roles. This time the wind theme is modified and takes up ideas from the string background. The closing section, A4, remains largely unchanged but the clouds soon gather and a dark, powerful atmosphere is generated.

Figures from the development, and in particular the syncopated chromatic figure of 'The Raven', as well as the powerful motives of tritone-plus-fifth and the descending seventh mingle in a final climax. In the coda the closeness of death becomes apparent as the life processes succumb to paralysis. The chromatic motion of the strings rocks backwards and forwards, broken only by the cry of the flutes and oboes, who intone the minor form of the third that opens the second group. There is a brief dialogue between various instruments; the horns respond to the woodwind thirds with a segment of 'The Raven' theme, until the strings move us to an A minor cadence. There are still a few steps before silence envelops us. Like a bird in the realm of the dead, a single flute intones a rising third – it is not too fanciful, perhaps, to see their initial notes, D, F sharp and G sharp as an allusion to the basic germinal cell of the symphony – while the descending augmented seventh on the oboe becomes weaker. The final words of the whole symphony are in one sense the dying cry of 'The Raven' for it is this motive that brings the music to rest.

It may be of interest to compare the above view of the movement with that of Gerald Abraham[1] in his perceptive but quite different analysis:

Tawaststjerna	*Abraham*
Introductory theme	Introductory bars
Exposition (A–B–A1)	First subject group
Beginning of development with	Second subject group
new material from 'The Raven' (C)	
Central part of development (A2)	Brief development (only the first
	19 bars of A2)
End of development (C1)	Second subject group (44 bars of
	A2 + C1)
Reprise (A3–B1–A4)	First subject group
Coda	Coda

Sibelius spoke of the Fourth as a 'spiritualized symphony'. In this case how is it that he gave it such titles as 'The Mountain' and 'Thoughts of a Wayfarer', most probably to the first and third movements, when after his inspiring trip with Eero Järnefelt to the Koli mountain, in late September – early October 1909 he played excerpts on the piano to Axel Carpelan? Both titles obviously serve as rough-and-ready signposts in much the same way as do Mahler's 'programmatic' indications in his First and Second Symphonies. The first calls to mind the atmosphere he describes in the Koli mountain. Ekman's description can be regarded as authentic:

It was a wonderful day. The wind sang; it was bitterly cold. At one moment the sun would shine on the two artists with a cold sparkling light, the next they were exposed to hailstorms and strong gusts of wind.

1 *Sibelius, A Symposium,* London, 1947, p.27.

Wherever they turned their gaze, they found inspiring impressions: autumnal Pielisjärvi with its bluish-grey waves, whose turbulent play was enlivened from time to time by a splash of sunshine, the cold, white cliffs, the scarred landscape round the hill, the view towards the Russian frontier across a limitless sea of forest, finally the wild vegetation on their rambles in the gloaming, while descending to the little lake of Herajärvi in the south-west, across the moonlit waves of which the travellers had themselves rowed in order to reach the opposite shore.

The landscape gave Sibelius the initial impulse or at least a background for the 'outer' programme.

In speaking of an 'outer' programme, it is worth bearing in mind that Schopenhauer's musical aesthetics played a vital role in the thinking of many composers in the German-speaking world at this period. For example, the original programme (later withdrawn by the composer) of the slow movement in Mahler's First Symphony, inscribed 'Funeral March in the manner of Callot', was derived from a story-book illustration, 'Des Jägers Begräbnis' of Moritz von Schwind. This engraving – possibly from an edition of *Des Knaben Wunderhorn* – depicts a procession of gaily dancing animals, accompanying the body of the dead hunter on his way to the grave. But in actual fact the details are not in themselves of importance or even of relevance – it is relevant only in so far as it serves to convey the general atmosphere. Mahler gave his First Symphony of 1893 the nickname 'Titan' after Jean Paul's novel but subsequently dropped it. However he did admit that it might serve as a kind of programmatic signpost on the journey, at least for the newcomer . . . but it cannot offer anything more than that! The outer programme cannot illumine the 'inner' essence!

My need to express myself symphonically begins where the darkest impressions rule: at that gate which leads to the other world, that world where things are not separated by time and place.

Mahler even makes himself the subject of such a programme:

I have called the first movement of my Second Symphony 'Feast of the Dead' and, if you want to know, it is the hero of the slow movement of the D major Symphony that I am bearing to the grave and whose life I view from the vantage point of a higher plane.

Carl Dahlhaus,[1] the eminent German musicologist, warns against the temptations of popular misconceptions. Biographical curiosity is no aesthetic yardstick. One demeans the stature of a symphony by reducing it to 'autobiography in sound', something that entails regarding the work as a

---

1 These references are based on Carl Dahlhaus, *Die Musik des 19. Jahrhunderts* (Neues Handbuch der Musikwissenschaft, Volume 6), Chapter V: 1889–1914, 'Die Moderne als musikgeschichtliche Epoche', Wiesbaden, 1980.

function of life instead of, on the contrary, seeing the life as a function of the work. In Dahlhaus's view the hero of these symphonies is neither Jean Paul's Titan nor Mahler himself but the aesthetic substance of the music, like the narrator in a novel or the empirical first person of a poem:

This subject cannot be identified either as the literary hero who has inspired it or the composer's own empirical experience. This programme is not to be found in some biographical documentary content, but rather charts more shadowy, abstract feelings comprised of a wide range of basic impressions: inner, hidden drives.

One can surmise that Sibelius experienced his 'mountaineering' (252 metres!) symbolically. He had ascended into his mid-forties, and could both look back on the past and look not without foreboding into the future. From the top of Koli he had been able to catch of a glimpse of Lieksa where he had spent his honeymoon. It was here that he had composed his setting of Runeberg's 'Under strandens granar lekte gossen' ('Under the fir trees the youth played'): he could view his life in perspective. Here the outer symbolism gives an impulse to an inner. If one looks at Sibelius's creative development, one can see that he was at a watershed. He could continue his path as a late romantic and develop the new classicism of the Third Symphony. Were there not enough elements in *Kullervo* and the first three symphonies on which he could build? He was well aware of the thinking of Debussy, Busoni, and the latest Richard Strauss, as well as Skryabin, to judge from a somewhat later diary entry. But if he was fully conscious of the fact that there was a non-atonal 'modernist' movement, he could not foresee that this movement would be placed by music historians in an independent category between late romanticism and *neue Musik*. The symphonic fantasy *Pohjola's Daughter* had placed him on the same level as a 'modernist' as Strauss. Now the moment had come for him to take the decisive step into the unknown, into 'Modernism'. The insight that he must broaden his symphonic horizon in new ways and go towards evolution and concentration in his musical language – that was the real impulse that the ascent of Koli had given him.

Is it possible that the anxiety that Sibelius had felt for some three years or more after the operation for his throat tumour left its mark on the formal conception of the Fourth Symphony? Dahlhaus rejects this view of a work of art as a 'function' of autobiography. In this special case he explains, almost ironically, that it is as if 'an advanced composition technique were to become more readily comprehensible by labelling it an expression of a darkening mood'. At the same time, he sees the danger of going too far towards objectivity by wholly eliminating the composer's empirical person from the aesthetic subject of the score. Even if I do not regard the Fourth as a 'death' symphony in the same sense as Tchaikovsky's Sixth or Mahler's Second, I still remain doubtful about Dahlhaus's thesis. Many years after the operation, Sibelius swung from one extreme to another, as in just before the New Year of 1910 when he noted in his diary: 'Back in the Himalayas! All is lightness and power. Worked like a giant.' But the following day, his spirits had been shattered: 'My throat! Oh, God!' However his spirits were soon restored by 'something new and big. Stop your doubts and work. You may well live a long time yet.' Is it not just as likely that these changes of mood have played their part in the conception of the Fourth Symphony, not so much in the formation of an 'inner' programme but as a factor in the dark orchestral colours and the almost chamber-like texture?

The central works that were composed in the proximity of the Fourth Symphony – *Night Ride and Sunrise, Voces intimae, In Memoriam, The Bard* and *Luonnotar* – are distinguished by predominantly dark colouring, ranging from the Mahler-like tutti in *In Memoriam*, to the aphoristic, almost Webern-like textures of *The Bard*. Together they form what one could call 'the dark period' in Sibelius's output, which begins after the Third Symphony in the autumn of 1908 and ends in the summer of 1913 with *The Oceanides*, whose impressionism is already foreshadowed in *Luonnotar*.

What, however, are we to make of the quotation from 'The Raven'? There is no question of any particular programmatic intention in the symphony so much as a piece of music (from figure F to figure H of the finale and again from figure 1 to bar 12 of page 58). Without knowing his conception of the complete orchestral song, it is impossible to form a view of the relationship between the voice and the orchestra. Sibelius had known and loved Viktor Rydberg's beautiful Swedish translation of the poem ever since his youth: it was included in the poet's *Collected Works*, which he treasured. Indeed, some of the imagery of the poem seems to pervade the First Symphony of 1898, particularly the violin cantilenas and the *pizzicato* motive. The whole atmosphere of the poem fascinated him, most of all the bird's 'hoarse cry': in August 1909, already before Aino Ackté had raised the subject of the commission, he had quoted in his diary, 'Quoth the Raven, "Nevermore" ', referring to the happiness he had felt at the time he was working on his Romance in C for strings (1903). An echo of this world that is gone beyond recall seems to resonate in the coda, with its resigned exchanges between wind and strings, the bird-like motive on the wind in minor thirds and the descending chromatic figure on the strings. In this desolate landscape the flute intones its thirds three times and the oboe replies with its descending seventh, which corresponds both to the original's 'Nevermore' and the 'Nie du Tor' of the German translation that Sibelius used for the setting. It is interesting to note that Sibelius's son-in-law, the conductor Jussi Jalas, compared this poignant exchange to the Apostle Peter's denial of Christ three times before the cock crowed, a view that the composer himself described as 'a far from impossible interpretation'.

We know from his 1914–15 sketchbook that an idea that at first presented itself for the Fifth Symphony could in the end surface in the Sixth, and that the final tragic E flat minor episode, which comes just before the finale's coda in E flat major, figures in the sketches for the final theme of the Sixth. Similarly, after he had placed the *pizzicato* theme of the Fifth Symphony's second movement in the right place, Sibelius began to develop it in the Sixth Symphony's second movement, as he then thought. It subsequently became its third. While carried away by his inspiration, he could not always discern the exact context in which it was to flourish. Something similar occurred in the case of 'The Raven'. Even though he was working on the finale of the Fourth Symphony, he agreed to compose an orchestral song for Aino Ackté with a view to taking it on their European tour, which was to commence in Munich on 17 February 1911. During the following weeks he tries to concentrate exclusively on 'The Raven' but cannot resist continuing his work on the Fourth Symphony itself. Subsequently it is clear that the symphony is not enjoying sufficient time to ripen and mature so he gives up the idea of the tour, as we have seen, much to Ackté's chagrin. He continued his work and suddenly it dawns on him that the melodic material he had planned for the ninth strophe of 'The Raven' sits perfectly in the context of the symphonic argument. The last bars in the reprise of the A section of the finale (page 47) lead seamlessly into what he has already written. In the climax leading to the coda, and the coda itself, the thematic material he had conceived in working on 'The Raven' is transformed into musical substance that has great tragic depth and that lends to the symphony a new and more searching perspective. Indeed he discovers that far from having abandoned the symphony for 'The Raven' he has been working on it all the time, and that the Raven's cry, 'Nevermore' had from the beginning served as its inner programme.

The two additional pieces Sibelius added to the *Kuolema* music, the *Canzonetta* for strings, and the *Valse romantique* for small orchestra, are, of course, on an entirely different plane from the symphony. The *Canzonetta* is in ternary form and has an engaging vein of melodic freshness:

Ex 141

Stravinsky expressed appreciation of this piece on his 1961 visit to Helsinki. 'I like that kind of northern Italianate melodism – Tchaikovsky had it too – which was part, and an attractive part, of St Petersburg culture.'[1] Two years later when he received the Sibelius Prize, he made a small tribute to the composer by arranging the *Canzonetta* for four horns, two clarinets, harp and double-bass. Its companion, the *Valse romantique* was perhaps intended as an E major pendant to the E minor of *Valse triste*. But already in its early stages of composition Sibelius found difficulty in returning to what he felt was an outworn theme. Immediately after the première, Sibelius once again succumbed to depression. 'That piece *Valse romantique*. Absolutely insignificant. Not in any sense "me" really!' Sibelius was not far off the mark, for he lacked Strauss's capacity to identify with the world of *Rosenkavalier* or Glazunov's feeling for the tradition of the Russian Ballet or even Ravel's hedonism that could produce the *Valses nobles et sentimentales*.

1 Igor Stravinsky and Robert Craft, *Dialogues and a Diary*, London, 1968, p. 225.

CHAPTER SEVEN

Scènes historiques

The Fourth Symphony brought in its wake a period of lassitude and a sense of emptiness. His struggles with the score had left Sibelius in a state of spiritual exhaustion. A diary entry of 23 May records his depression, though matters were not helped by bleak weather, which had seemed to banish the prospect of spring. The gloom soon lifted and his spirits were restored a few days later when a change of wind brought the smell of the sea to the meadows round Järvenpää. Once again he could view his economic worries with greater detachment and humour. He drifted into a kind of *dolce far niente* and strove to take life more easily but with no less style.

In this unproductive state of mind, his thoughts turned to practical matters: it was high time that he gave his attention to the house. A June diary entry finds this exhortation: 'must force myself to find the energy and inclination to carry this through', and he set about hunting for the builders he needed to enlarge the kitchen and to convert the attic and make log walls. The family desperately needed more living space, for on 20 July Aino gave birth to another daughter, Heidi, the last of the five daughters, not counting Kirsti who had died in early infancy. Living on top of each other and in such close proximity presented its difficulties: 'The wear and tear of constantly being in contact takes its toll on our nerves; there is friction and subsequent insensitivity.' The constant drain on his resources that the building work entailed, the incessant hammering and muddle, prevented him concentrating on his real work, and he sometimes wondered whether all the sacrifices he was making for the house were worth while. He showed evident irritation with those around him:

> In all relationships between the sexes, there is a moment when the woman, hapless and vulnerable, is dependent on the generosity of the man; his love is then at its lowest ebb but the gentleman in him must be uppermost. Yes, indeed! My God! This is my unfortunate destiny. I am building myself a workroom – small, very small, and on top of me are all the children whose games and noise ruin everything . . . You are a veritable *Pechvogel*! Get away from it all!

In the autumn Sibelius moved into his new workroom in the attic, from where he had a good view of the lake, which in later years was obscured from view on the lower floors by the growing trees. Now, when he came down the stairs, he was greeted by a much greater sense of space, since the wall between the living room and the dining room had been removed so that the two formed one handsome expanse. All these distractions that occupied his summer are reflected in an uneasy sense of restlessness. One can discern a growing awareness that, with the symphony behind him, he is embarking on a new chapter in life. He relaxed by playing movements from the Beethoven trios, which brought back memories of his youth, and watched the bonfires and festivities of Midsummer's Eve from the balcony in Ainola.

23 June 1911. Ruminated on the days of my youth, 'les aventures de la jeunesse', the scent of burnt juniper twigs, all creates a wonderful poetry. In the back of my mind are new works – the actual writing remains to be done. Will I live long enough to see everything through? I asked a wise owl who promised me another 23 years!! *O juvenes, terque beati.*

Life had lost none of its pain, and in moments of nervous anxiety, he was still aware of the taste of metal in his mouth – something that had afflicted him in his youth when he had played the violin in public.

In August his eldest daughter, Eva, became engaged. Her fiancé, Arvi Paloheimo, was an up-and-coming lawyer, the eldest son of a successful industrial magnate who had a lively interest in the arts, which his son shared. Sibelius was sympathetic to his daughter's choice; indeed, in later life Eva became his trusted confidante especially concerning 'les aventures du compositeur', as he coyly put it, and other delicate matters that he would not want to discuss with Aino. Eva inherited most of the outgoing and epicurean qualities in her father's personality, and the knowledge that she would soon be leaving home pained Sibelius more than he would care to confess even to himself. He composed an *Etude*[1] for her as a souvenir from home, and when his mood shifted and he found himself 'i minore', he ascribed his depression to her imminent departure.

Now the flame flickers uncertainly on Eva and Arvi's altar . . . Strange that it is I who eat my heart out. Take yourself in hand – properly. Don't you see the strength, power and vitality that you possess. You must look at Eva from that point of view. Put an end to your pettiness. Away with the degenerate upper-class attitude which has fortunately not fallen to your lot.

The 'fortunately' has ironic overtones since Sibelius's feelings about his background were by no means straightforward. It would be untrue to say

1 The piece in question was published as Op. 76 No. 2.

that he suffered from an inferiority complex because, unlike Aino, he was not of aristocratic stock, but at the same time he occasionally reacted as if he did. Once at his brother Christian's house, viewing a picture of the Sibbe's ancestral home, he observed his feelings of pride at his family origins with a twinge of embarrassment, for it was obvious that such responses were faintly ridiculous. 'My great-grandfather lived there! My name was latinized from Sibbe, as is well known; it is an ancient Swedish name, at least 1500 years old!' (A diary entry on New Year's Day, 1912.) On another occasion Christian had noticed in a German clinic that a Sibelius had been active in Russia during the seventeenth century. Jean was altogether delighted with the news: perhaps he was of the nobility after all. The news gave substance to one of Sibelius's most secret fantasies, that the Johan who had, according to family tradition, come from afar and married the daughter of Sibbe's manor, was in fact of noble birth. Indeed, more than a fantasy, it was something of an *idée fixe* and Sibelius once again took himself to task in his diaries: 'Stopped all the agonizing over not being upper crust: that nonsense is all over.' All these speculations sprang no doubt from a need to give voice to certain inner tensions. The musical aristocrat in him reacted violently to any exhibition of aristocratic pride or arrogance, and his antagonism was particularly marked if they surfaced in any of Aino's relatives. In this respect, perhaps, 'that nonsense' was not all over.

Sibelius closely followed everything that was written about him – or what was not written! After a concert in Stockholm by a Finnish Male Choir, the *Dagens Nyheter* snubbed him by writing nothing about his work but praising Toivo Kuula and Selim Palmgren. Sibelius reacted by quoting some lines of Anna-Maria Lenngren in his diary: 'Say, Seraphs, have I not the right to plead when Gyllenborg neglects me, and now, as is the wont of this world, another reaps the praise?' The German *Musik Pädagogische Blätter* savaged his Op. 61 songs, maintaining that they represented a retrograde step and comparing them unfavourably with Sinding. Sibelius noted: 'I have not developed to the taste of the German critics . . . Possibly I have gone my own way too far for them to follow. But surely in this our age, this must count as a strength? Sinding goes his own merry way along with all the others.' The generally negative attitude of the review had more effect on him for coming at a time when he was himself seized with self-doubt.

And then, suddenly, once again his thoughts were turned in the direction of opera. In May he heard from Georg Boldemann, a German admirer living in Copenhagen, who sent him an opera libretto whose action was set against a military background in eighteenth-century France. Boldemann was a dilettante, a businessman married to a wealthy sister of a Stockholm banker, Aschberg, who spent his spare time writing plays. He had translated a number of Arvid Järnefelt's novels – and indeed later on his son was to marry Järnefelt's daughter, Maija. Boldemann's enthusiasm for Sibelius had been fired as early as the turn of the century and among other things, he even succeeded in interesting Max Fiedler in Hamburg in the then unpublished Second Symphony. Like Adolf Paul before him, he cherished ambitions of collaborating with Sibelius on an operatic venture, for he hankered for the prestige this would bring him. The plans came to nothing: his libretto was nothing if not conventional and Sibelius, to get himself in the right frame of mind, threw himself into a study of Strauss's *Elektra* only to reaffirm his instinctive feeling that opera was not his medium: *'was in mir nicht ist* – my inclination is towards the symphonic poem. I find the operatic mode banal. Had I been brought up in a stage family or had the theatre in my blood, things might have been different.' Yet, for all that, his next venture was to be music for the stage, a piece for Adolf Paul's new play, *The Language of the Birds (Die Sprache der Vögel)*. This was a wedding march, which it would seem he enjoyed composing, though his diary entries record that he longed for his cigars, a good bottle of burgundy and bemoaned the passing of his youth – *'Tempi passati*. It makes one want to weep tears of blood.' Of the music itself he writes, 'It may not be stupefying but it is interesting in the manner of modern commissioned stuff. It is natural and *zweckmässig* in its scoring – and not without poetry.'

He also composed another bagatelle during these summer months: *Homesickness*, a cantata for women's voices to words of Walter von Konow. But the rest of his energies were directed towards a rescue operation and he devoted the whole of September to revising three pieces – *All' Overtura*, *Scena* and *Festivo (alla bolero)* – from the Press Pension Fund music that he had composed in 1899. *Festivo* filled him with a certain naive delight: 'Das ewig musikalische zieht mich heran. This sort of thing consumes me!'

It was more than mere exhaustion after his labours with the Fourth Symphony that promoted work on the *Scènes historiques*. In the symphony he had charted a new course and entered a new world. He had skirted the furthermost borders of tonality and was inevitably at a loss to know whether to go further along this same path. Having gone thus far, he drew back. So, too, did many of his contemporaries who had strayed to the frontiers of tonality. After *Elektra*, Strauss returned to the more sumptuous world of *Der Rosenkavalier* while Debussy, after the elliptic utterances of the *Préludes* turned in his last years to the classicism of the late sonatas. Not even Stravinsky followed up the radicalism of *The Rite of Spring* by further erosion of tonality, anymore than did late Skryabin venture very much further after the Sixth and Seventh Sonatas. It remained for Schoenberg to pursue atonality and to take its consequences to their logical conclusion.

Sibelius's diaries reflect something of his dilemma. 'Am worried about my capacity to come with something really new. I even doubt my way of working – so far removed from the kind of thinking of the German school! As far as I can see, they have made the art of composition into a science.' Goldmark had once told him that there was far too much *Mache*[1] in his E major Overture; perhaps he in turn found this too much in evidence in the symphonies of Mahler, Strauss's *Elektra*, Reger's chamber music and those works of Schoenberg that he knew. At the same time he was fearful of the dangers of mere spontaneity and excessive simplicity. Yet it was this that proved dominant in the next work to which he turned. In October he wrote a cantata, *Men from Land and Sea*, to words by the Bothnian folk poet, Ernst Knape. The work fired his enthusiasm: 'The intractible, inexorable power that is the God-given voice in my music is something "they" can't turn up their noses at.' But soon doubts overcame him: the more that he tried to improve the piece, the more he sacrificed its spontaneity.

The early autumn months brought little of inspiration to Helsinki's musical life. John Forsell, the Swedish baritone sang *The Ferryman's Brides* 'not at all badly', as Sibelius noted in his diary, 'though he does not penetrate far below the surface of my music'. Sigrid Schnéevoigt played some of the Op. 58 piano pieces, and Kajanus conducted a Svendsen concert. At home in Ainola, things were far from happy. Sibelius had taken care of his sister, Linda, whom he had invited to Ainola during the summer to stay for a few days to give her some respite from the mental home where she was temporarily confined. The visit proved to be quite a strain, and he soon imagined that he could discern in himself the same symptoms of nervous disintegration. Aino had gone to stay with the Paloheimo family in order to get a rest, but on her return home, Sibelius found her thoroughly worn out, full of self-denigration and often close to tears – there were even thoughts of suicide. But, as usual, it is difficult to know how much store to set by his objectivity; he was prone to project his own feelings of depression on to those around him. Yet, suddenly, in the midst of all his domestic gloom, he could record that all these misfortunes were to him

> like water off a duck's back. Nature is so full of poetry. Strindberg speaks of the world as a haunt for the souls of the condemned. Maybe it is, but music is surely from the spirit world, which is why we can't explain its meaning.

The provinciality of the capital suddenly became stifling and oppressive. The artificiality of the Helsinki upper crust was lampooned in a poem of Eino Leino which made great play of their snobbery and 'refeened' speech mannerisms. It fortified his longing to return to the real world outside; the cranes had already sped southwards and their cries ('sounds most deeply attuned to my innermost soul') lured him in their wake. His destination was Paris but his itinerary took him over Berlin. There he went to the opera

1 Contrivance, artificiality. *Tr.*

207

where not even the legendary Emmy Destinn could put him under her spell: 'She "sings" beautifully enough but without charm.' A little later, he wrote to Carpelan,

I have been here two days. Must get out of it. Everything is lacking in charm. This evening I am going on to Paris . . . How terribly alone we all are! Alone and misunderstood. And then afterwards, who knows what happens to us? I'm beginning to think that it is best when we are at our most human – when we hate, love, come to blows and caress.

Even on the day of his arrival in Paris, he went off in search of his youth:

Came here and found my old haunts. But the young hard-drinking and smoking 'Jean' is no more. Is life all over now? Has it forever lost its zest?

To revive youthful memories and restore his spirits, he was tempted to indulge in a little adventure – or, perhaps in mere fantasy, it is difficult to be sure which! Two lines have been removed from his diary but the entry continues,

. . . but trying to talk to such a goose – impossible. And the sad fact is that they are all – without exception – geese. How infinitely beautiful, lofty and noble Aino seems when put alongside them.

But on an empty sheet opposite this in the diary he notes,

One could argue that the feminine temperament embodies qualities that are incompatible with the way in which the masculine mind functions. Not that I believe this to be so, any more than it has ever inhibited me, for God's sake. And the conversation has been of the best with the finest of them. Never mind that the undercurrent is passion . . . after all, work in whatever form is health-giving, that's a cert. Ah, that rhymes with flirt. You can see from all this diary scribble that the subject of smoking and alcohol are studiously avoided. Note the form, 'avoided'. Can anything strike a chillier note.[1]

In other respects he lived without thought of the morrow and spent extravagantly. He ordered suits from the legendary tailors Stroem at Chaussée d'Antin, and shirts at the equally fashionable David, and spent his time meeting Finnish and Scandinavian friends – the painters Magnus Enckell and Juho Rissanen, the writer Wentzel Hagelstam and the Swedish composer Emil Sjögren. His touchiness occasionally posed problems for his friends but it probably worried him even more, 'Must learn to keep your feelings to yourself. Otherwise it will be unbearable to be with other people . . . if I could only control my expression but my skin is too thin.' His funds, which he had raised by borrowing against Ainola as security, were

1 31 October 1911.

almost exhausted after only a month. He moved from his comfortable hotel to a cheaper one but felt very 'down-graded' and thought the hall porter looked positively like a cutthroat. In spite of the fact that he was expecting to take delivery of a piano the following day, he moved out and went to a favourite old haunt, the Hôtel de la Grande Bretagne in the rue Caumartin. 'Voilà la solitude. Either in the forests of Finland or in a great city,' to quote his words to Rosa Newmarch.

In mid-November Mrs Newmarch joined him in Paris. She noted with some concern on her long walks that her normally generous companion never offered her refreshment, nor, when he was exhausted, suggested taking a taxi. Towards the end of her stay, he confessed that all this time, he hadn't as much as a single franc in his pocket, but that now his remittance had come; and, clad in evening dress, the pair of them dined in style. A day or so later, Sibelius saw her off at the Gare du Nord. Mrs Newmarch records that Sibelius followed Paris musical life with keen interest, even if he does not seem to have made any major discoveries on this trip. He found Stravinsky's *Scherzo fantastique* (1908) 'lively enough', but then he was hearing it in the immediate wake of a rather academic symphony of Guy-Ropartz, a work written in the shadow of d'Indy. In Louise's aria from Gustave Charpentier's opera of the same name, he was charmed by the bold leaps in the vocal line, and he thought the C major Symphony of Dukas 'a marvellous piece'. Franck's tone poem *Psyche* seems to have bored him, however, and he was not taken with his biblical scenes, *Ruth* and *Rebecca*, with their monotonous rhythmic patterns – 'one note per stave and absolutely symmetrical phrase lengths'. Surprisingly enough, Beethoven's *Missa Solemnis* gave him little joy. He thought its instrumentation old-fashioned and there was far too much in D major. Moreover, he grew tired of the vocal writing, particularly above the stave – 'high Gs, As and Bs all the time. It doesn't sound natural.' Nor did he respond to his youthful favourite, the 'Trout' Quintet, which seemed far too long, but on the other hand, the 'Death and the Maiden' Quartet restored his spirits. From a recital of 'Le Lied moderne', he took a taxi in order to be in time for the third act of Massenet's *Manon* and the following day he went to a performance of François Boieldieu's *La dame blanche* ('a masterpiece of its kind'). But his great operatic experience of this visit was on 1 December when he heard Gemma Bellincioni in *Salome*. 'The bejewelled, perfumed, naked public revelled in the dreadful, perverse text. The music and in particular the orchestration is marvellous.' Sibelius presumably transposed adjectives from the heroine to the public in his diary entry, as a 'naked' public, particularly in early December, is hardly a possibility.

While he was in Paris he spent a good deal of time at the home of Emil Sjögren. Here he met the critic, M. D. Calvocoressi, best known for his study of Mussorgsky and his memoir of life in the Diaghilev ballet in whose administration he had served. Calvocoressi was a member of Ravel's circle of friends and it was his texts that the great French composer used in the *Cinq mélodies populaires grècques*. It would seem that he planned to write an article on Sibelius though this never came to anything. For Sibelius, the encounter was frustrating. Here was an important figure who could have introduced him to Ravel and many other influential French musicians, but the evening was spent in listening to a handful of his own songs performed by a second-rate American singer, Minnie Tracey, and generous doses of Sjögren's own compositions. After a time he had had his fill: 'Left in a bad temper, my ears ringing with all this Sjögren . . . is it to suffer this sort of thing that one comes to Paris?'

Had he, on the other hand, come to the French capital to rework his own compositions? In his precarious financial position, he turned to such chores; he wrote a new version of *Har du mod?* (1904) for Breitkopf und Härtel, though this did not go far to keep the wolf from the door. A little later he turned his attention to a much more rewarding task: a reworking of his choral suite *Rakastava* (1894) for string orchestra. The outcome was a pure gem, the string textures being as refined as those of the Fourth Symphony, and in working on this score, he secured the dissemination of this music to a far wider audience than could possibly be achieved in its choral setting, hampered inevitably by its Finnish text. Things did not, however, seem to be going his way. Work on *Rakastava* had not brought the solution of his stylistic dilemma any closer. A letter from Mrs Newmarch related that the *Canzonetta* and *Valse triste* had been coolly received in London under Henry Wood. Sibelius suddenly felt that fate was turning sour and wanted to get away from Paris: 'Are my fears becoming a reality – that is, is my art now in decline – Aino must help me.'

Sibelius returned home for his forty-sixth birthday. Christmas was drawing nigh – a period 'entirely dependent on money and lots of it', as he noted in his diary. He felt trapped in the web of middle-class expectations:

> My domestic harmony and peace are at an end because I cannot earn sufficient income to supply all that is needed. A constant battle with tears and misery at home. A hell! I feel completely unworthy in my own home. A donkey who cannot carry its pack as far as its goal. Not even a senator's salary would be enough!

His stream of self-reproach went on.

> Poor Aino! It can hardly be easy to manage the house on so little. It makes me more than aware of the truth in the old saying: don't marry if you can't provide for your wife in the style to which she was accustomed before. The same food, clothes, servants – in a word, the same income. If you are an impractical devil like me, model your home completely on the style of your wife's: the same expenses and so on.

In a way these musings are not quite fair since in matters of life-style and servants, Sibelius was every bit as demanding as his wife. When he was complaining of their outgoings, she quite rightly rebuked him: 'It is you who wants to live like this!' Contrary to his protestations in letters from the early 1890s, he had middle-class expectations of comfort; the artistic struggles were far too absorbing to be compounded by material hardships.

'There's an earthy fragrance about it. Earth and Finland,' wrote Sibelius in describing *Rakastava*, which reached its definitive form in January 1912. Strangely enough, he had difficulty in placing this exquisite piece. Breitkopf und Härtel were unenthusiastic: the public was accustomed to big orchestral canvases from Sibelius's pen and felt some reserve in accepting a work just for strings and percussion, particularly since it drew on much earlier material. Sibelius felt quite hurt by their attitude:

> I must frankly confess that I do not share your views. Admittedly, I have from time to time misjudged the quality of my earlier works, pleasant associations and memories can easily prove deceptive. Even if the suite in question is newly composed, it belongs to an earlier period since it derives from material that I have already used in an earlier composition. But in my view, it fully justifies its place in my output as Op. 14.

He turned to another publisher, Zimmermann, but again to no avail. Then his thoughts turned to Lienau, who had expressed regrets during the previous autumn that their association had come to an end with a touching phrase, 'Aber so sind die Herren Komponisten.'[1] However, he declined *Rakastava* on the grounds that works for string orchestra were, generally speaking, no longer in demand. Eventually, the Helsinki publisher Lindgren accepted it and turned to Breitkopf und Härtel to get the work printed – which prompted a reproachful letter from the Leipzig publisher to the composer. Their pained surprise that he should have gone elsewhere cut little ice with Sibelius: 'The work in question is the one which you rejected as inferior!'

'How many more of these pinpricks do I have to put up with?' he asked himself. Another was to come which struck a raw nerve: in the Christmas issue of *Nuori Suomi*, the writer Ilmari Kianto (the poet Calamnius) spoke of him as 'fat and juicy'. For years he had retained his youthful figure, but now he was beginning to become a little corpulent. In one diary entry he apostrophizes himself, 'Wonderful, food-loving Ego!' Even Carpelan noticed that his idol was no longer as slim as he should be, and was beginning to run to fat. At lunch at Ainola on one occasion, he leapt suddenly to his feet, caught hold of Sibelius, whose fork was poised in hand, and shouted for all to hear, 'You are not to have another potato!' Sibelius flew up from his chair and threw his serviette to the ground. A stormy exchange followed, which ended with Carpelan taking himself off.

1 'Thus it is with composers.'

He was pursued by one of the daughters and eventually persuaded to return, and the ruffled feathers on both sides were soon smoothed over. During 1912 Sibelius did a number of sittings for the painter, Antti Favén, a talented if superficial artist whose drawings are generally more successful than his paintings. His portrait of the composer is in fact rather gaudy, with its violet and crimson shadows across the face. It provoked quite a scene between Aino and Sibelius. 'Favén depicts characteristics that kill my beloved wife's feelings for me!' he wrote. The sittings went on and on and distracted him from his work. Was he, one wonders, also pained by a recognition that there was some truth in what he saw. He noted the 'flabby muscles', and thought the finished article was 'a disaster . . . It makes me look like a butcher.'

The autumn brought political shadows that were to have far-reaching implications for Finnish musical life in general and the Helsinki orchestra in particular. As Finnish citizens were not subject to conscription into the Tsarist Army, Finland made an annual contribution to the Russian Defence budget instead. However, a wrangle took place over this provision; the Riksdag putting such difficulties in its way that the government responded by making alternative savings, including a punitive cut in cultural subsidies. Among other things, the Helsinki Philharmonic lost all its state grant. In response to this measure, Kajanus went to St Petersburg to plead the orchestra's case with Glazunov and he obtained a meeting with Kokovstov, the President of the Council of Ministers who promised to take up the matter with the Governor-General of Finland, Seyn. There is no doubt whatsoever that Kajanus acted in a spirit of complete altruism but his intervention was much resented by certain nationalist elements and aroused strong feelings, particularly among the Swedish-speaking community, who saw him using his personal influence in the Imperial capital to further his own ends. As a result he became the victim of a highly vocal campaign and his concerts were boycotted. Indeed, feelings ran so high that at the first of the season's concerts the management feared demonstrations and as a result the leader of the orchestra, Sitt, substituted for him. In the remaining concerts during the spring, his place was taken by Selim Palmgren.

In Sibelius's own circle, opinions were divided: Yrjö Hirn denouncing him while the poet Eino Leino was on his side, as for that matter was Sibelius himself. Of course, the situation had unpleasant resonances, for it called to mind Kajanus's unscrupulous use of his St Petersburg connections at the time of his appeal in 1897 against Sibelius's appointment to the University.[1] 'Kajanus has again appealed to St Petersburg,' Sibelius noted with just a shade of bitterness, 'and will bow and scrape to Kokovstov and Seyn.' But when he ran into Kajanus on the street in Helsinki, he realized how much strain he was under; he was 'looking the worse for wear and

1 See Volume I, p. 192–3. *Tr*

drink'. Kajanus's fight for his and his orchestra's security prompted him to realize how much Kajanus had done for him, most recently in Turin where, during the previous summer, he had conducted the First Symphony. He demonstrated his solidarity by pointedly attending a Kajanus rehearsal of *Night Ride and Sunrise*.

But right from the start Sibelius's sympathies had been with Kajanus and when, after a holiday abroad, Kajanus returned to Helsinki in March they dined together. Sibelius put his name to a petition in support of the Philharmonic out of gratitude for all that they had done for him, for much of his success had been the result of their loyal advocacy. Kajanus paid a visit to Ainola, as we see from a diary entry: 'Strange to have him here in the house. He has now gone to St Petersburg to listen to Glazunov who is his latest love'.[1]

There is a hint of envy here: Kajanus, who was after all nine years his senior, had been puzzled by the Fourth Symphony and seemed not to follow him into its new world. But when Glazunov had come to Helsinki in 1910 to conduct his Seventh Symphony, Kajanus – along with the rest of the Finnish musical establishment – had been altogether captivated. Glazunov's music gave no offence either on account of its idiom or any inner spiritual depths. 'In spite of my enormous reputation, there is a move to denigrate my creative achievement. Not least on the part of Kajanus – at one time a friend of my art – and now of another. A strange soul or perhaps demon! In any event no ordinary man.' In voicing these darker thoughts, Sibelius was forgetting that it was not Kajanus who had changed, but he himself who had become something quite different from the young man of the 1890s. On one occasion he wondered whether he had been wise to be drawn into the quarrel about the orchestra, and when Kajanus reassured him, hailing the orchestra as 'laying the foundations of the international reputation of Finnish music', he felt a twinge of pique.

In January 1912 Sibelius was asked whether he would be willing to accept the position of Professor of Composition at the Akademie für Musik und darstellende Kunst in Vienna. The vacancy arose from the retirement of Robert Fuchs with whom Sibelius himself had studied during his year in Vienna. It seems that Richard Strauss was the first to have been approached and when he turned it down the offer went to Max Reger. Fuchs himself was presumably the instigator of the present invitation, though Sibelius was not a big name in Vienna. When his Violin Concerto, together with that of Max von Schillings was performed at a concert of pupils from Otakar Sevčik's master class, it drew a contemptuous reaction from some sources. Somewhat later, in December 1910, Ferenc von Vecsey played the concerto in Vienna, and Weingartner, who had already introduced the First Symphony to Viennese audiences two years earlier, gave the Second with the

1 7 March 1912.

Philharmonic Orchestra. Given the rough treatment meted out by the Viennese press to new symphonies, whether Teutonic or not, Sibelius got off relatively lightly. Julius Korngold, one of the more progressively inclined critics, complained of 'rhapsodic forms and shadowy contours' but welcomed the symphony as a worthwhile new acquaintance. Max Kalbeck, a Brahms admirer of the old school, thought he discerned a funeral procession emerging from the mists of the *Andante*! However, the foundations were being laid for a Sibelius presence in Vienna.

News of the academic offer was soon published in the Helsinki newspapers and also gained currency in the international press. Sibelius's first reaction was undoubtedly coloured by his irritation with the controversy that was raging over Kajanus and the orchestra. 'Am toying with the idea of the Chair – it would be wonderful to get away from the plebeian mob who, even though they are compatriots, lose no chance of belittling my work.' He probably had little notion of the effect that the continuing speculation about his future was having on those around him. Some weeks after news of the invitation had broken, Leevi Madetoja wrote from Berlin: 'The great honour bestowed on you by this offer must surely be very tempting, but your absence from the country would constitute an irreparable loss for Finnish culture, and I venture to be selfish enough to believe that we may yet keep you with us at home.' Werner Söderhjelm went to Ainola to talk the matter over with Sibelius and discuss his own financial plight. Judging from Sibelius's own diary, the composer turned down the various suggestions that arose except for one: an increase in his state pension. When he had written from Vienna, Wilhelm Bopp had gone into detail about the terms: a professor of seventh rank would command 6,410 francs per annum. The director's letter had come in mid-January and Sibelius's response on 5 February was evidently not completely negative. But by the end of the month he was seized by doubts concerning the post and on 1 March he telegraphed Vienna to turn the offer down. As his diary records, 'I can't go on drifting further into debt for the sake of honours. Several of my compatriots and friends have expressed surprise that I should have turned down Vienna. They don't understand my patriotism and love of my own independent way of working.' Even if he had at first been beguiled by the temptations of the offer, he soon grasped what the realities would entail: he was no teacher, he would have been quickly drawn into the Viennese pastime of intrigue – besides he had no ability or desire to adapt at this stage in his career to an entirely new environment and way of life. The position eventually went to Franz Schreker. In Finland itself, the outcome was greater pressure to raise Sibelius's state pension. This bore fruit the following summer when it was increased from 3,000 to 5,000 Finnish marks, though the rise was effectively offset by increased inflation.

The Fourth Symphony now appeared in print and was glowingly reviewed in *Die Musik*. 'As an artist, Sibelius has now attained a creative maturity and stature that can no longer he gainsaid.' The uniformly positive tone of the review was totally at variance with the reception that the symphony itself was to encounter in the German-speaking world. Indeed, it was not until a half-century later that the work was to come into its own, in the hands of such conductors as Karajan and Maazel. Its publication prompted an inspired, lyrical outburst from Carpelan's pen: 'I am possessed; I throw my arms round everyone I meet; I have had a glimpse of the eternal life!'

At the turn of the year Sibelius himself was beginning to emerge from the orbit of the symphony. Already, just before Christmas, he had embarked on a new orchestral work, *La Chasse* and by February 1912 his plans had begun to take a more definite shape. There was to be a second set of *Scènes historiques*, to consist, like the first, of three pieces. The first was called, *At the drawbridge;* the second was *The Falconer*, and the third, *La Chasse*. The *Falconer* was soon changed, first to *Knightly Love* and finally to *Love Song*. Work on the three pieces proceeded slowly and he had to work hard to generate the right atmosphere: 'Ordered lots of fruit from Helsinki. Have thoroughly aired the upper floor of the villa. Eventually I managed to muster up the requisite concentration – at least to begin with. I'm still far from happy with my work methods or my capacity.' In a way the *Scènes historiques* with their world of medieval chivalry was related to another project, plans for a setting of the *Song of the Goths* and other stanzas from Rydberg's poem *Dexippos*, from which the *Song of the Athenians* comes. Sibelius sketched out a theme for the song itself but by the middle of February, he had abandoned the whole scheme, '*Dexippos* impossible from an artistic point of view. Melodrama! To hell with it!'

Meanwhile Paul Juon, the Russian-born composer now domiciled in Berlin, came to Helsinki to give a concert. Sibelius had come to know him through the good offices of his former publisher, Robert Lienau and attended his programme. According to Sibelius, Juon remarked how little the Finnish composer was played in his own country. Even if the remark was based on a casual impression rather than a more thorough-going examination of concert programmes, it left its mark on him. 'Were I pianist or an executant of some kind, it would help . . . when I think of Busoni's enviable position as an artist, I understand my own fate. My infinitely tragic fate!' The self-pity was not all that serious, for he continues, 'Is there anything really tragic about you, you old joker?'

At the turn of the month (March–April), Sibelius gave three concerts of his own music, mostly 'old and a few unimportant new compositions': there was the Fourth Symphony, *Rakastava*, the second set of *Scènes historiques* and the *Impromptu* for women's voices and orchestra, which at the last of the three concerts was replaced by *Night Ride and Sunrise*. Kajanus presented him with a garland as a mark of 'gratitude for the work of twenty years', a reference to his début in 1892 with the *Kullervo* Symphony. Both the critics and the public seem to have responded more warmly to the symphony than they did at its first performance, but Sibelius himself was disturbed by the poor quality of the orchestral playing, particularly the clarinet: 'Mistakes in abundance!'

The *Scènes historiques II* were ready for the printer on 18 April but already, before the concerts, new ideas had come to him. 'A fifth Symphony. A sixth: *Luonnotar*. Let's see if these plans work out.' His plans were constantly changing. By the beginning of May, he was 'in a period of expectation' and his invention was holding fire. ' "Erste Phantasie für grosses Orchestra, Op. 67"!! "Zweite etc". Perhaps that was the solution! – Opera?! Symphonies?! You must keep calm and not allow things to run away with you.' At times, it seemed to him that all his symphonic activity was a waste of time: 'How little, infinitely little understanding have my symphonies met with in the world at large!' He took some comfort in Weingartner's thoughts on culture in broader terms: 'To forget one's own little ego and discover one's role, small but necessary, in the overall pattern of things.' Sibelius reminded himself of Liszt's words that it was important for one's own development to sort out one's relationship with the work of contemporary composers.

More domestic tensions surfaced to strain his patience. After a bitter quarrel between Saimi Järnefelt and Aino he decided to move 'lock, stock and barrel' to Paris. It must have struck him as obvious that while the children were still growing up, this idea was totally impractical. But he wanted to get away from Järvenpää at any cost. 'We cannot put up with things as they are here any longer, Aino and I. Everything conspires to wear one out.' To his surprise he found that Aino was by no means unresponsive to his plans. He even went so far as to go into Helsinki to see an estate agent about the possibility of putting Ainola on to the market, but of course, he soon came to his senses. He quickly realized in his heart of hearts that he was going to spend the rest of his days there, come what may, and he was pained to find that news of his plans to move had leaked out. That all this was a passing fancy became all the more evident later the same summer when he had a stable built near the villa and bought a horse, and the following autumn he actually bought more land from his neighbour, Westermarck, for the sum of 2,500 Finnish marks.

In his diaries he ruminates on the question of the artist and money:

Your wife gives up nothing, nothing of her self, her clothing or her inner life. Nor should you. But if I were not to make sacrifices, life would be much the poorer. Yet the result is that you don't generate the right climate for your creative work or, put it another way, without the income you can't compose. Work all that out. Impossible for me to harmonize my concern with what is right for me as an artist and the necessity to ensure income. Surely, though, I wasn't sent into this marvellous world just to pay off debts, to give what little I earn from the

216

fruits of all my spiritual struggles, my genius, to people who merely live off the interest of their capital. Take for example, my Second Symphony. It has brought fame and credit to Finland on countless occasions. Yet it has cost me more than 18,000 marks and I have earned from it 1,500! My debts mount with every symphony!

There is some justice in this outburst. Finland undoubtedly needed Sibelius as its standard bearer: his work had served to draw attention to her plight as a Tsarist vassal and bolster her growing sense of national awareness. By now he was probably the best-known Finn. Yet those who profited from the image he was helping to create made all too little contribution to his own well-being.

Now he was torn – or so he thought – between symphony and opera. He was still toying with plans to set Boldemann's libretto though he wanted to transpose the action from eighteenth-century France to the Sweden of the 1780s, with officers in Gustavian uniforms, a Polish count and with the heroine becoming a Russian-Karelian. But the very next moment he was outlining his views about abstract opera:

> I can see quite clearly that any opera I write will be without words, the scenery will be architectonic and the singers will merely intone on vowels – above all, there will be no words! Everything will sound beautiful, lyrical and colourful but there'll be no complex plots and sub-plots.

Boldemann can hardly have been surprised the following autumn when he learned that Sibelius had abandoned the project. Two years earlier he had explained his view that opera as an art form was really inferior to absolute music. Sibelius's imagination was now consumed by embryonic motives that could well be for a fifth symphony, and his whole mind was possessed by what his inner ear could dimly make out. Yet suddenly he threw everything to one side and began writing a set of sonatinas for the piano 'on account of my heavy debts that have to be repaid'. He realized that he stood at a crossroads:

> Shall I give myself to these small pieces which will pay the food bills, or go on with deeper things and become a pure idealist? The latter is no doubt the right course . . . but impossible to put into effect. But perhaps the two courses can in some way be reconciled.

He finished the Three Sonatinas, Op. 67, at the beginning of July. In one sense they belong more to the idealistic rather than the 'opportunistic' side of his work. But perhaps Sibelius took the view that his creative irons were rusting when he was occupied by miniatures but in any event he continued with smaller projects. He spent a week in Kuhmoinen in the depths of the country, fishing, bathing and relaxing, and at the same time he reworked the choral piece *Har du mod?* and composed a tune for the bells of the Berghälls Church of Helsinki.

After this he intended to write a number of serenades for obbligato solo instruments and orchestra. This idea came to fruition later in the Two Serenades for violin and orchestra, Op. 69, but the idea of a serenade for two clarinets and another in the manner of a Mozart serenade, to which he had assigned the working number 'VIII' in his diary, came to nothing.

Sibelius could mollify his conscience with the straightforward thought that he simply could not afford to go on writing symphonies. For a popular work, such as the *Scènes historiques II* or the Three Sonatinas for piano, Op. 67, that took him a month or so to complete, would bring him in 3,000 Reichsmarks, while the Fourth Symphony on the other hand occupied his energies for more than eighteen months and was rewarded by a mere 4,000 Reichsmarks. At times one is tempted to speculate as to whether the impossible financial predicaments into which Sibelius drifted were the product of some compulsive drive, as – if we are to believe the late Edward Lockspeiser[1] – was the case with Debussy. Was he subconsciously driven to burden himself with hurdles in the belief that in overcoming them he would rise to greater artistic heights? Given the evidence of the diaries, it would seem that this was not really the case. He heaped troubles upon himself and they weighed heavily on his day-to-day life; as he put it, he lived with 'humiliation and poverty, that's to say, in luxury without money'.

At the end of 1912 he wrote despairingly, 'I wish for no more than to be able, untroubled by material anxieties, to devote myself completely to the composition of bigger works. But – as things are now – this is impossible.' Without doubt, this has the ring of truth, but one must at the same time question its premiss. After all, the Fourth Symphony had been composed at the same time as he was working on other pieces. Now, ideas for new symphonies and tone poems were forming themselves in his head, and yet he seems fearful of allowing them to take him over. In May 1912, he had taken the view in his diary that there was no solution to the problem of form, other than allowing the motives to dictate its shape. At the same time, he was beginning to view atonality with some degree of fascination:

> Arnold Schoenberg's theories interest me even if I find him single-minded to the point of prejudice. Perhaps I wouldn't if I were to get to know him better.

But only a month later he was writing in sceptical terms of modernism:

> Whatever path you choose, Glorious Ego – don't sacrifice the life-giving warmth and vitality that lies at the heart of your music. You won't be any 'greater' by outdoing – or trying to outdo – your contemporaries in terms of a revolutionary 'profile'. Let's not join in any race.

1 Edward Lockspeiser, *Debussy: His Life and Mind*, Volume I, London, 1962; Volume II, London, 1965.

Even so, the Fourth Symphony had 'outdone' most of his contemporaries in terms of a radical profile, yet he doubtless feared that in this kind of race the horse rather than the rider would soon take charge.

During the first four days of October, attention shifted from London's musical life to that of Birmingham. For the third year in succession, Granville Bantock was the driving force behind the Birmingham Festival. The main conductor was Sir Henry Wood and the soloists included Moritz Rosenthal and Pablo Casals. Seven oratorios formed the central body of the programmes – from Bach's *St Matthew Passion* to Elgar's *The Apostles* – and new works had been commissioned from Elgar, Bantock and Walford Davies. The two novelties from abroad were Skryabin's *Prometheus* and Sibelius's Fourth Symphony. Sibelius arrived in London on 24 or 25 September in time for a rehearsal at the Queen's Hall. While in Birmingham, he stayed with Bantock, as he had done on his earlier visit in 1905, and together with Mrs Newmarch he took a trip to Stratford-upon-Avon where he was enchanted by the splendid oak trees and all the relics of Shakespeare.[1]

Mrs Newmarch found him far more tranquil and at peace with himself than he had been on his earlier visits. Then she had fears that his moral and creative powers would in some way dissipate themselves; now she discerned a greater sense of concentration on his musical objectives and a marked change in his way of life – no tobacco or alcohol! 'Without intending to flatter you,' she wrote, that 'unlike poor Elgar' he now radiated 'une belle atmosphère'. Her letter, dated simply 'dimanche', was presumably penned on the 6th immediately after his departure. There were no dramatic developments during his rehearsals during which Bantock acted as interpreter and Sir Henry called out instructions to the players from the wings. Delius was present at the rehearsal and sat with Mrs Newmarch who heard him say time and again that this is 'no ordinary music'. Skryabin, on the other hand, felt that not enough time had been allotted to the preparation of his *Prometheus* and withdrew the work. The two composers, incidentally,

1 Sibelius's diary contains entries (18 September and 1 October) concerning his visit to England. From Stratford-upon-Avon he wrote to Aino (29 September) mentioning that he was with Mrs Newmarch and he mentions this in another letter to Carpelan. In her Sibelius book, Mrs Newmarch speaks of this as having taken place during the composer's later visit in February and March of 1921. Another mistake that should be corrected occurs in Ekman's study, in which he records that Sibelius told him that he had also given concerts in Liverpool, Manchester, Bournemouth and Cheltenham as well as in Birmingham. Mrs Newmarch may well have been influenced by this herself as she speaks of him as conducting in four or five other cities during this trip. The fact is that Sibelius must have confused the two visits, for the concerts in question took place on his 1921 visit. In 1912 he rehearsed on 26 September one or two days after his arrival, went to Birmingham where another rehearsal took place, visited Stratford-upon-Avon on 29 September, conducted the symphony in Birmingham on 1 October and left England on 3 October. He arrived back in Helsinki on 6 October and took a rehearsal with the Philharmonic Orchestra the following day.

never met either on this occasion or at a later date.

At the concert itself, on 1 October, Sibelius shared the programme with Elgar, who conducted his cantata *The Music Makers* before it was Sibelius's turn to present the symphony. According to *The Times*, the legend prefacing *The Music Makers* –

O men, it must ever be
That we dwell in our dreaming and singing
A little apart from ye

– was more apposite to the symphony than the cantata. Its orchestration struck *The Times* as little short of astonishing given the fact that Sibelius did not use larger forces than did Brahams:

. . . it is music which stands far apart from the common expression of the time. Yet it is not a self-conscious apartness, and the composer could not have used such a motto, because he lives so much in his own world, thinks his own thoughts, and translates them into sound so spontaneously, that he is under no temptation to measure himself against his hearers. [. . .] Sibelius brings a wealth of contrasted material; each instrument has a personality of its own; and that is why, although he uses an orchestra no bigger than that of Brahms's First Symphony, the orchestration is almost disconcertingly new. He scarcely ever makes instruments of different colours do the same thing. Sometimes, therefore, their personalities clash in the most glaring way, because they are following different trains of thought independently.[1]

Ernest Newman saw the greater severity and concentration of the symphony as part and parcel of a more widespread stylistic trend: Schoenberg, he argued, was trying to do much the same thing but without the same success. Perhaps without realizing it, Newman was sowing the seeds of one of the most bitter polemics of the post-war years. In a somewhat later article in *The Nation*, monitored in the Swedish-language Helsinki press, Newman wrote that Sibelius's new symphony, Delius's *Sea Drift* and certain new works of Strauss put most of the programmes to shame. The symphony was 'the hardest nut to crack'; it was seldom smiling yet was without any Tchaikovskian self-pity; indeed it was a voyage of spiritual exploration and so inward-looking that it is not easy to follow without guidance. Other press comment was either guarded and respectful, as was, for example, the *Musical Times* or directly uncomprehending, as was the *Standard*: 'Mr. Sibelius's music could be described as written in cypher and unfortunately he has omitted to provide us with the code.' The *Illustrated London News* summed up the general view that Sibelius had with the Fourth Symphony contributed the most important novelty of the Festival.

1 *The Times*, 3 October 1912.

Sibelius stayed in Birmingham only a day or so after his concert, for he was due to take an orchestral rehearsal in Helsinki. A large number of admirers left photographs of him at the concert hall in the hope of getting them autographed. Before he left, he was asked – presumably by Bantock – to write a sacred work for the 1913 Gloucester Festival. Mrs Newmarch did not warm to the idea:

> I have a horror of Festival commissions. This is the way we ruin so many of our best composers in England . . . Elgar is going quickly downhill under the strain of more or less commercial projects; Bantock writes far too much with the result that half of what we hear of his sounds a little facile; does it surprise you to learn that I would not want to see you turned into a composer *en vogue*, as happened to poor Dvořák twenty years ago?

As far as she was concerned, his next work should be nothing less than his 'Fifth'.

When Sibelius had embarked on the revision of *Rakastava*, he faced a far more difficult challenge than he had in the case of *En Saga*. Less than a decade separated the definitive *En Saga* from its original while *Rakastava* was nearly twenty years old and Sibelius's style had undergone enormous development and change. Particularly after so radical a work as the Fourth Symphony, a marriage between the old material and the new style might seem hazardous indeed. Yet the outcome could not have been happier. The composer rethought the material in new psychological and technical ways without allowing the results to break out of the existing framework.

In the first movement, *The Lover*, the syllable per note setting gives way to a far more flexible, freer and ethereal polyphony whose individual strands are no longer bound by metric accents:

Ex 142

From a whispering triplet figure in the inner parts Sibelius weaves atmospheric and mysterious sounding interludes:

Ex 143

In the second movement, *The Way of the Lover,* Sibelius sets in motion a kind of *perpetuum mobile* which in its momentum and sound world call to mind the *Vivace* movement of the *Voces intimae* quartet:

Ex 144

This is the movement that least departs from the text of the original. Also in the third movement, *Goodnight – Farewell!*, the folk-like simplicity of the farewell song is retained, but the tenor solo over sustained chords is replaced by a richly worked-out transition:

Ex 145

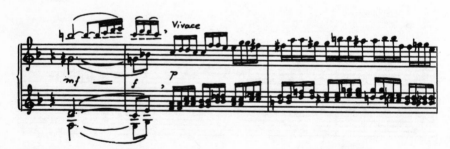

All this leads to darker-hued chords, which lend the idyllic, rustic melancholy of the original a much greater intensity. Accordingly, the final farewells are more extended without being long drawn out and their effect is more poignant:

Ex 146

Even though the naive and erotic atmosphere of the original has been transformed into something less tangible and more refined, there is still an earthiness, a scent of Finnish soil here.

The three tone poems that comprise the second set of *Scènes historiques* are vivid, life-enhancing pieces and in some ways balletic in inspiration. The first, *La Chasse*, evokes much of the spirit and atmosphere of a royal hunt: the Prince and his devoted companions are pictured in their glittering attire in the forest. Right from the opening horn figure, E flat, F and A, the tritone of the Fourth Symphony, and the echoing fanfares over a pedal E flat, we feel something of the power and mystery of the forest as well as the drama of the hunt:

Ex 147

The piece derives much of its special character from the changes between the hunting calls and the onomatopoeic galloping episodes. By comparison with the world of *Rakastava* with its fragrance and sense of mystery, the second movement, *Minnelied*, has the air of a ceremonial court love song. The orchestral texture, and in particular the writing for the harp, remind one a little of the incidental music of Strindberg's *Swanwhite*, though the sonorities are more sumptuous. The melodic line, love-lorn in feeling and almost elegiac in tone, is supported by a richly embroidered texture:

Ex 148

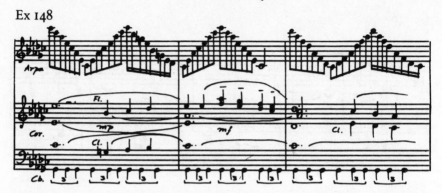

After this *pas de deux*, the final movement, *At the drawbridge*, might well accompany a harlequinade. The violins strum in the manner of a guitar and the two flutes outline a delightful idea in parallel thirds whose charm and grace are only occasionally obscured by distant, threatening clouds:

Ex 149

A second theme, which derives from it, has an engaging syncopation and moves us to B major:

Ex 150

Despite outward appearances, it would be misleading to call the *Scènes historiques* pastiche, for Sibelius's imagination is so steeped in the medieval chivalry and ceremonial that this fantasy world became reality for him. Perhaps he needed this romantic refuge after the harsh realities of the world of the Fourth Symphony.

In the first of the Three Sonatinas, Op. 67, in F sharp minor, we renew contact with the asceticism of the symphony and one could describe its layout and design as equally *dépouillé*. The first movement begins pensively with a melodic cell in D major (the relative major of the submediant – B minor):

Ex 151

The second group acquires its special colour from the diminished fifth and the sense of a tritone D–G sharp as well as the change to the Phrygian mode:[1]

Ex 152

The resemblance to the contours of the second and third movements of the Fourth Symphony is quite plain. Another point of contact is some of the changes of character, the psychological metamorphoses. An ascending figure of thirds in the bass at the very end of the second group (page 3, bars 4–7) is transformed into a dynamic triplet idea in the development and is alluded to in the coda. The questioning, pensive character of the main theme is underlined in the reprise by new dissonant harmonies.

The *Largo* movement serves as another demonstration of Sibelius's power to blend organic unity, a sense of inevitable melodic growth and continuity while at the same time maintaining the character of an improvisation:

1 Much of the Phrygian character is weakened by two disastrous printer's errors. The bottom note in the last bar of the first page should be a D (analogous with the G in the reprise). The second note in the first bar of page 3 should be D and not D sharp, according to the autograph. The composer made these corrections in his daughter Katarina's copy of the Sonatina.

Ex 153

The reprise of this idea fully scored – again a reminder of the third movement of the symphony – as it were forms the climax of the movement. In the final *Rondo*, the right hand glitters impressionistically over the melody in the left:

Ex 154

As was the case in the outer movements of the symphony, Sibelius juxtaposes chords a tritone apart, in this instance C sharp and G, as a means of generating tension:

Ex 155

Wilhelm Kempff underlined the almost bitonal impression this creates by generous pedalling. The movement comes to an end in the iridescent haze cast by the main theme in its major form.

Sibelius may well have written the Second Sonatina, in E major, in a moment of contrapuntal exuberance. The first movement has something of the spirit of a two-part invention – or indeed canon:

Ex156

The *Andantino* with its cello-like cantilena forms a lyrical foil against the background of polyphony that distinguishes the outer movements and that lends the finale a special charm.

In the Third Sonatina, in B flat minor, the thematic substance of all three movements derives from the descending intervals of a third, fourth and fifth, all in the dominant area. In the first movement these intervals lend the music an intimate, melancholy flavour (F–D flat, F–C, F–B flat) –

Ex 157

– while in the slow movement they acquire the character of a funeral march:

Ex 158

The finale presents them in the form of a playful rondo theme:

Ex 159

But the movements also have other thematic cross-references, as, for example, the final element of the second group with a counterpoint going in contrary motion:

Ex 160

(a)

(b)

(c)

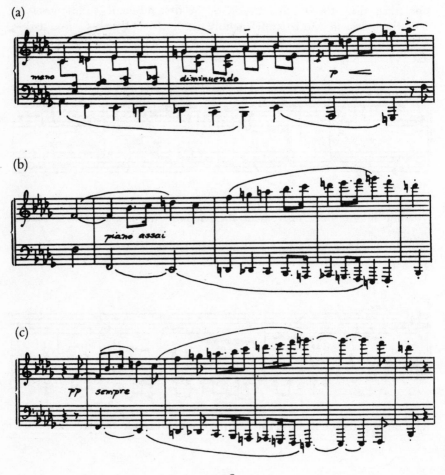

The first movement could aptly be described as a sonata-form design but without development, albeit that this is an anomaly. The second with its modulations, sequences and fugato is predominantly developmental. From it there is a transition to the vivacious final rondo. In view of the thematic unity the three movements could well be thought of as comprising an organic entity thus: exposition – reprise – development – transition passage – scherzo-like rondo. And once this design is perceived, one becomes aware of its prophetic relationship to the definitive version of the first movement of the Fifth Symphony.

The Two Serenades for violin and orchestra are of roughly the same difficulty as the two Beethoven Romances. The first, in D major, has a wonderfully lyrical and touching main theme whose special intensity is heightened by the sharpened Lydian fourth:

Ex 161

Note the flattened Mixolydian seventh in the oboe part – again the same combination of modal elements as we find in the finale of the Fourth Symphony! The solo part seems to spring from the very spirit of the instrument, so natural is his feeling for it. Sibelius secures a marvellous effect by ending the first main section on the orchestra in B major and then bringing back the main theme in D major against a dark chromatic background from the strings! And how ecstatic this theme sounds in the very closing pages, offering the soloist every opportunity for expressive, glowing tone.

Its companion, the Serenade in G minor – which Sibelius had originally intended to call 'Romance' – is suffused with melancholy brooding. Its main theme climbs expressively against a poignant harmonic landscape:

Ex 162

The iambic character of the second idea seems to come from much the same
stable as the finale of the Violin Concerto:

Ex 163

Stylistically, the Two Serenades are much further removed from the
Fourth Symphony than are the Sonatinas. It is as if the composer is casting a
nostalgic glance at his youthful love affair with the violin, and perhaps, even
that occasion when he himself performed a Beethoven Romance.

CHAPTER EIGHT

The Bard and Luonnotar

The position of the Philharmonic Orchestra, threatened earlier in 1912, became even more precarious as the year wore on. A new orchestra called the Helsinki Symphony was founded and Georg Schnéevoigt was summonded from Riga to be its conductor. Kajanus was distinctly out of favour in Swedish-speaking circles and his future looked bleak. He was not even considered for the new appointment and his old orchestra was now without any state support. Ten of its members went over to the 'opposition', but the bulk of them and in particular the Finnish-born musicians, remained loyal and even went so far as to announce their intention to play on, if need be, without salary.

Kajanus showed his fighting spirit. He arranged a loan using the orchestral library as security and also organized a lottery to raise money. And so, by the beginning of the autumn, the battle lines were drawn and plans for the season were announced. Of course, the situation was little short of grotesque. Helsinki, a town of some 150,000 souls, could hardly sustain two orchestras, and the public inevitably divided into two camps: the Swedish-speaking patrons supporting Schnéevoigt, while the Finnish-speaking audiences rallied to Kajanus, who adopted a low profile so as not to exacerbate the situation. He conducted only two of the ten concerts.

Sibelius himself viewed the situation with distaste: 'The orchestral feud pains me, particularly since I can't outwardly declare for either party because of indifference.' None the less, he showed his colours by allowing Kajanus to enlist his services for the first of their Celebrity Concerts at the Finnish National Theatre. His diary still reflects something of his old ambivalence: he speaks of Kajanus as 'devilish calculating' and grumbles that Kajanus's entry in *Riemanns Musiklexikon* 'lists my *Kullervo* among his works'. Of course, the work in question was Kajanus's own *Aino* Symphony and the following day Sibelius notes that he has allowed unworthy thoughts to run away with him:

> As far as Kajus is concerned, he is fighting for his life as well as his place in our musical history. That it is part of his scheme to put me in the

shadow is as certain as it is unconscious. But I have an important card in my hand: my works are at least printed!

Sibelius's suspicions would seem entirely groundless, indeed almost paranoid, given the consistent loyalty Kajanus had shown him, most recently by conducting his works, not only in Finland but in Turin, Christiania and Pavlovsk. Deep down no doubt, he still saw in him 'the old friend in spite of everything', but obviously there were twinges of the mistrust engendered by the events of 1897. With Schnéevoigt, on the other hand, he had a far more superficial relationship. Schnéevoigt seems not to have taken offence at Sibelius's guest appearance with the rival orchestra, and he conducted a number of Sibelius works during the season including three performances of the First Symphony during the autumn and one of the Second during the spring. Sibelius found his reading of the latter 'virtuoso-like but sentimental', an epithet that could well be extended to cover his conducting in general. He was endowed with excellent technique and had plenty of temperament but not unimpeachable taste. Kajanus may not have been his equal technically, and was not a particularly good orchestral accompanist, but there is no doubt of his greater depth. Even if Schnéevoigt was better known outside Finland and enjoyed some measure of international recognition, it is Kajanus whom we see as the more searching artist and the greater interpreter of Sibelius.[1]

Sibelius himself did not suffer as a result of the orchestral feud. During the 1912–13 season he was played just as much as he had been before, though his plans to bring the two orchestras together for a concert under his own baton came to nothing. For his concert with the Philharmonic on 11 October, Sibelius chose a long and demanding programme: the Second Symphony, movements from *Swanwhite* including *The Harp*, which he had just revised for a production at the Deutsches-Theater, Berlin and both sets of the *Scènes historiques*. Opinion divided along predictable party lines. The Swedish-language *Hufvudstadsbladet*, irritated by the frenzied shouts of 'hyvä' (bravo) from the Finns in the audience, spoke of 'a certain want of vitality' and noted that the woodwind sounded 'feeble, uneven and occasionally ugly'. *Uusi Suomi*, for the rival camp, was full of praises. Sibelius noted in his diary that he was caught in the crossfire of the language war: 'I conducted – it seemed to me – well, but the press is partisan.'

All these petty squabbles were soon forgotten when at the end of October, Busoni came to Helsinki to give two piano recitals. The first included Bach's Chromatic Fantasia and Fugue and Beethoven's C minor Sonata, Op. 111, which prompted an ecstatic diary entry from Sibelius, 'An

---

1 No doubt Kajanus's pioneering gramophone records of the First, Second, Third and Fifth Symphonies, *Tapiola, Pohjola's Daughter* and *Belshazzar's Feast* account for this view, particularly when compared with Schnéevoigt's interpretations of the Fourth and Sixth Symphonies. *Tr*

unsurpassable artist – an unforgettable evening!' Busoni seemed to be much taken with the Fourth Symphony and keen to break a lance for it in Europe. He wrote a touching note to Sibelius just before his second recital ending with a promise 'to play as well for you tonight as I possibly can', and if Sibelius's reaction was anything to go by, it must have been one of the most memorable of all piano recitals. 'Busoni played the *Hammerklavier* Sonata. I shall cherish the memory of this performance all my life. Never has the greatness and power of Mankind seemed more evident and convincing. Kraft ist die Moral der Menschen. Beethoven has said.'

An unfavourable notice of the Fourth Symphony in *Monthly Musical Record* prompted further bouts of self-questioning and depression but life went on. In November he sent Two Rondinos for piano, Op. 68, to Universal Edition in Vienna, which was subsequently to draw a pained reproach from Breitkopf. The selfsame month he sent them his First Serenade for violin and orchestra and after some hesitation they accepted it but paid only 50 per cent of the sum he had asked.

At the beginning of the autumn the Danish publisher, Wilhelm Hansen, had written to ask whether he would undertake a commission: to compose music to *Scaramouche*, a pantomime by Poul Knudsen. He accepted in the belief that only a few dance movements would be required: it was only later when he had embarked on the project that he realized his mistake. Meanwhile Hansen organized a concert of his music in Copenhagen. The composer suggested a wholly orchestral programme but Hansen demurred, suggesting that a soloist – a singer – should be engaged, particularly as they were proposing to include something as uncompromising as the Fourth Symphony. At the end of November Sibelius set off for Copenhagen and, given the problems posed by the symphony, he had sectional rehearsals but even some of the violinists would stop in the middle of a passage, thinking they had got lost or made a mistake.

The concert did not find Sibelius at his happiest. He felt exhausted and one critic described him as 'an anxious, haunted creature whose right hand clutched a baton that trembled like an aspen leaf in the wind, while the left flailed the air nervously'. He saw him as 'perhaps a self-tormented figure, hyper-tense and introverted' who gave the impression that it was 'a physical endurance to appear in public'. Charles Kjerulf, on the other hand, wrote of him in quite different terms:

> Tall and pale with a melancholy face whose fine lines and furrows almost suggest runic lettering . . . Sibelius's conducting mostly consists of big gestures and outstretched arms – there is something about him that suggests a bird in flight – the music seems to take wing and waft away. Closer scrutiny reveals that he almost trembles with nervous tension – the music from deep within his being pulsates, like the machine room of a ship, causing the whole vessel to vibrate. There is nothing particularly elegant about his beat – and he is not beautiful to watch as was Johan

Svendsen – and even less can he be described as a virtuoso conductor. Yet he is completely at one with his music and his orchestra – and he leads them as a father would a child, envelopping them in his arms like an embracing lover.[1]

In the symphony Sibelius did not have the public with him. It was not until the second half, which comprised the second set of *Scènes historiques*, a group of songs with the Norwegian soprano Borghild Langaard as soloist, and *Night Ride and Sunrise*, that the ice was broken. After the concert, the Society of Danish Composers gave a dinner at the Hotel d'Angleterre in his honour at which most of the leading figures in Danish musical life were in attendance. Carl Nielsen and Louis Glass made speeches while Sibelius, himself no speechmaker, gave a short but warm reply of thanks. The male choir, Belcanto, sang his *The Broken Voice*. Under the palms in the Winter Garden he met his old friends from Berlin, Fini Henriques and Schnedler-Petersen, and on the surface all was as well as one could possibly wish. Yet underneath Sibelius sensed that there were tensions in the air: between his admirer, Charles Kjerulf, and other less positively inclined critics, and between Carl Nielsen and himself. He was conscious of the fact that he was coming from one small country as 'Jean-le-Grand' to another, which had its own 'Charles-le-Grand', and matters were not helped by the fact that he enjoyed a growing international reputation, which Nielsen did not yet rival.

There was some measure of justice in what must now seem paranoid, or at best insecure responses on Sibelius's part. The Copenhagen press did not show anywhere near the same understanding of the Fourth Symphony as had their English colleagues two months before. The *Berlingske Tidende* can serve as a typical example:

> Sibelius has shrunk from reality, partly on grounds of his temperament, partly because of a kind of unproven necessity. He prefers to move towards the periphery where music almost ceases to be music . . . and when he has to sustain the larger forms, he purposely avoids passages where we can verify his procedures. It is as if he himself was conscious that in his technical equipment there are gaps that must be kept from view. It is the capacity to keep his material together, to work it out, to hammer and chisel so that everything is clearly focused and in its place, that is lacking. His music becomes merely fantastic sketchings in a grey and mystical world.

Only Charles Kjerulf seems to have grasped 'this great piece of chamber music for orchestra'.

The reviews reached Sibelius on 8 December back in Finland and ruined his birthday: 'The demons are out in the Copenhagen papers. Am abused in a scurrilous fashion. I cannot maintain my good spirits in face of this.' His

1 *Politiken*, 4 December 1912.

diary entry goes on to cast aspersions on Nielsen, whom he describes as 'a false friend', which reflects on his own judgement. No one could describe Nielsen as 'false' or hypocritical for, in spite of his warmth and naturalness, he could be direct to the point of sharpness. Indeed, it was his candour and unwillingness to be anything other than straightforward that posed problems for some of his relationships, as, for example, his breach with his lifelong publisher as late as in 1926. One should not, of course, attach any great significance to an entry made when the Copenhagen visit still left an unpleasant taste in his mouth. He maintained good relations with the Danish composer but these never developed in the way that his friendship with the Swedish composer Stenhammar had flourished. Nielsen for his part had laid the basis for closer contacts at a personal level, and in February 1909 had written to Sibelius after having heard a performance of the Second Symphony, which Stenhammar had conducted in Copenhagen:

> I am an enormous admirer of the strange and unique power that radiates from your symphony, and I am thankful for the great impression that is still with me – several days after the concert – and from which I cannot get free.
>
> In general your symphony is all embracing – at one moment it is powerful in temperament, wild as in a violent conflict, and, at the next, tender and gentle in its melancholy stillness. But your music must be judged as something apart: it is not to be weighed on a set of pharmacist's scales but on a highway along which one can drive a coach and horses, with man and beast under the open skies in sun and wind, where there are people moving around and where nature unfolds itself in its grandeur and peace. Such is the impression I have of it at present and I once again beg you to accept my warmest thanks and greetings.[1]

In some respects this description of the Second Symphony bears as much witness to Nielsen's recent development as it does to the Sibelius. At about this time he had been occupied with his Third Symphony, the so-called *Sinfonia espansiva*. The 'espansiva' of the title can be thought of, in Robert Simpson's words,[2] as meaning the 'outward growth of the mind's scope and the expansion of life that comes from it'. In some ways the two composers were moving in different directions: the sense of Nature and its power were still strong in both, but the Sibelius that Nielsen had met in Copenhagen was no longer the figure he had admired from the Second Symphony. Sibelius's perspectives had altered: his sights had moved on to the horizons of an inner world, and this element of introspection would have presumably been alien to the Danish master, at least at this juncture. In any event, when he held the appointment of Chief Conductor of the

1 A letter dated 7 February 1909.
2 *Carl Nielsen, Symphonist (1865–1931)*, London, 1952, p. 46.

Copenhagen Music Society during 1915–27, Nielsen conducted neither the Fourth Symphony nor any other of Sibelius's later works but contented himself with *En Saga* and the Second Symphony. Perhaps Sibelius had realized during their encounter in Copenhagen that they were set on a different course, and perhaps he felt that the Fourth Symphony had disappointed Nielsen. This in itself would have been sufficient to create a barrier between them and would account for the diary entry, for Sibelius divided mankind into two: those who understood the Fourth Symphony and those who didn't.

The turn of the year found Sibelius still torn with doubts as to his future plans. He was weighed down by the knowledge of so many incomplete projects and by the realization that he had composed nothing of real importance since the Fourth Symphony. Had he been right, he wondered, to turn his back definitively on the operatic scene when he had rejected Boldemann's libretto? In any event another opportunity had presented itself in November, when Juhani Aho had offered him a libretto. This was based on his novel *Juha*, which had appeared in 1911 and had prompted a commission from Aino Ackté for him to fashion a workable libretto. Despite her experiences with 'The Raven', Ackté was eager to see Sibelius undertake its composition, for she felt confident that he would produce something that was both powerful and refined. Aho found Sibelius far from unresponsive and his diary records that at the beginning of November he took the project seriously. *Juha* is in many respects a Karelian counterpart of Janáček's *Jenůfa*, and of all the operas he considered, this was undoubtedly the most promising. But eventually he was to find its rural *verismo* uncongenial and the idea lapsed, only to be brought to fruition in the early 1920s by Aarre Merikanto.

A second idea surfaced from his old friend Adolf Paul. His dramatic career had been far from uneventful: his play, *Teufelskirche* had been banned almost immediately after its première, and he only narrowly escaped a charge of blasphemy. *King Christian II* was revived in Berlin but was thought hopelessly old-fashioned and even Sibelius's incidental music was ignored. But Paul went on without apparent concern, even though he could hardly find enough at times to feed himself and his family. He occasionally sent appeals to Sibelius: 'You have so many wealthy patrons – ten for every finger – can't you soften up one up for me?' These did not go unanswered for even in the midst of his own problems, Sibelius managed to arrange a little something for him. During the autumn of 1910, Paul's *commedia dell'arte, Blauer Dunst,* was given in Hamburg, and for this production Paul himself composed four short pieces, which he asked Sibelius to orchestrate. Sibelius evidently went along with this idea and suggested that they should be credited to 'Jean Paul'. Paul was surprised and gratified that his august friend should bother with such mean chores, though it is only fair to say that it is not known what part Sibelius actually played in this affair. Paul dreamt of great riches for his friend and wrote at the end of the year of Janne 'completely gilded, one large living lump of gold'. The Vienna Burgtheater mounted a production of *The Language of the Birds* but without Sibelius's music.

Paul's fantasies about Sibelius as a potential operatic gold mine did not abate, and he now came up with a new idea: that *Blauer Dunst* itself should be recast in the form of a libretto. Strangely enough, he suggested a third party should be brought into the enterprise and to this end he approached the Swedish poet and travel writer, Count Birger Mörner, with the proposal that he should prepare a Swedish version of the German original. Early in December 1912, he wrote to Sibelius:

> At long last, I am delighted to be in a position to present you with a libretto that will suit you and that will soon tempt your muse to inspiration: Birger Mörner is a delightful man and I only had to mention your name and say that you wanted *Blauer Dunst* as an opera, for him to be overjoyed and immediately set to work. Go on, dear Janne, do it. Just say you will. Promises cost nothing.

Paul asked for a reply by return of post, even though he had not seen any of the projected libretto apart from the hero, Lorenzo's monologue and about thirty couplets. Although Paul's offer came at a crucial moment, during the fallow period following the Fourth Symphony, when Sibelius's sense of direction was uncertain, and when a successful opera would have brought him welcome financial rewards, his resolve faltered. A *commedia dell'arte* with a Spanish setting was hardly his style, and in any event if he were to tackle such a project it would be better to do it straight into German so as to facilitate its acceptance on the Continent. Above all, was Adolf Paul, despite their long friendship, a dramatist of sufficient stature for such a collaboration to be successful – or to be taken seriously? The same old doubts that had occupied him earlier in the year resurfaced: 'Plans for opera. Am dubious about the whole genre. Can I hope, at the age of 47, to compose something good enough when success in a dramatic enterprise is to a large extent the product of stage experience? Yet, on the other hand, I believe – and so do others – in my dramatic potential.'[1] Paul telegraphed to press for an answer: Sibelius wired back on 22 December, 'Yes. Ready by September.' He soon received the first two of the opera's five acts, and write to Mörner asking for the rest. 'It would be good if I could be in receipt of the remainder of the text as soon as possible. As you well realize, I sincerely admire your work.'[2] The following day he urged Paul to 'bring as much pressure as you can on him. I am delighted with his way of writing. It's real Swedish and full of poetry.' By this time Paul was convinced that he

1 9 December 1912.
2 4 March 1913.

had won the composer over. 'With a new opera from you I shall be able to take any publisher you care to name.'

Had he known that Sibelius's thoughts were becoming more consumed by a new tone poem than by *Blauer Dunst*, he might have been less euphoric. His next step was to send two copies of a contract to Ainola assigning the composer 60 per cent of the income from the work. Sibelius kept both contract and duplicate without signing either. In April, the Swedish press carried reports of 'operatic plans by Paul and Mörner', which Sibelius tartly noted in his diaries. By this time, the situation itself has something of the *commedia dell'arte* about it: the fussy author dreaming of making his fortune, Mörner writing for dear life to get the remaining acts into shape, blissfully unaware that Sibelius's admiration was more for his title than his verse, while the composer was busily throwing dust in their eyes and turning his thoughts elsewhere.

By the following month Paul was beginning to sense the truth: 'Are you intending to compose it . . . or have you already composed it, or don't you give a damn about it?' However, it wasn't that Sibelius 'didn't give a damn' about opera but that his concerns for it lay at the level of fantasy. Like some Prospero, he toyed with the idea of his characters singing wordless arabesques, of the castles of legendary times echoing to vocalise, but the next minute all this would fade and symphonic dramas with vital, full-blooded musical characters would take the stage. After the Fourth Symphony, Sibelius had attended a performance of *Salome* – and this put operatic ambitions firmly in their place.

However, the operatic corpse still twitched. In October, Birger Mörner sent him a little book of poetry and, in his note of thanks, Sibelius mentioned that he had still not received the rest of the libretto, presumably the missing fifth act. He also added, 'You would be willing – would you not – to make any adjustments I should require as far as metre is concerned, when I come to the actual composition?' That was the end of the affair. Mörner was later to learn through Paul that the whole enterprise had fallen through, as Sibelius hadn't cared for the fifth act. His mind was now firmly set on other projects: between the New Year and the first week of February 1913, he composed four piano miniatures 'in the lighter vein I reserve for Pelle Westerlund', a Helsinki publisher. He sold all four, together with a *Valsette* written for a Christmas publication, to Westerlund, who lost no time in offering them to Breitkopf und Härtel at a considerably higher price!

Breitkopf in their turn saw to it that Sibelius was made aware of this development and asked why he bothered to place these miniatures with smaller publishers instead of offering them directly to Breitkopf – to their mutual benefit. These were the golden years of the amateur pianist and the market was able to absorb enormous quantities of suitable material whereas orchestral music involved much greater risk for the publisher. One can only assume that Sibelius was reluctant to be represented on the Continent by pieces that were so obviously inferior and uncharacteristic. A work such as the Serenade No. 2 in G minor for violin and orchestra, on the other hand, was an entirely different matter; that he despatched to Breitkopf the same month.

News of the progress of the Fourth Symphony in the wider world brought him various shocks that spring. 'It is, of course, too delicate and subtle for this squalid world,' he had noted in his diary the previous autumn. He was undoubtedly on target in his prognosis, at least in the short term. In Vienna, Weingartner who was now conductor of the Philharmonic Orchestra, had included the symphony as one of two foreign novelties in the 1912–13 season: the other was a piece by Louis Charles Bruneau. But on 19 January, Sibelius learned that all was not well. 'Weingartner will not perform my latest symphony, even though it has already been put into rehearsal.' A few days earlier, Stenhammar had conducted it in Gothenburg, though as yet Sibelius was unaware of the public reception it met. Just as well, perhaps, as he was anxious as to its fate in Berlin, where Busoni planned a performance with the Philharmonic. 'Am deeply worried since it begins the programme, and Busoni is no conductor. He can't possibly conduct that work. Oh, dear!'

By February he had news of the symphony's reception in Sweden. Stenhammar wrote,

I was unwise enough to put your symphony into one of our subscription concerts. The public for these is largely made up of people from the middle classes who lack any deep musical interest and we therefore aim to attract them with the inducement of famous soloists – or occasionally, composer-conductor celebrities such as, for example, Jean Sibelius two years ago! But it is one thing to offer them *Valse triste* and *The Swan of Tuonela* conducted by the composer and quite another to give them the Fourth Symphony under the baton of their permanent conductor. What happened has, as far as I know, no precedent in the annals of Gothenburg musical life – for, at the end of the symphony, the timid, polite applause was drowned by loud hissing. I can't deny that after the initial surprise had worn off, it seemed quite stimulating and that I felt a certain pride on your behalf – a feeling that cooled somewhat when I heard that the offenders were officers from the artillery garrison here. What however remains – and cannot easily be explained, is that the applause itself was virtually negligible and the audience was totally bewildered, and that our stupid critics, who have hitherto borne your colours aloft, suddenly turned tail and denounced you in the most ludicrous and uncomprehending fashion.[1]

When a few weeks later Stenhammar conducted the symphony for the

1 Letter dated 6 February 1913.

more discriminating Wednesday concert audiences, it was given a demons-
tratively warm reception. All the same Sibelius took the news badly: 'I am
sick at heart and totally taken off balance . . . [The next sentence in the diary
entry is inked over] . . . a bullet would be the best way out for me, yes, a
bullet!' Not even Eero Järnefelt tried to brush off Stenhammar's news as a
mere bagatelle but, on the contrary, took the reverse quite seriously. But it
all soon passed over: Sibelius was not one to allow his spirits to be long
dampened by a bunch of officers and businessmen, particularly 'as such
great figures among my contemporaries as Weingartner and Busoni believe
in this work'. All the same, Weingartner had not been as supportive as he
should. The Fourth Symphony and Tchaikovsky's Sixth had been the two
works in the Vienna Philharmonic subscription concert on 15 December,
and had been widely advertised in the press and on posters throughout the
town. Only two days before the concert was due to take place, the new
symphony was withdrawn on the somewhat transparent pretext that the
bells required for the score had not arrived in time. In actual fact, the
orchestra had quite simply refused to play it at rehearsal, and Weingartner
had lamely given in and replaced it with Weber's *Euryanthe* Overture and
Beethoven's Eighth Symphony. As a gesture of compensation, he put in
The Dryad at a later concert, which caused neither a ripple of protest nor, it
must be said, any great success. The episode was not to pass without
comment.

Richard Specht, writing in *Der Merker* thundered,

> If the orchestra had accepted the symphony, it was their confounded duty
> and responsibility to perform it, and not damage the reputation of an
> established composer by a sudden bout of contrariness. Again, if
> Weingartner had accepted the work, it is altogether indefensible that after
> such a vote of no confidence that he should not throw his baton aside and
> leave the rehearsal, after a suitably fierce outburst.[1]

The Fourth Symphony has not been publicly performed in Vienna up to the
present time.

There was no news from Busoni in Berlin, and Sibelius presumed that the
work had suffered a similar fate:

> It is vital not to lose your nerve – and above all your head. They don't see
> me – at least, not the world's leading musicians – as a spent force. But
> *nous verrons.*'[2]

He was glad to be in the country and out of reach of curious eyes, but it was
already obvious that he was getting back on an even keel:

> Am planning *Der Barde* – *Tonstück* for orchestra – or, more properly,

1 *Der Merker*, January 1913.
2 Diary, 21 February 1913.

15. Carl Nielsen in 1911.

16. A letter from Carl Nielsen written after a performance of Sibelius's
Second Symphony in Copenhagen.

17. 'Jubal' by Ernst Josephson which inspired Sibelius's song,
Op. 35, No. 1.

18. Wilhelm Stenhammar. Painting by Robert Thegerström.

19. Announcement of concert with the Fourth Symphony,
conducted by Weingartner.

20. From the slow movement of Voces intimae.

21. Part of the Fourth Symphony in its quartet form.

22. Sketches for the Fourth Symphony.

25. Sibelius with his daughters Margareta and Heidi in 1912.

Tondichtung. There is my strength. Favén has been here and the house is fragrant again with the scent of cigars. Perhaps the sun will shine once again on my own path.' Two days later and he is again optimistic. 'Am now in calmer waters. Wonderful day. The sun shines as much outdoors as it does in my heart. I am working full out: this is my fate! Oh, come now, Jean Sibelius, put an end to all this scribbling. It's enough to make you weep!

It was only later that he discovered that Busoni had been forced to abandon the Berlin première on financial grounds, but in April he received a telegram from him announcing that he had just conducted the symphony in Amsterdam 'mit grosser Freude'. And not only pleasure, it would seem, but also with success if one is to judge by the review in *Het Algemeen Handelsblad.* 'One cannot but acknowledge the freshness of the musical ideas and their individuality and appreciate the independence of mind that distinguishes the composer, who distances himself from any kind of shallowness or striving after effect.'[1]

The first American performance took place in March and was given by the Philharmonic Society Symphony Orchestra under Walter Damrosch. Before he raised his baton, the conductor, maliciously described by detractors as no mean orator, turned to the audience and made a short speech: he was not sure whether they would like the piece, which was receiving its first – and perhaps last – performance for, as far as symphonic form was concerned, it was the most extraordinary he had so far encountered but, nevertheless, he considered it his duty to perform it. Even if some members of the audience left between movements and everyone seemed quite relieved when it was all over, there was still a respectable amount of applause. Critical opinion was divided: Henry Krehbiel in the *New York Herald Tribune* summed up his distaste by declaring that Sibelius had become 'cubist', while W. G. Henderson in the *New York Sun* was less negative. He thought that Sibelius had aligned himself with the futurists and was 'as dissonant as the worst of them', yet at the same time, the Fourth must be regarded as a remarkable symphony. *Musical America* hailed the work as deeply convincing and extraordinarily powerful: 'There is something Mephistophelian about this craggy music; it had a wild authenticity and individuality.'

'What do I care for wordly things?' wrote Sibelius, shrugging off these reviews. New plans for composition were welling up in his mind: he was toying with an idea for a short orchestral piece, *The Knight and the Naiads,* obviously drawing for its inspiration on Josephson's poem. 'Duke Magnus'. But things turned out differently and the result was *The Bard,* on which he worked throughout March. He conducted its first performance at a concert by the Philharmonic Orchestra at the end of the month but was

1 *Het Algemeen Handelsblad,* 31 March 1913.

distressed by the mediocre quality of the playing. It was relatively well received but did not excite the enthusiasm of Breitkopf, who thought it sounded more like the opening movement of a suite rather than an independent orchestral piece. Sibelius decided to recast it as 'a fantasy in two parts, or an *Intrada and Allegro*'. By June it had grown into a triptych, but a bit later in the summer he arrived at the definitive solution: '*The Bard* should be much as it was to begin with. But the end should be in the tonic and not the dominant.' Presumably Sibelius refined the original and made it more concentrated.

With a few exceptions during the 1890s. Sibelius had always managed to spend some time abroad each year, ever since his first visits to Berlin and Vienna. Even if he could not manage to go further afield, he at least crossed the Baltic. The year 1913 was the first exception during the new century and the uninterrupted contact with Finland and its claustrophobic musical life took its toll on his nerves. He had no opportunity to distance himself from Helsinki and see it in perspective, and had neither the stimulus of being in a great metropolis nor of conducting a first-class orchestra. Instead he had time to brood on imagined threats: Kajanus became an object of a certain envy. In spite of his own reputation abroad, he could still feel threatened by the attention Kajanus received. There was a petition launched to get a state pension for life for Kajanus, and a number of influential figures in Finnish cultural life signed it. Kajanus's contribution to Finnish music and its dissemination abroad and his work on behalf of younger colleagues was stressed. Sibelius signed it as a matter of course, and in so doing signed, as he thought, his own death warrant as a composer. 'With this, they are turning values upside down and have put my own creative work at naught. Thus, they – these bastards – have, in their efforts for Kajanus, reduced me to nothing.' That he should see Kajanus's improved standing as a threat to his own emerges in his letters to Carpelan. The latter lost no time in pouring oil on troubled waters and immediately destroyed Sibelius's letters.

> Everyone knows that Kajanus is no real composer and less a founder of our Finnish national music . . . It goes without saying that you are the only composer of international standing, and the father of Finnish nationalism in music. That is an axiomatic truth which is moreover underlined by the very fact that you yourself have signed the petition. Everyone understands this – of that you can rest assured for the present and the future.[1]

This was the reassurance that the occasion called for. In May Sibelius wrote enthusiastically of plans for a new concert on 8 February 1914, of which the programme was to be '*Intrada* (presumably *The Bard*), the Violin Concerto, and a Dramatic Fantasy for orchestra.' Perhaps he had hoped to

1 23 April 1913.

have a new fantasy or symphony ready for the new year, but in any event his plans were to take a different course. Interest for his music had been growing in the United States during the past few years, and one can even encounter examples of his influence in such works as Horatio Parker's award-winning opera *Mona* (1912), which was mounted at the Metropolitan Opera that year. 'Mon Dieu, the whole piece, among other things the end of one act, is by me,' Sibelius declared after going through the score in the spring of 1915. Donald Grout speaks of it as a kind of up-dated *Tristan* in his *A Short History of Opera*.

Parker had been entrusted with the task of editing an anthology of songs for schools, and in the spring of 1913 he set off for Europe to persuade various well-known composers, among them Reger and Gabriel Pierné to contribute. He sent three poems to Sibelius and by the end of June, the composer had set them ('Autumn Song', 'The Sun upon the Lake is Low', and 'A Cavalry Catch'), subsequently publishing them as *Three Songs for American Children*. In August, Horatio Parker wrote with a new offer, a commission from Carl Stoeckel and Ellen Battell-Stoeckel for a new symphonic poem, whose duration was not to exceed fifteen minutes, to be given its first performance at the 1914 Music Festival in Norfolk, Connecticut, which the Stoeckels financed. The fee was to be 1,000 dollars. An invitation for a concert tour, which he declined, and membership of the National Music Society left him in no doubt that his star in America was in the ascendant.

Meanwhile he decided against going to the Gloucester Festival in the autumn as he did not feel disposed to compose the choral work that they had asked him for. However, as fate ordained, he was to be represented there by a new piece. During 1912 he had promised Aino Ackté an orchestral song, presumably to mollify her after the fiasco with 'The Raven'. When she was engaged for two concerts in Manchester in the autumn, she wrote asking Sibelius for a piece that she could present in her programme alongside the final scene from *Salome*. Later on she told the composer that she would also be giving the new work at the Gloucester Festival, and so after finishing *The Bard*, Sibelius turned his attention to the new piece. From about 17 July he began sketching *Luonnotar*, 'tone poem for soprano and orchestra', and by the middle of August he was in a position to send Ackté a copy of the score, presumably in a voice and piano reduction. '*Luonnotar* is brilliant and magnificent,' she wrote. 'It has swept me off my feet – but at the same time, I am so very frightened that I will not be equal to its demands, for it is madly difficult and my otherwise sure sense of pitch may fail me.'

Before she left for England, Ackté went through the score with the composer. 'She sang well, but – how far off is the ideal, when I have to press on with the work and not allow it to grow to maturity and devlop its own patina.' On 10 September he noted: 'Today *Luonnotar* is to be performed in Gloucester!?! Afterwards I shall work over it again. It is much in my mind at present.'

The Times wrote that even if the English translation gave only an approximate idea of its poetic content, it was obvious that Luonnotar was the product of a highly individual imagination and a work of some stature. The rhythmically free vocal line was based, so they thought, on a folk-derived melodic style, but unlike other composers who shackle folksong with all sorts of restrictions, Sibelius sets it free, and as in the Fourth Symphony one is conscious of the exquisite orchestral atmosphere. At the end of October, Sibelius sent off the final version of the score to Breitkopf und Härtel. They decided not to risk publishing it in full score and contented themselves instead with a piano reduction.

The summer of 1913 had been a happy one at Ainola dominated by the marriage in June of his eldest daughter, Eva, with Arvi Paloheimo, an event that was celebrated in great style. There were other domestic distractions: perhaps as a reaction against the exigencies of financial stringency, Sibelius had the wild idea of building a wall round Ainola, and then he planted a hedge to protect himself from the vulgar gaze. Both the wedding and the building involved considerable expense, but the creative impasse in his life had resolved itself, and once again life was full of savour. Katarina filled the house with her practice – 'Nothing is more conducive to meditation than hearing a child practising scales in thirds,' he noted. Ruth, the second of the daughters, was enjoying some success and made her début that autumn at the Finnish National Theatre in a play by Minna Canth.

The Scaramouche commission gave Sibelius much trouble. At the turn of the year 1912–13, he had received a new version of the scenario with some additional dialogue. The prospect of the pantomime being spoilt by the insertion of spoken passages worried him but the publisher, Wilhelm Hansen, reassured him that the dialogue was intended only to serve as a guide for the actors. Later on, he discovered that Knudsen had virtually plagiarized Schnitzler's The Veil of Pierrette and appealed in vain to Hansen to ask Knudsen to start afresh. But the fateful moment came when he discovered that he had bound himself contractually to compose a full-length pantomime not, as he had thought, two or three dance movements. He now insisted on the agreement either being annulled or its terms modified in his favour, and stressed in a letter to Hansen that his international reputation was at stake: 'If I am to be held to the terms of the contract, the music must be good – there can be no other alternative for me.' He felt that he had fallen into a trap:

I've completely ruined things for myself by signing the Scaramouche contract. Was in such a temper about it today that I smashed the telephone. My nerves are in a terrible state. What is left for me now? Nothing! I have allowed myself to be weighed down by one stupidity after another.[1]

1 Diary, 21 June 1913.

In September, at the time of the first performance of *Luonnotar*, he had another go at *Scaramouche* but by the end of October he was once again depressed and assailed by fears that the pantomime would never be finished. However, finished it was, though not before 19 December. Two days later he despatched the score to Hansen with a covering note:

As you see, the original scheme has grown into a comprehensive work. To get it right has cost me much thought and work. In the form it now takes, I believe it will be successful. Generally speaking, I have thought of the stage as being full of activity – it's not a work for actors who stand around waiting for gestures from on high.

Something about the tone of his letter does not quite ring true, and we are tempted to wonder whether he was as sure of its success as his words imply. As it so happened, the première was not destined to take place for almost a decade: the Royal Theatre, Copenhagen, mounted a production in 1922.

The foreign press gave Sibelius no peace, and negative as well as positive reviews were being reproduced in the Helsinki papers. He found it particularly galling to be compared with younger Finnish colleagues. When Toivo Kuula conducted some of his own music in St Petersburg in November, the Russian press hailed him as having achieved something that Sibelius and Palmgren had not succeeded in accomplishing, 'the creation of a truly national Finnish style'. On an earlier occasion the St Petersburg press had been quite dismissive and said that Finland had not produced one great composer, and that Sibelius, relatively speaking the greatest of them, lacked the most important prerequisite for a composer: a cultural tradition. Palmgren's Second Piano Concerto 'The River' was given in Berlin by Ignaz Friedman and the composer conducting, to great acclaim – 'which delighted me in that I predicted it', but when afterwards Hugo Leichtentritt wrote that 'in a curious way' he could be compared with Sibelius, the latter was plunged into a black mood.

The year brought yet another volume from the indefatigable pen of Walter Niemann, *Die Musik seit Richard Wagner* in which he touched on the question of Sibelius's standing compared with such masters as Chopin, Grieg and Tchaikovsky and wondered to what extent he would achieve the same measure of recognition:

Perhaps in England, where there is sympathy for many different styles, but hardly in Germany. Sibelius has the depth and warmth of the genuine musical innovator and the power and momentum of a national tide. But compared with Grieg and Chopin, his music is not as varied and rich in spirit. In his largest works, the same main ideas are repeated over and over again . . . besides in recent years he appears to have come under the influence of Russian and French impressionism.

However, the most important event was the first performance of the

Fourth Symphony in America. After eight rehearsals, Karl Muck and the Boston Symphony Orchestra gave three consecutive performances, though the conductor appears to have made little sense of the score.[1] A number of critics showered the work with invective, others drew parallels with Debussy – among them Olin Downes. Sibelius had to be content with his lot as a difficult composer. When *Voces intimae* received its first performance in Stockholm, it was called 'a fantasy on feverish dreams'.

In October 1913, Nielsen paid a visit to Helsinki to conduct a concert of his own music. Sibelius was in attendance: 'Today I heard Carl Nielsen's new symphony [No. 3, the *Espansiva*]. A good piece but without, as I see it, compelling themes. But he's a real artist, this man.'[2] The frenetic rhythm, the well-defined blocks of sound relieved by pastoral contrasts, the sheer joy in music-making, the way in which Nielsen distances himself in the symphony from the metaphysical legacy of late romanticism must have served as a challenge or a warning – in much the same way that Nielsen had evidently reacted a year earlier to the Fourth Symphony of Sibelius. Yet who knows? Perhaps the example of the *Sinfonia espansiva* did not go completely unheeded, for by the time he had come to wrestle with the Fifth his attitude was far more outward-looking.

The last few weeks of 1913 were overshadowed by a domestic crisis: his brother Christian was taken seriously ill, suffering from anaemia and exhaustion. For Jean the news came as a hard blow; the very thought that his brother's health could fail had never entered his head. It was he who was the weaker of the two; it was *his* alcohol problem, *his* pains and nervous anxiety that had occupied them. Both seemed happy to accept their allotted roles of the egocentric artist and altruistic psychiatrist. It was now his turn to wait in the hospital corridor only to be refused admittance. Christian pulled through even if his anaemia lengthened his period of recuperation. During the latter part of November, Christian spent some of his convalescence in Järvenpää to his brother's delight. 'Christian is with us at Ainola every day to the great joy of the family. If only he is fully restored to health. For me this is all quite incomprehensible. He has always been the strong one.'

Throughout the summer and autumn there had been no word from Axel Carpelan. Suddenly a letter arrived, albeit cold and impersonal in tone, expressing concern at the news of Christian's illness. Sibelius responded at once and in the warmest terms: 'Thanks once again for your kindness and for the joy these welcome lines from your hand gave me.' The whole tone of the letter is a plea for their relationship to continue as before; but answer came there none, and a week later he confided to his diary: 'Everything is

1 He returned the copy of the score to the library with a note, 'Bless me, if I know what he means.'
2 Diary entry of 23 October.

over with Axel because of Kajus.' In any event the reasons for his silence remain unspoken, for Carpelan's own explanation that he had simply been too tired and depressed to write hardly rings true.

This is not the only cloud on the horizon. Once again Sibelius's finances were not in good order and he presumably went in search of funds. One of the two guarantors of the credit that had been mobilized on Sibelius's behalf was the industrialist August Ramsay. He was completely unmusical and never went near a concert, a down-to-earth businessman whose working day would begin at half-past six. Even if his life-style could not be further removed from that of the composer, he saw it as his obvious patriotic duty to support Sibelius. Whatever took place between them when they met in September remains in the realm of conjecture: all we have is a diary entry, 'August Ramsay insulted me. May God have mercy on him.' Perhaps the composer asked for further help only to be met with the argument that he had no automatic entitlement to open-ended credit merely because he had written the Second Symphony and *Finlandia*. If earlier precedents were anything to go by, Sibelius would have relapsed into silence and would have gone away without further ado. 'I simply agreed – couldn't in the end justify my creative existence!' he noted in a similar situation where he had felt crushed.

Sibelius never forgave Ramsay and his diaries often return to the theme of Ramsay's insult. He even indulged in fantasies of a duel in the dawn mists and makes scornful references to Ramsay's 'tradesman's mentality'. The last day of 1912 found him in a distinctly pessimistic frame of mind: 'My sanity is failing, not least because of the loss of all my friends. Why? The fault is all my own . . . Poor lonely Ego with your morbid temperament! Everything is going to pieces.'

Once towards the very end of his life, Sibelius was suddenly asked over the telephone whether his tone poem *The Bard* had been inspired by Runeberg's poem of the same name. Somewhat irritably he replied that it wasn't, and with that the questioner let the matter rest. Sibelius never went into the subject of his source of inspiration, apart from saying that the title refers to a skald of the Ancient Scandinavian world and is not drawn from the *Kalevala*. For my part, however, I would think it unlikely that Sibelius would have called this work *The Bard* without having Runeberg's poem in mind. Runeberg formed part of his daily diet and Sibelius always had his poems to hand, and *The Bard* is undoubtedly one of his most magnificent poems. Furthermore Sibelius could readily identify himself with the Bard – as, indeed, could Runeberg himself – having grown up in 'the heart of the valley'.

He dreamt not yet of his future
And no one sensed his goal.
His world was narrow; yet he found its greatness
And beauty was aroused by the spring.

On his progress through the world he captivates slaves and kings, queens and maidens with his song:

Time came when winter touched his locks
And age paled his cheeks;
And so once more he took his lyre
And plucked sonorous chords – and died
Rendering up his soul to the spirit from which it came.

The elegiac mood of the tone poem as well as the dark E flat minor of its closing pages calls to mind the final moments of the Bard of Runeberg's poem. Did Sibelius see himself as the dying poet? This might explain his reluctance to discuss possible programmatic inspiration for the piece; the fears of 1909 left deep scars and it is unlikely that he would want to touch upon them. He would certainly be reluctant to confess that the dying poet Runeberg portrays could be himself.[1]

The tone poem falls into two sections, *Lento assai* and *Largamente*, the latter evolving organically from the former. As Robert Layton puts it, 'the change of mood between them might well be compared to the shift in emphasis in the second part of a sonnet. Both parts are related in feeling, but the second and slightly shorter section raises the emotional temperature a little.' To what extent its form resembles the reworking he was planning for an *Intrada and Allegro* is uncertain. In most respects *The Bard* breathes the same air as the Fourth Symphony; it is based on meagre scraps of ideas that are subject to a sophisticated organic transformation. The texture is even more chamber-like than is that of the symphony; indeed, many pages of the score are two-thirds empty. There are the occasional wisps of colour from the wind, and the odd pedal notes from the horns, so that when, towards the end of the work, the lines are more firmly etched and the harmonies fill out, the effect is all the more striking. The harp plays an important obbligato role.

The opening bars contain all the melodic substance of the piece: a rising motive of a major third and minor second –

1 There is another indication of Sibelius's preoccupation with Runeberg at the time of *The Bard*. Some months later he composed a short piano piece, *To Longing* to which he attached no Op. number. This is so unusual a title that one wonders how it occurred to him until one opens Volume I of Runeberg's *Collected Works* where that title occurs in heavy type a page or so after the final stanzas of *The Bard!*

Ex 164

– to which the harp immediately responds with a descending figure:

Ex 165

There is a ritornello-like formula from the harp (descending seconds). The *Lento assai* section is virtually held together, almost narrated, by the harp. Its sonority seems to symbolize the fine thread on which life hangs and gives brief glimpses of the pathos and melancholy that envelops the poet. The main theme, moving step-wise, assumes a more pensive and intent character.

Ex 166

The second theme (the 'tremolo' motive) with its characteristic final fifth is related to the first by the descending intervals of a second:

Ex 167

This second theme is gently outlined in the string tremolo only to return in bolder relief (and slightly varied form) in the *Largamente* section.

Tone colour plays a structural role in *The Bard*, and one can view the *Lento assai* section as a kind of dialogue between the harp and various chamber-like instrumental groupings. In its treatment of ideas the section falls into an ABA pattern, and the *tremolando* strings eventually return us to the musical material of the opening. In the *Largamente* there is a considerable heightening of tension. What was at first shadowy now appears more firmly etched; gentle wisps of ideas and fragmentary motives give way to bolder outlines. The harp abandons its role as a leading protagonist in the argument and confines itself to impressionistic gestures. The timpani and bass drum lend their weight to a nervous tonic pedal (on A flat, which subsequently becomes the mediant of F minor) over which the wind develops a figure derived from the 'tremolo' motive and which is repeated sequentially.

Ex 168

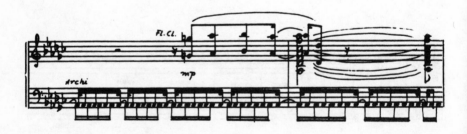

This builds up to a powerful and indeed poignant outburst. The tritone figure on flutes and clarinets (F flat – G flat – A flat – B flat) (page 17, bar 3) calls to mind the slow movement of the Fourth Symphony:

Ex 169

It is as if the pain has become insupportable. But release approaches and over a string *tremolando* there is a rising figure of fifths and fourths on the brass:

Ex 170

Sibelius is on record as having said that the calls of the Ancient Scandinavian *lur* or long horn were much in his mind here. The effect is archaic and primitive, yet at the same time imposing and even awesome. It is as if the Bard's death knell is sounding. There is a short epilogue that is subtly related to the very opening; three string chords embody the inversion of the opening idea in the cellos and double-basses:

Ex 171

The harp ritornello intones its final farewell before the strings bring the tone poem to a close in E flat major. *The Bard* is very much a child of its time and finds Sibelius carrying a stage further the chamber-like treatment of the orchestra that he had begun to develop in the Fourth Symphony and *The Dryad*. Indeed in his pursuit of the aphoristic line and the elusive sonority, striving, as it were, for the unseen and ineffable, he almost reminds one of the aesthetic aims of Webern.

Luonnotar, tone poem for soprano and orchestra, is inspired by the fable of the creation of the heavens as related in the *Kalevala* (*Runo* I, lines 111–242). The daughter of the Heavens, Luonnotar – also known as the Spirit of the Air (Ilmatar) lives alone in the emptiness of space. Eventually she comes down to the earth and for 700 years roamed the oceans as the Mother of the Waters, swimming from north to south and west to east. Then a great wind arose that drove the waters into fury, and in her distress she calls upon the Father of the Heavens, Ukko, for his help. Then came a gull, brave bird, flying from horizon to horizon in search of a nesting place, be it in the wind or on the waves. Then, Luonnotar, Mother of the Waters, lifts her knee from the waves on which the gull makes her nest and begins to hatch the eggs. Luonnotar's knee becomes hot, she convulsively shakes her limb so that the nest rolls into the waters and breaks into pieces. From the egg beauty was created, the top becoming the sky, the top of the white the shining moon; from the yolk the sun was born and the mottled part of the shell formed the stars in the sky. The legend of the gull's flight over the waters and the image of the Creation taking place in the way described in the *Kalevala* is widespread not only among the Finno–Ugrian peoples but in the mythology of cultures as diverse as those of the Near East, India and Peru. In adapting the Genesis story from the *Kalevala*, Sibelius made a number of changes, including transposition of the verse order, and, in so doing, makes the narrative less easily understood. Taken on its own the text does not fully convey the complete background on which he drew for inspiration.

In *Luonnotar* Sibelius uses the major and minor second both as a structural element and a colouristic device. These intervals are all-pervasive and can be found even in the timpani. There is a 'modern' feeling about the sound, partly on account of elements of bitonality and cluster-like harmonies. The orchestration is for the most part spare and chamber-like but with unexpected and striking effects of sonority. The rising winds over the seas are illustrated by some finely calculated swirls from the two harps over timpani thunder. The soprano line is built on the contrast between two different elements, one epic and narrative and the other atmospheric and magical. The tone poem is conceived in a kind of free sonata form. The orchestral introduction is a fine-spun string tremor (F sharp minor), which can well evoke the emptiness of the universe before creation:

Ex 172

The soprano entry brings us the first element, the epic and narrative, and its billowing lines seem to envisage the sense of space the *Kalevala* so eloquently describes:

Ex 173 'There was a Maiden, daughter of the heavens, the beautiful Luonnotar, who wondered about her life'

The descending Phrygian second (G – F sharp) is harmonized by triads of C major and F sharp minor. Here, as in the case of the Fourth Symphony, the modal implications of the line produce tritone relationships.

Another parallel between the symphony and the present work can be found in the tonal relationship between first and second groups. The second does not appear in A major, which woud be one of the logical keys, but rather in B flat minor (the relative minor of the dominant major, i.e. C sharp enharmonically changed to D flat). B flat minor here serves as kind of surrogate dominant in place of C sharp minor. The second group itself is comprised of a series of pathogenic sighs over a double pedal of tonic (B flat and F) and 'dominant' (C sharp = D flat and G flat). This is related to the 'wailing' runes of Karelian folk music.

Ex 174 'How pitiful is my life'

There is a short interlude of a development-like character that introduces a kind of 'fate' motive from the clarinets, a variant of the opening idea:

Ex 175

Then from the rustling string writing emerges a relatively playful flute idea:

Ex 176

The whole passage evokes the gull's flight across the waters. Although the music touches on some distant key-centres, the development is unusual in that it departs from classical precedent in being largely centred on the tonic, F sharp minor, albeit with a strongly Dorian inflection. It is possible that this key represents the purely narrative and would remain constant as in any runic chanting. Only towards the end of the development, when the gull's search proves fruitless and dramatic tension then mounts, does the key centre move to the dominant (C sharp minor) – and subsequently E flat.

The dramatic high point comes in the main section of the reprise, which depicts the gull's desperation at the prospect of building its nesting place on the wind-tossed waves. Contrary to convention Sibelius begins his restatement not in the tonic, F sharp minor, but in the dark, dramatic regions of his surrogate 'dominant', B flat minor. Even vocal considerations must have weighed with him here, for this transposition a major third higher means that the soprano is in her most effective register. After the appearance of the 'fate' motive, which is repeated three times, the writing both for voice and orchestra mounts to one of the most passionate climaxes in all Sibelius:

Ex 177 'the waves would swallow it.'

The 'fate' theme in augmented form is heard sequentially on the full orchestra – note how C flat, the Phrygian second of B flat minor, becomes the dominant of the key a tritone away (F flat = E major). Harmonic tension is not yet spent, for the second group begins in G sharp minor, the key of the supertonic, as if to pave the way for the mystery of the Creation. When the egg rolls into the sea and splinters, the tonality sinks to F sharp minor. The Heavens appear, the stars and the moon shine in the firmament – and the orchestra sounds almost like an antecedent of the space visions of the 1960s:

Ex 178 'stars in the sky.'

The haze has enveloped the landscape – the two superimposed and undulating fifths (F sharp – C sharp and D–A), incidentally the same pattern as in the slow movement of the Fourth Symphony, the harp appoggiaturas and the double-bass pedal point at the tritone, C, a symbol of cosmic gravitation – clears in the transparent, tranquil light of F sharp major.

The magical closing bars of *Luonnotar* bring to an end the inward-looking metaphysical period of Sibelius's development, which had begun in 1908 with *Voces intimae* and reached its most concentrated and powerful expression in the Fourth Symphony.

*

255

Turning finally to some of the smaller pieces that deserve a passing mention we come to the Two Rondinos, Op. 68 (1912). The First, in G sharp minor, calls to mind the atmosphere and key of the *Andantino* of the Third Symphony. The interval of the second and the tritone play a major part in its melodic thinking, as they had done in *The Bard*. It has a certain delicacy and charm, and its keyboard layout is at times not unreminiscent of the Liszt *Consolations*:

Ex 179

The Second Rondino, in C sharp minor, is perhaps more deserving of its title. After a ritornello with a tremolo tenth, an unusual phenomenon in Sibelius, a finely chiselled idea emerges. It is playful in character and from a pianistic viewpoint belongs to much the same species as do the Sonatinas:

Ex 180

In 1913 Sibelius grouped together five of the pieces that he had sold to the publisher Per Westerlund at the beginning of the year and added five more. These ten comprise Op. 40 and are all slight but not without interest. The *Valsette* is a sober little piece with a transparent texture; the *Pensée mélodique* is distinguished by some attractive modulatory sleights of hand; the *Petite Sérénade* has a charming tune and the *Polonaise* is a skilful blend of the festive, the characterful and the melancholic.

CHAPTER NINE

America and The Oceanides

Early in 1914, Sibelius went to Berlin for a month to work on the orchestral piece that Carl Stoeckel had commissioned for America, and to listen to new music. The day before his departure he wrote a letter to Carpelan:

> As I am leaving the country tomorrow after a most painful year, my heart prompts me to write a few lines to you. I understand now what it means to suffer the slings of misfortune. No one knows what it is like to be under the daily scrutiny of the world press and to have daily reminders of it for good or ill. I have made mistakes no doubt – more than others, but then who is to cast the first stone? I pray that the coming year, in spite of your frail health, that your spirit will be its usual, lively self.

To judge from the tone of his letter Sibelius remained somewhat wary and was unsure to what extent their relationship was still strained. Whether or not this was the case, he struck just the right tone. Sibelius's description of his own troubles seems to have released Carpelan from his sense of isolation and inertia. He hoped that Sibelius had undergone his 'baptism of fire' in a way that would cleanse and purify him.

> Suffering is an essential ingredient in life . . . I have always thought that pain would also reach you in the end, and that from its furnaces, a greater, nobler and more beautiful Sibelius would emerge. Your finest and greatest work should see the light of day in your fifties.

Perhaps Carpelan had intuitively sensed that Sibelius had left the world of the Fourth Symphony, *The Bard* and *Luonnotar* behind him and was moving into altogether lighter regions.

At the outset of his Berlin stay, Sibelius had the first inkling of a reaction against late romanticism and himself: 'The latest thing here is "Back to Mozart". Those who know least about Mozart shout the loudest.' Strauss's retreat from the expressionism of *Elektra* to the more readily accessible *Rosenkavalier* had already found responsive echoes. No doubt this reaction sprang from the feeling that a further erosion of the classical major–minor key system would weaken the formal structures that had evolved in the past two centuries. In any event Sibelius's appetite for new music proved insatiable. Only a year earlier he had bemoaned his declining interest for the music of others: 'The loss is mine,'[1] he wrote. Now he went to concerts almost every day and devoured even works of composers of the second and third rank.

January

12. Yesterday heard d'Albert + Nikisch . . . My 'reputation' embarrasses me. Avoid new acquaintances with all their false smiles . . . Heard this evening Zöllner's Symphony III. Without compelling ideas. In substance, no inspiration but technically good.

13. Saw *Kadra Sufa* a film aiming for sensation rather than art. In the evening heard Scharrer's Overture. He is still a beginner.

15. Heard an interesting violin and piano Sonata by Weissman[2] [*sic*] and in the evening a Symphony of Ziell that was beneath criticism.

18. Heard today Lendvai's *Masques* in the shadow of Strauss together with Weissman's Piano Concerto which plagiarizes me. *Quosque tandem!* I don't understand why the critics don't say so!

He also told Carpelan that he thought the Zöllner symphony was much influenced by him. He succumbed to loneliness, thought he was lacking powers of concentration and longed impatiently for Busoni who was soon expected to return to Berlin. Rather against his will he went the following day to von Vecsey.

19. Was with von Vecsey who played in the new style of the times. Whatever will become of this man? Heard a Violin Concerto of Juon which he himself has acknowledged to be influenced by me, which it certainly is.[3]

20. Heard the Brahms E minor and F major Cello Sonatas together with a piece of Tovey for two cellos. Subtle but not new.

21. Heard d'Ambrosio's Violin Concerto!! Both the work and the soloist supremely mediocre.

22. Heard Rudolph Tobias's *Kalevipoeg*. Oh dear!

23. Heard Busoni's Two Elegies, Ansorge's Piano Sonata, Dohnányi Four Rhapsodies.

The Ansorge he found full of Brahms and Liszt, while the Dohnányi struck him as 'good, though a little feminine'. Sibelius summed up his first ten days in a letter to Carpelan:

1 Diary entry 21 January 1913.
2 Julius Weismann (1879–1950) was a pupil of Josef Rheinberger among others and wrote six operas, one to a libretto of Georg Büchner, a symphony and two violin sonatas. *Tr*
3 A glance at the score leaves no doubt that this is the case.

If you want to hear and come to terms with what is going on in the way of composition, Berlin is the ideal place. I am sitting at a café table just after a concert and writing this letter with an altogether impossible pen . . . Of the new pieces I have noticed just how many have been influenced by me.

After having heard Holländer's Violin Concerto No. 3, he began to feel that he had had enough. Delius he thought 'a poet', though he was not convinced that he really understood the orchestra, and a performance of Spohr's *Gesangsszene* Concerto (No. 8) touched a vein of nostalgia. He was reminded of his own early years as a violinist with all the joys and sorrows.

His composing proceeded slowly. He arranged scenes from *Scaramouche* for the piano and with mixed delight and embarrassment confessed to Carpelan that he had just finished a setting of Rydberg's poem, 'Vi ses igen' ('We will meet again'): 'You smile – ! Yes, but one becomes sentimental now and again.' After a while he began to plan the American commission and at first thought of Rydberg's *Fantasos and Sulamit* as a programme. He had toyed with this theme before but fortunately abandoned it again, for *Fantasos and Sulamit* is not a particularly inspiring text.

The flood of new music began to irritate him. Nikisch conducted among other things two typical Kapellmeister pieces, Scheinpflug's *Comedy Overture* and Gernsheim's Violin Concerto in which the soloist was Henri Marteau. But the great musical experience on this occasion was the Fifth Symphony of Bruckner which moved him to tears: 'What an original and profound spirit, a personality steeped in religious feeling. And that deep religion has been got rid of at home as no longer relevant to our time.' However, his next concert, with banal novelties for soloists, chorus and orchestra by Humperdinck among others, struck him as a waste of time. 'It is as if these new cultural figures, composers, are incapable of writing anything vital based on the old Gregorian modes. That is more possible for me and others who have enjoyed more peace and solitude,' he told Carpelan. He developed the same thoughts in his diary; 'It is as if I who am closer to the Gregorian modes because of my heritage and upbringing, am somehow made for them. Thought a great deal and composed.'

At last the dialogue between the two friends had been resumed. In a perceptive letter Carpelan took up the question of the supra-national in Sibelius and challenged the view of Taine and others nurtured on Darwinian evolutionary theories that the most important formative element in Man's individuality is environment. He argued that it was the individual who is mysterious and irreducible and that it was environment that is constantly undergoing change. In the final analysis the individual personality can be understood only in terms of itself rather than as the product of various other forces, whether environmental or genetic. For Sibelius, whose fate it was to be regarded as an expression of nationalist sensibility, these words struck a sympathetic chord:

If Niemann and others were steeped in Finland's history and landscape they would have a much fuller perspective, but the more deeply they look into the innermost depths of your personality, the more thoughtful and admiring they will become. The great artist attains universality because of the depth of his individuality and being, whether he is born here or Kamchatka.

Undoubtedly this served to bolster the composer's self-confidence:

Whenever I hear new works by colleagues, I become more and more convinced that my music has infinitely more natural feeling and life than this work-a-day *Erzeugnisse*.

He went to a piano recital, however, which inspired altogether different reactions: it included Debussy's *L'Ile joyeuse* and *La fille aux cheveux de lin* as well as pieces by Emile Blanchet and Rudolf Ganz, who was also the executant. For the first time during his stay his spirits rose: here was something important in music. He had made precious little headway with the new commission but his diary leaves no doubt that he sensed that this new work would be something of real substance. Sibelius was rarely to be seen at piano recitals, and if he was, it was for the sake of the repertoire rather than the pianist – unless, of course, the pianist was Busoni! Doubtless he had gone to the recital of 23 January for the sake of Busoni and Dohnányi's music,[1] and likewise attended Ganz's programme on account of the Debussy. *L'Ile joyeuse* was, of course, inspired by Watteau's *L'Embarquement pour Cythère* and for one so well versed in Greek mythology as Sibelius, it must have conjured up visions of the enchanted isle where Aphrodite was born. In any event it would certainly have brought the Mediterranean before his eyes, and one wonders whether this served as an impulse in his own creative path.

Later that spring he was to compose *Soft West Wind*,[2] an impressionistic miniature for the piano, as well as his most impressionistic orchestral work, *The Oceanides*, albeit in a first draft and under a different title, *Rondo der Wellen*. The definitive tone poem, however, refers to the nymphs who inhabited the streams and rivers of the Mediterranean in Homeric mythology.

During the following days he was to be pulled in the direction of expressionism rather than impressionism, as his Berlin diary shows:

January
28.   A song of Schoenberg made a deep impression on me.

---

1 The diary does not mention the pianist. It was in all probability Conrad Ansorge.
2 Published as Op. 74 No. 2.

February

1. Heard Mahler's *Das klagende Lied*, a wonderful piece, together with some poetic quartets [four-part choral pieces] of Brahms.

4. Mahler's Fifth Symphony and Schoenberg's *Kammersymphonie*. This is a legitimate and valid way of looking at things I suppose. But it is certainly painful to listen to. A result achieved by excessive cerebration. People whistled and shouted. Not for weak minds or so-called talented composers. They would certainly misuse it. There is something important there all the same, even if it is not yet fully realized.

The following day he wrote to Aino and described the Chamber Symphony as the musical equivalent of cubism.

8. At the morning concert I heard the Philharmonic in Mahler's *Kindertotenlieder* and Korngold's Sinfonietta. He is a young eagle.

9. Heard Duparc's songs, Korngold's Trio and Schoenberg's Second Quartet, Op. 10. It gave me a lot to think about. He interests me very much.

The encounter with Schoenberg obviously brought Sibelius face to face with his own artistic crisis. Should he continue to explore the world of the Fourth Symphony even at the risk of breaking the tonal barrier and moving into the realm of atonality? Would his concept of sonata form and the symphony be able to survive an atonal harmonic language and melodic vocabulary? For three years he had hovered on the brink – albeit perhaps subconsciously. Now was the moment of truth.

In the *Kammersymphonie*, the superimposed fourths and the high norm of dissonance must have produced ambivalent reactions and Schoenberg's approach to form – a free sonata form in one continuous movement comprising exposition–scherzo–development–slow movement–finale (reprise of the exposition ideas) – touched on his own thinking. The Second String Quartet, however, with its *Tristan*esque sound world and its transparent, almost Mozartian textures, struck a singularly responsive chord and not the least of its fascination was the sense of 'air from other planets' that it so successfully portrays.

Two days after hearing the Schoenberg Quartet, he went to the Opera: 'Was at *Elektra*. Strauss is a genius.' His response is revealing, for it was Strauss who stretched the boundaries of tonality to their uttermost limits without venturing beyond and without undermining the classical major-minor tonal system that kindled his enthusiasm. For all that, his fascination with Schoenberg persisted and when in the following June he was questioned in New York by the *Musical Courier* about his views of his contemporaries, he said: 'There is one composer whom I greatly admire and that is Arnold Schoenberg.' And he added, 'I don't mind saying that I have a pretty high opinion of my own compositions too!'

By the end of Jauary he had come to grips with his new tone poem, so much so that on the last day of the month he was so engrossed in composition that he did not even attend – or perhaps did not care to – a performance of his Violin Concerto at the Singakademie with Wittenberg as soloist. However the sour reviews poisoned the atmosphere for him for some days and encouraged suspicions that his fellow countrymen and other Scandinavians in Berlin – Selim and Maikki Palmgren, John Forsell and others – were conspiring against him. Hardly had he recovered from this episode than another performance of the concerto, probably with von Vecsey as soloist, received an equally hard critical drubbing. Sibelius undoubtedly took it to heart: 'It is as if Burmester's "es schadet deinen Ruff" is coming true. To be treated with such contempt at my age is wounding. I must reconcile myself to being out of the game but nevertheless go my own way forward.' His spirits were not improved by learning from a Danish admirer, Gunnar Hauch, that Nikisch had not been optimistic about Sibelius's long-term prospects in Germany

He buried himself in his work and in concert-going. 'Inside me more polyphony and concentration . . . This evening heard Nielsen's *Ouverture* [*sic*], together with [pieces by] Peder Gram and Stenhammar, but the best thing was a piano sonata by Jean Huré.' His appetite for new music seems to have remained voracious. He heard Max von Schillings's *Junger Olaf* and parts of the opera *Molok*, a symphony by Strauss's protégé, Bischoff, Bossi's oratorio, *Jeanne d'Arc*, Xaver Scharwenka's *Frühlingserwachen* and chamber music by Grzegorz Fitelberg. Here was a cross-section of what was happening in the Berlin musical life of the day. He was put into a bad mood on seeing Breitkopf und Härtel's window display, which had works of Busoni, Palmgren and Mahler but nothing of his! 'But still what does it all matter!' he noted in his diary.

On the brighter side he was able to take up his old friends from the 1890s, among them Adolf Paul. He had become ill during the closing months of 1913 and sent Sibelius a touching letter of farewell with the now familiar refrain of their collaboration in a *commedia dell'arte* once again rearing its head. Sibelius had no inclination to be drawn into such a project but on his arrival in Berlin he had, by way of reassuring his friend as to his warmest feelings, gone directly to the Paul household. Here, everything was the same: creditors besieged them and bankruptcy loomed large on the horizon, but the first performance of a new play in Hamburg would save the situation and besides Paul was standing by to write a book on Strindberg. He had appeared himself in a number of Strindberg stories under various guises and pseudonyms – Ilmarinen, Anjala and so on, none of which showed him in a particularly sympathetic light – and as a result had developed a healthy phobia about the recently deceased playwright, which surfaces in his book. But still he worshipped Sibelius and they had splendid times together.

Theodore Spiering had just returned from New York and was now working with the *Neue Freie Volksbühne*. He expressed interest in the Fourth Symphony and Sibelius spent some time with him going through the score, which he thought suited him. Unfortunately he wasn't able to bring the idea to fruition as he left Germany immediately on the outbreak of the war later that year.

By now Sibelius was beginning to feel homesick and was longing to get back to his 'den' and get on with his new work, but he did not wish to leave Berlin without having seen Busoni. He went to his recital on 12 February and packed his bags the following day, and took the Berlin–St Petersburg express, sharing his compartment with a lieutenant in the Guards and a minister of state.

As usual he found that it was not so easy to adjust to life at home after having been used to a foreign city. He felt that he was disturbing Aino and the children in their piano playing and homework and was almost an intruder, and in his turn was irritated by the activity in the house. However, his consideration for the family's welfare and progress had soon to give way to his need for absolute quiet. The American commission was looming large on the horizon. To make matters worse he had become hoarse in Berlin, and his old fears of throat cancer were rekindled, only to disappear in time.

He got down to work in earnest. A new set of piano pieces, Op. 74, was finished: to the *Eclogue* he had written in Berlin, he added three new pieces, *Soft West Wind, At the Dance* and *In the Old Home*. To his setting of Rydberg's 'Vi ses igen' he added a pendant, 'Orion's girdle', to words of Zachris Topelius. The autographs were both in the possession of Breitkopf und Härtel by the time war broke out and disappeared during the 1914–18 conflict. By the beginning of March *The Oceanides* was under way, though by the middle of the month he was far from sure whether he would finish it in time.[1] This was his usual reaction when things were proceeding well. He reassured the Festival organizers in Norfolk and wasted no time or energy in worrying over Peterson-Berger's bad review of *The Dryad* and *Night Ride and Sunrise* ('no real inspiration seems to have touched Sibelius in these pieces'). After a ten-day silence in his diary, he noted on 30 March, 'Op. 73 finished' and a few days later he sent off a copy of the first, D flat major version of *The Oceanides* to America.[2]

On 12 April, he received a letter of invitation from Horatio Parker asking him to conduct *The Oceanides* and a number of shorter works for the handsome fee of 1,200 dollars. And on the selfsame day another piece of

---

1 *The Oceanides* was first conceived in three movements and ran to seventy pages of full score. The first movement, comprising the first twenty-five pages, has not so far come to light. The autograph of the remaining two survives and is in the possession of Helsinki University Library.

2 After Sibelius's visit, Stoeckel deposited the autograph of the D flat major version, which was superseded by the definitive score, in Yale University Library.

good news came: he was to be given an Honorary Doctorate of Philosophy at the University of Helsinki. He was delighted, 'Evoe! Evoe! Venus Bacchusque omnesque dei!' Yet another honour arrived later the same month, when on 20 April, Horatio Parker wrote that the Senate of Yale University had decided to confer on him an Honorary Doctorate of Music at a ceremony on 17 June.

Although he may have been showered with public honours, his private circumstances were less happy. After his return from Berlin he felt that Aino had in some way lost faith in him. He knew that he did not possess all the qualities that she looked for in him, and he feared, too, that she was changing: 'She is withering away before my very eyes. She should be with someone of a different temperament.' After it had become clear that he would be going to America, it seemed to him that Aino lost her usual equilibrium. It only needed a bagatelle, such as his forgetting to pay for the rental of the piano, for her to flare up.

> Aino seems easily to lose patience with me – I who out of sheer fatigue at having to struggle for money forget to settle every account (hundreds of bills, debts, loan repayments, altogether mounting to 100,000) – all this makes life impossible for me. What a release it would be to put an end to it all. The idea has often, quite often gone through my head. I can't earn enough to support my family, let alone pay off my debts. And America. The new work is beginning to flow nicely.

Not that he took his suicidal thoughts all that seriously, and he was soon writing enthusiastically to Carpelan of his progress on *The Oceanides* 'Isn't it just like me to rework the tone-poem – at the moment I am ablaze with it.'

To what extent is *The Oceanides* an impressionistic work? Its impressionistic elements are largely centred in the orchestral sound world, and to a lesser extent in its harmonic vocabulary and rhythmic patterns. Take the very opening bars.

Ex 181

The irregular motion of the violins in their triplets over distant timpani rolls evokes a static vision. Like Debussy, Sibelius avoids the stabilizing effect of a firm tonality by using the mediant, the dominant and submediant – the timpani's interval of a second (B–A) gives a subtle and refined touch. The effect is of a vibrant tonal mist shrouding the sea's seemingly infinite depths. The flutes playfully bring the 'oceanides' to life.

Another parallel with the Debussy of *L'Ile joyeuse* is the use of open-sounding parallel fourths without any superimposed thirds. The first idea resolves on to a D major triad, which then dissolves into a slow trill of parallel fourths moving in different rhythms.

Ex 182

In the coda these fourths on tremolo strings over a wide compass lend the texture a greater sense of space and depth:

Ex 183

A different kind of impressionistic effect surfaces at the beginning of the second group (on page 8 of the score). A powerful sense of the swell of the ocean is conveyed here by a motive divided between oboe and clarinet over strings and harp glissandi:

Ex 184

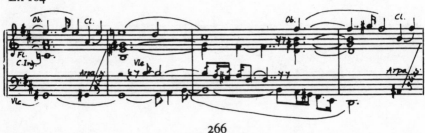

The cellos describe a contour with characteristic tritone inflections. But even if the texture and the modal element in the bass line is impressionistic, the overall effect is not. In the chromatic harmonies, there are reminders of the chords of the ninth we encounter in the First Symphony, albeit in a more complex and sophisticated context. It is largely on this count, its anchorage in major–minor harmony and the relatively sparing use of modal and whole-tone formulae, that *The Oceanides* belongs to the world of late romanticism rather than impressionism. Moreover the frequent recourse to sequential writing is a post-romantic trait, but there is no doubt that the sound world evoked in the following passage is strongly impressionistic:

Ex 185

Debussy makes a comparable modulation in *Sirènes* from F sharp major to A major, but whereas he continues step-wise to C major, thus underlining its whole-tone basis, and moreover creates an archetypal impressionistic effect with his parallel fifths, Sibelius proceeds with greater circumspection.

Structurally, *The Oceanides* evinces parallels with and differences from impressionist procedures. The 'oceanides' theme is pointillistic in conception and appears a number of times as an isolated phenomenon in an alien landscape while the second-group figure, suggesting the ground swell of the ocean, proceeds on classical lines both in its organic growth and tonal organization. In common with *La Mer*, and perhaps with more recent pieces such as Messiaen's *Oiseaux exotiques*, the overall shape of *The Oceanides* seems to mirror nature itself. One can imagine Sibelius depicting the sea from dawn to midday in a series of episodes where the 'oceanides' or nymphs play, **A**, and the ground swell of the ocean becomes more powerful, **B**, thus –

A (D major) – **B** (modulating, ending in the area of D minor–F major) – **A1** (F major) – **B1** (ending in E flat–G flat) – **C** (modulating and ending on the pedal A which becomes the dominant of D major) – **A2** (indeterminate D major) – Coda

– and here C serves as a development drawing on material from both **A** and **B**. But all these different episodes are subservient to a grander design and one can visualize the wind increasing from light to gale force as it lashes the ocean. In the **A** section the oceanides play in the morning light, while the **B** section brings the ocean's depths and perhaps the God of the Sea himself before our eyes, while in the return to **A1** the winds begin to gather force:

Ex 186

The harp glissandi call to mind the evocation of the wind in *Luonnotar*, and as the waves mount in the strings, the play of the oceanides becomes wilder. The glockenspiel is heard and together with harp and clarinet outline the theme that is embedded in the string textures (pages 17–18). Both from the viewpoint of sonority and function, this calls to mind the Fourth Symphony and serves as a reminder that Sibelius spoke of a stylistic relationship between the two works in one of his letters. The transition to the next section **B1** is effected by an episode where the strings shed thematic concerns and merely occupy themselves with portraying the movement of the waves. Like the shore scenes in Britten's *Peter Grimes*, a sustained wind chord comes to symbolize the limitless expanse of the sea. The **B1** section brings the storm nearer and the development, **C**, begins with an expectant atmosphere and when the storm draws near, over a pedal point on the dominant minor (A) the oceanides are swamped as the second group evoking the sea itself rises sequentially:

Ex 187

The waves build up to a mighty climax, whose impact always exceeds one's expectations, but the final vision that the coda brings before the listener is the immutability and vastness of the ocean waters into which the oceanides themselves do not venture.

'We'll see now how things will work out in America. I have much against me but on the other hand I have many advantages too.' He was in good spirits as he set off on 19 May to board the Norddeutscher Lloyd steamship, *Kaiser Wilhelm II*. On the following day at 6.08 pm they passed Cherbourg pier and though Sibelius remained in his cabin, going through the orchestral parts of his new work, he found time to enjoy the voyage and admire the view. According to the logbook, winds were light to moderate and on only one occasion did they encounter stormier weather. Sibelius was disappointed not to see a whale and had to content himself with a shoal of flying fish which passed the liner.

In the Sunday edition of the *New York Herald Tribune*, Henry Krehbiel had paved the way for his arrival with a long article headed 'Finland sends musical envoy'. On board Sibelius had received a welcoming telegram from Maud Powell, who had given the first American performance of the Violin Concerto, and once the ship had docked, he remained in his cabin a while so as to avoid – or at least postpone – the inevitable encounter with the press. Most of the important dailies and the musical press were represented but with the help of his host, Carl Stoeckel, the occasion passed off both painlessly and quickly, and he was rushed off to the Essex Hotel where a suite had been reserved for him. Here he was presented to Mrs Battell-Stoeckel:

He took her hand and kissed it three times with reverence and formality as well as with grace. As to his personal appearance, I should think he might be five feet ten or eleven inches in height, with a compact and well-filled body. His frame was well-built and proportioned and he had an air of distinction. He was very particular about his clothes and linen and shoes, all being of the best make and cut. His hair was clipped quite close and altogether unlike the generally accepted impression of foreign musical composers. If I had passed him on the street, I would have rated him as a prosperous professional gentleman, like a doctor or civil engineer.[1]

Stoeckel was a gourmet but in Sibelius he had met his match:

We went to Delmonicos for supper, knowing that this place had some admirable arrangements for securing fresh caviar. We ordered some of this delicacy which pleased Sibelius, who was good enough to say that it was finer than any that could be obtained in Russia at the hotels there. We had some broiled salmon as the composer was fond of fish in any form, followed by roasted guinea hen, with Delmonico potatoes, and for the composer lettuce and tomato salad.

Sibelius watched with fascination how his host mixed an orange salad with tarragon dressing but refrained from tasting this typical American mixture. Stoeckel noted that throughout the meal Sibelius confined himself to mineral water and also that on their return journey along Fifth Avenue, he seemed to know the names of many of the famous New Yorkers whose residences were pointed out to him.

The next day Sibelius and his host visited the New York offices of Breitkopf und Härtel, where an exhibition of scores and pictures had been mounted to celebrate his arrival. 'He took no notice of this attention and did not see the exhibition until I asked him to look at it.' Sibelius affected the role of a world figure to perfection. How upset he had been only a few months earlier when he had found no score of his displayed in Breitkopf's windows in Berlin!

On Tuesday the rehearsals began in Carnegie Hall. Clad in a spotless white flannel suit, he climbed the podium to the applause of the seventy-five hand-picked musicians of the Festival Orchestra, drawn from the Philharmonic and Metropolitan Opera House orchestras. Before him Henry Hadley had rehearsed his tone poem *Lucifer* and while he was waiting, Sibelius carefully studied the orchestra. It amazed his host how quickly and correctly he picked out the best instrumentalists in each section, and he did not go wrong once. He began the rehearsal with *Pohjola's Daughter*. At first he was a little nervous but that soon passed, and it became evident that he had completely mastered the players. A little later he turned to the new piece, which was completely unlike anything else the musicians had played before. 'At first,' wrote Stoeckel,

I think they did not understand it at all from what they said. The next morning, after having run through it three times, they were thoroughly

1 Carl Stoeckel, 'Some Recollections of the Visit of Sibelius to America in 1914', MS in Yale University Library, p. 34.

delighted with it and remarked that the beauty of the music grew with each rehearsal. Although the rehearsals were supposed to be private, there were a score of newspaper men and reporters of musical papers present. Some of them tried to pump Sibelius as to the meaning of certain passages in his music, but he would not say anything definite, answering always that everyone must use his own imagination for his works. He was glad, however, to indicate to some of the conductors who were present the tempi of his symphonies and other works, humming them or playing them on the piano from the score, when he remarked that he was not a pianist and only played as a composer played. It was mighty good playing though, full of feeling, strength and nuances. While playing on the piano he remarked that he was originally a violinist and had even played solos on that instrument but from a fall his bow arm had stiffened up so that he could not draw a full bow length.

The next morning before the rehearsal he made a number of changes in the score. During the crossing, he said, he had learned more about the ocean than he had from watching the sea from the shore in Helsinki. He was totally absorbed in *The Oceanides*: 'It is as if I find more and more of myself. The Fourth Symphony was the beginning. But in this, there is even more. There are places that make me go mad. What poetry!!!' In writing to Carpelan he made a point of stressing still further the connection between the symphony and the new score:

America's best critics have written warmly about my Fourth Symphony . . . and this new work is in the same style, although it is a 'tone poem'. The ocean has really inspired me. I am beginning – so it seems to me – to approach *cher-maître* status. A little portly (good living), not nervous, demanding particularly where the orchestra is concerned and perhaps a little impertinent.

On the Friday afternoon Sibelius and Stoeckel took the train to Norfolk. When Sibelius saw Grand Central Station he declared with wonder, 'What a place for a concert if only one had an orchestra of two or three hundred people!' During the journey he was fascinated by the name of the Housatonic river and intoned these Indian-sounding syllables many times. They arrived later that evening at the White House, the Stoeckel's mansion, which had been built by Mrs Stoeckel's grandfather, Joseph Battell in 1798. He was given the 'Old Blue Room' on the first floor, which had previously served as the library. Sibelius called the White House, 'Poetry's Refuge'.

Carl Stoeckel was the son of a Bohemian immigrant organist who had become the first professor and first doctor of music at Yale University. Even if he was not an active musician, there was much in him that was reminiscent of the German-trained musician, though more of the wealthy American businessman and patron of the arts. In his youth he had been the secretary of an extremely wealthy businessman, Robbins Battell, whose daughter Ellen he eventually married. Sibelius clearly grasped the situation:

> Stoeckel is of German descent but his wife comes from a well-born French-Huguenot family who settled in the New World two centuries ago, and their house is one of the oldest in America. They all have a good background. All the men have worked their way up and are 'self-made men' but all the wives are aristocrats.

In the Battell household, there was a good collection of American painting that had been acquired over a century or more. To a present-day visitor the ground floor is furnished in the *fin-de-siècle* manner with a strong art-nouveau element, and is in its way impressive if somewhat ornate. However, the rooms where Sibelius lived on the floor above retain much of the charm of the early part of the nineteenth century, an American equivalent to the Gustavian style of Sweden and Finland that Sibelius loved so much.

Sibelius's pleasure at his reception in America comes over clearly in a letter to his brother Christian:

> Here I am, living in state and in the lap of luxury. I am presented as a great celebrity, and at times have some difficulty in maintaining the right 'profile'. I have an enormous reputation here in America, and I believe that the proposed tour (as yet secret) of between forty and fifty concerts would be a great success. I could pay off my own debts and yours besides . . . My new work – by the way, not *Rondo der Wellen* now but *The Oceanides*, is altogether superb. (We are familiar with my modesty!) This Norfolk is a mixture of Finland and Italy or Algiers. Negroes and whites. Methodists, Quakers, Lutherans.

To Christian he confessed that he was frankly enjoying his new role as a celebrity but to Aino he presented another face, one which was not quite so at home in his new environment and more in tune with her ascetic Tolstoyan way of life. 'We will have to see whether I can cope with all this luxury until the 20th or 22nd. The novelty of it appeals to me as I was not brought up in this style.' In any event Sibelius seems to have acclimatized himself to the Stoeckels' life-style more easily than did Vaughan Williams and his wife, who were invited there eight years later in connection with the performance of his *Pastoral Symphony*. Vaughan Williams reacted against being dependent on his patron even for a few days and said gruffly that he understood Mozart. Besides, unlike Sibelius, he detested long restaurant meals and late nights and again, unlike Sibelius, he had no language problems and could do his own sight-seeing without Mr Stoeckel. But for all these minor irritants, both Vaughan Williams and his wife thought the Stoeckels 'very kind people'. Mrs Vaughan Williams described life in the White House, 'They live in the style of the *ancien régime*, horses rather than cars, Swiss servant girls, an English gardener and an English maid. There is a very happy atmosphere in the house. The meals are far too rich and wine flows all the time.'[1] Sibelius was much happier surrounded by luxury: 'I love it. At last I have enough servants. Negroes, whites and girls of all colours.'

The weekend at the White House proceeded apace. Out of courtesy to his hosts, Sibelius attended the service at the Congregational Church. He mistakenly sat on a pew reserved for war veterans and was turned out, and listened from another part of the church to a long sermon, not a word of which he understood. But his interest was aroused by the hymn tunes of New England; otherwise his time was taken up by the social round, and he met among others Horatio Parker's daughters and went to some choral rehearsals taken by Richard Paine, one of the celebrities of the day. Among the sights, he was much taken with the birthplace of Harriet Beecher Stowe.

The Norfolk Festival was in every sense the Stoeckels' creation. Not only did they finance it but they were its driving force artistically. Mrs Stoeckel's father, Robbins Battell, had been an accomplished flautist and an amateur composer, and thanks to him a lively choral tradition had been built up in Lichfield County. He had been responsible for a performance of Handel's *Messiah* as early as 1851. Now under the patronage of Carl Stoeckel, the choirs had reached an international standard and the Litchfield County Choral Union was a pillar on which the Norfolk Festival rested. But Stoeckel and his adviser, Horatio Parker, wanted to give the Festival additional prestige by commissioning new works by living composers of stature, many of whom were also invited to conduct them. Horatio Parker had been represented by his *King Gorm the Grim*, George Chadwick by his *Noel and Aphrodite* among other things, and Henry Hadley by his Fourth Symphony, 'North, East, South, West', based on American folksong. Others who had been so honoured included Samuel Coleridge-Taylor of *Hiawatha* fame, and Max Bruch.

The concerts took place in 'The Music Shed', a huge wooden edifice that could accommodate an audience of about 2,000. At the inaugural concert in 1906, the legendary Wagnerian soprano, Lilian Nordica had sung 'Dich teure Halle' from *Tannhäuser*. The 1914 Festival began on 2 June with the traditional opening – a chorale by Robbins Battell, after which there were two works, Hadley's *Lucifer* and Bruch's oratorio *Arminius*. Stoeckel noticed that Sibelius did not appear to care for *Arminius*, but that *Lucifer* made a more positive impression on him. The following day, after a brilliant performance of *Messiah*, Sibelius and Hadley had a long talk. Sibelius had planned the rehearsals in 'The Shed' quite systematically. Tuesday morning he devoted to *Pohjola's Daughter* and *The Oceanides*, both

1 Ursula Vaughan Williams, *R.V.W. A Biography of Ralph Vaughan Williams*, London, 1964, p. 144.

of which were new to the orchestra. The next session he gave over to the better-known pieces, paying special attention to the blending of the wind section, which he wanted to be rounded, smooth and powerful without rough edges.[1]

The concert, on 4 June, brought the Festival to a climax. As on all the mornings he spent in the White House, Sibelius rose fairly early and was shaved by a barber, specially engaged for the purpose at his request![2] At the final rehearsal he concentrated exclusively on the smaller pieces on the programme. The audience included a number of conductors and other musicians, and all seemed to augur well. After some preliminary nervousness, which he assured Stoeckel would pass once he mounted the podium, he took up his baton. The podium itself was decked out in the American and Finnish colours, and the Finnish coat of arms, the Lion, was also displayed, much to the composer's satisfaction.

As a conductor, Sibelius was graceful but at the same time powerful, recalled Stoeckel: 'He did not bother about beating one, two, three, four. His gestures were more reminiscent of someone reciting a great poem.' The concert began with *Pohjola's Daughter*, after which came the *King Christian II* Suite, *The Swan of Tuonela*, *Finlandia*, *Valse triste* and finally, the new work *The Oceanides*. Both as a composer and conductor, Sibelius appears to illustrate the paradox that the best style is no style at all. His baton technique followed no predetermined procedure but adapted itself to the changing musical circumstances. In *The Oceanides*, for example, he did not beat out the crotchets at the beginning of the work and achieved the most ethereal *ppp*, afterwards building up climax upon climax. After that tremendous moment which Olin Downes called 'the crash of the great wave' subsided, he whipped up a climax almost twice as powerful, which none of those present could easily forget. But in the coda he secured once again the deepest quiet.

For Sibelius it was, of course, a joy to discover players who could do justice to the sound world he had envisaged:

> The orchestra is wonderful!! Surpasses anything we have in Europe. The woodwind blend is of such an order that you have to put your hand to your ear to hear them in *ppp* even if the cor anglais and bass clarinet are there. And even the double-basses sing.[3]

Obviously Sibelius had managed to secure excellent ensemble from these musicians and a good rapport with them; not only were they drawn from the two New York orchestras but, according to Sibelius himself, some even came from the Boston Symphony Orchestra.

1 Stoeckel, op. cit., p. 16.
2 His tremor probably prompted this request.
3 Letter to Carpelan, 5 June 1914.

After the final work, the public gave the composer an ovation, the like of which I have never seen equalled anywhere,' wrote Stoeckel. 'The calmest person in the hall was presumably Sibelius himself. He bowed several times in that distinguished way that was typical of him, and arranged the laurel wreaths around the podium.' Afterwards he sank exhausted into an arm chair at the back of the Stoeckels' box with tears in his eyes; then they listened to the second half of the programme: Wagner's overture, *Die Feen*, Coleridge-Taylor's posthumous *The Prairie*, Alma Gluck's solo and finally, Dvořak's 'New World' Symphony. At the very end the chorus and orchestra played the Finnish anthem 'Vårt Land' ('Our Country') and 'America Forever'. 'He was deeply moved . . . and took my hand saying, 'Finland thanks you and your wife. I take the playing of the national anthems not as a mark of honour to myself but to my country.' He saw 'Vårt Land' as an augur of freedom and an unforgettable moment, and the whole concert had brought Finland alive in the eyes of all those who were there. He had been reminded on his way to 'The Shed' of his role as 'Finland's musical envoy' and he felt satisfaction at the results. Ironically enough, the telegram he sent after the concert to Christian was written out in Finland in only one language – Russian!

Sibelius returned in a horse-drawn carriage to the White House where the first to congratulate him on his deportment as a conductor was Walter Damrosch, no less. At the supper party he sat next to Horatio Parker and George Chadwick, the Rector of the New England Conservatory in Boston. Sibelius spent the following Sunday in New York and read with delight Krehbiel's article on the Norfolk Festival which largely centred on Sibelius. Krehbiel compared *The Oceanides* to Aeschylus and the fettered Prometheus:

Ye virgin sisters, who derive your race
From fruitful Thetis, and th'embrace
of old Oceanus your sire, that rolls
around the wide world his unquiet waves.

But as he had taken the theme of nationalism at the Norfolk Festival as exemplified by Parker, Hadley, Coleridge-Taylor and now also Sibelius and Dvořák, he dwelt on *Pohjola's Daughter*: 'The Finnish composer stands before the world as a nationalist in art and presents his ideal or vision of his country much in the same way as Tchaikovsky does for Russia, Dvořák for Bohemia, Saint-Saëns for France, Elgar for England and Richard Strauss Germany.' It was presumably the first and last occasion on which Sibelius was compared with Saint-Saëns!

Olin Downes wrote that during the last fifteen years there were few occasions when he felt himself in the presence of a genius of world class: when Richard Strauss had conducted his own compositions in Philadelphia and Boston in 1904; when Toscanini conducted *Tristan und Isolde* in Boston in 1910; and now, most recently, when Sibelius had conducted his own works in Norfolk. *The Oceanides* he thought contained

> the finest evocation of the sea which has ever been produced in music. Even if Sibelius uses a different and more powerful idiom than Debussy's, he is more closely related to Debussy's sea than to Wagner's. Handel's or Mendelssohn's or Weber's or Rimsky-Korsakov's oriental conception of the high seas are all too distant to qualify for inclusion in this context. Instinctively faithful to his extraordinarily developed feeling for form, proportion and continuity . . . Sibelius gives a shape and melodic interest to a work, which is in its essentials preoccupied with colour and harmony. But to a greater extent than in any other work, he emerges as an arch-impressionist who does not work with lines and the co-ordination of sound-blocks but rather with free sonorities which reflect natural phenomena. Nevertheless he holds himself closer to the coastline of tonality than does Debussy and suggests by so doing a picture of limitless and eternal power.

Stoeckel was at pains to see that Sibelius met the leading musical figures of the day. He telegraphed an invitation to a dinner in Sibelius's honour in Boston on Monday, 8 June, to several important composers such as Hadley, Chadwick, Frederick Converse and Charles Loeffler, the critics Hale and Elson and the choral conductor, Richard Paine. He reassured himself in advance as to the quality of the caviar but was on his arrival displeased to note that the wine glasses were coloured. They were soon replaced by pure crystal. Stoeckel was delighted at Sibelius's pleasure at the sight of the Johannisburger Schloss and Chambertin in the glasses and the whole picture of the table with its candelabras and the grand piano in the background struck him as being like a painting of Sargent. They spoke German and French, and Sibelius seemed completely at ease: 'He did not in any way monopolize or lead the conversation and simply replied to suggestions and questions which were made to him by the other men.' The atmosphere seems to have been thoroughly agreeable and Sibelius was later to conduct a correspondence with one of the composers present, Henry Hadley. The only anti-Sibelian there was Charles Loeffler, known for his oft-cited remark: 'Sibelius? Sibelius! My dear Downes, to tell you the truth, I prefer music without cod-liver oil.' The following day Sibelius was taken over the New England Conservatory where he could hear from several rehearsal rooms the sounds of his Romance in D flat being practised. His attention was really captured however by one student violinist practising his scales, to whom he listened most intently.

Soon the time came for his departure from the White House. On 12 June there was a banquet for 250 people who were served by 50 waiters brought in from New York as – to quote Sibelius – in Norfolk it would seem nothing was quite top-drawer! The guest-of-honour was ex-President Taft and Sibelius took the opportunity to speak to him about the situation in Finland, with which Taft appeared to be thoroughly familiar. Afterwards he told Mrs Stoeckel that the whole occasion was at one and the same time the most aristocratic and yet democratic that he had even known. The following day Stoeckel took his guest by car to Rochester, Buffalo and Niagara. Sibelius revelled in the journey, enjoying the flowering acacias and walnuts as well as the sensation of being driven around in such a lordly fashion in a luxury limousine and surrounded by untold comforts. Everywhere they went, they had been preceded by servants whose job it was to see that all was in order.

They arrived the next day and visited the America Falls before crossing over to Horseshoe Falls on the Canadian side of the border:

> As he viewed the great spectacle there was an expression on his face of one who is experiencing profoundly religious emotions. He evidently did not wish to be spoken to.

The following day they dressed themselves in sou'westers and oilskins and went on board a little steamboat at the foot of the Falls:

> Sibelius was deep in thought during the entire trip and I saw that he did not wish to converse, for which he thanked me afterwards, saying that he had been trying to get an impression of this great natural phenomenon for representation in some musical work, but he said, 'I have given up the idea. It is too solemn and too vast to be represented by any human individual.' We went then to a photograph shop where he purchased several pictures of the Falls. He found fault with the majority of the pictures because there were human figures in them or buildings. He said that such a great natural object should be taken entirely by itself, free from every contamination of any semblance of humanity. He spoke with such reverence of Niagara Falls whenever he referred to it, that I could not help thinking that he might have inherited, in a faint way, the old Scandinavian feeling of the great phenomena of nature being the dwelling places of divinities.'

The sight of Niagara had prompted Mahler to say that he placed a work of art higher than natural beauty. This is no more than one would expect. One is more surprised by Vaughan Williams's assertion that he was more impressed by the Woolworth skyscraper in New York than by Niagara: 'Man's work astonishes me more than God's.' Sibelius responded to Niagara in more pantheistic fashion – which did not prevent him from being inspired by the sight of New York and the dynamic power of its architecture:

> It is gigantic and impressionistic but at the same time strangely symbolic. A mixture of beauty and ugliness, hot and cold, frenzy and calm, power and suggestiveness, so that I feel as if I am reeling in the clouds . . . I

would love to get to know some of the interesting people in this witches' cauldron. They are presumably as dynamic as their creation.

But he scarcely met any such people. Ivan Narodny in *Musical America* complained that he came into contact with only the society world of New England in much the same way that Gorky had encountered America only through the window painting in his studio on Staten Island. At least where Sibelius is concerned, his assertion is not wholly true: the composer also met many fellow musicians and professionals in Norfolk and Boston. But it is true, of course, that he did not meet many representatives of New York musical life with the exception of Damrosch and Krehbiel. He and Stoeckel came from Niagara just in time for caviar at Delmonicos, and on the next day went straight to Yale University at New Haven, where preparations were in hand for the Encaenia. Three weeks earlier he had been given an Honorary Degree at Alexander University in Helsinki. This posed certain problems for his hosts at Yale:

> My robes at the Encaenia are those of a doc. phil. hon. causa which are black with a blue border. A Barett hat. When I get the mus. doc. I am given a pink mantle round my shoulders. Wear the cross of the *Légion d'honneur*.

During the solemn ceremonies the procession went into Woolsey Hall to the sounds of *Finlandia*. Indeed, during the whole of the Encaenia, Sibelius's music was played, including – of all things – *Valse triste*! The public orator hailed him as one of the leading contemporary composers: 'What Wagner did for the Old German sagas, Dr Sibelius has done in his own glorious fashion for the Finnish mythology . . . He has translated the *Kalevala* into music's international language.' The first to congratulate him afterwards was ex-President Taft.

At the banquet that followed, Sibelius cast a delighted eye over the delicacies spread before them and whispered in Horatio Parker's ear, 'I was so preoccupied by the doctorate and so frightened that I might commit some blunder that I quite forgot to take breakfast!' Just before the train's departure for New York, Parker presented him with a score of his opera *Mona*.

That evening Sibelius was the guest of the Stoeckels for the last time at Delmonicos or 'liebe alte Heimat' as he had christened it. They began with a generous portion of the most exquisite caviar which had just arrived from Russia via Paris, and finished with champagne, which Sibelius diluted with soda water. The following morning, 18 June, the Stoeckels drove him to the Hamburg–America line docks, where the *President Grant* was ready to sail. His somewhat abrupt departure was due to the fact that he had to conduct a concert in Malmö. Through his connections Stoeckel succeeded in getting Sibelius an officer's cabin on the boat, which was fully booked. As a last sign of attention, he had bought presents for the whole of the Sibelius family: a jewel ring for Aino and toys for the children. Sibelius appeared subdued and withdrawn, and Stoeckel did his best to cheer him up. They went on a tour of the luxury liner and when the time drew near for departure, they were all quite upset. Sibelius kissed Mrs Stoeckel's hand numerous times and hugged his host. A few hours before departure, he had written to Carpelan: 'If by any chance something should happen, tell Aino that right up to the very end I have behaved in such a fashion that she could be proud of me'. Surprise at the note of self-dramatization is tempered by the thought that the *Titanic* had sunk only two years earlier and its unexpected fate had sent shock waves round the world. The *President Grant* arrived safely enough but a note of foreboding was sounded during the trip when the ship's telegraph broke the news of the assassination at Sarajevo. From the *President Grant*, Finland's 'musical envoy', sent a telegram of thanks to his host, which he answered. Without doubt there had been something of *A Thousand and One Nights* in the lavishness of Stoeckel's hospitality. Like some Haroun-al-Raschid, he had granted all of Sibelius's wishes.

After Sibelius's departure, Stoeckel penned 'Some Recollections of the Visit of Sibelius to America in 1914', thirty-four typewritten pages which he deposited in the Yale University Library. The account contains one or two lapses of memory. Stoeckel places his arrival in America two days too early, and has to make up an extra day in New York and another in Norfolk before he gets to the Festival, and he forgot Sibelius's brief visit to New York on 7 June! However he is an intelligent observer who contents himself with narrative rather than speculative notions. His first sentence departs, perhaps, from his usual factual style: 'My first impressions and also my last of Sibelius as a man and artist are those of the two principal attributes of greatness: simplicity and modesty.' It would appear that Stoeckel himself was neither self-important nor in any way ostentatious. He could easily have turned the Norfolk Festival into a star-studded event but instead he built on the musical life of Litchfield County of which he was so loyal a patron and at the same time stimulated contemporary composers to write for him. That caviar assumes so important a role in his account of the visit springs from his pleasure at finding a fellow gourmet. Even a year later the chef at Delmonicos could recall the foreign visitor who really understood and appreciated caviar.[1] 'Very nice and simple' was Vaughan Williams's verdict on the Stoeckels;[2] Sibelius took the same view: 'Highly cultured. Free of pretence.'[3]

*

1 According to Stoeckel in a letter to Sibelius on 11 January 1915.
2 Ursula Vaughan Williams, op. cit., p. 143.
3 In a letter to his brother Christian, 1 June 1914.

Aino and their daughter Ruth were waiting for him on his arrival in Copenhagen. He waxed lyrical over his journey: 'I have seen and experienced more in six weeks than I normally do in many years,' he told the Danish paper, *Politiken*.

> To tell the truth I was amazed to encounter so highly developed a musical culture in the New World. I had imagined that American musical life did not extend far beyond the boston and ragtime . . . If all goes well, I shall set my sights on a return trip over the Atlantic. I have promised faithfully to go back and give a whole string of public concerts.

But the First World War was to scotch his plans and its shadows were already being cast over the concert in Malmö. In connection with the Malmö Exhibition, each of the countries involved – Sweden, Denmark, Germany and Russia – had mounted a concert. Sibelius had been engaged for a concert on 4 July but on his arrival in Malmö he learned that it had been cancelled. Perhaps the Swedish impresarios were fearful that in the tense political climate of the day, a Sibelius concert would be interpreted as a pro-Finnish and anti-Riussian gesture. To save face, they had included a number of short Sibelius pieces in a Russian concert conducted by Vasily Safonov the previous week.

Aino had wired to ask that in the programme Sibelius should be billed as a Finnish composer – but in vain. The concert promoters in Malmö were evidently overcome by 'phantom nerves', at least that was the expression used in the Helsinki press. In 1900 during the days of Bobrikov, the Helsinki Philharmonic Orchestra had appeared representing Finland at the Paris Exhibition without a word of protest from the Russians. Why should things be any different now, when Sibelius as the leading Finnish composer, who had conducted his own works in Moscow and St Petersburg, appeared at the Baltic Exhibition with a similar programme? But politics are rarely understood by musicians and a world war was beginning to threaten. Sibelius was outraged: 'The concert was cancelled under my very nose,' he wrote to Carpelan, and he was doubtless displeased at the loss of his fee of 1,000 Swedish kronor.

On his return home he was greeted as a conquering hero by the Finnish press, and one wonders to what extent their (and his) enthusiasm was justified. After all, when one looks at it in the cold light of day, he did not conquer any of the major American musical centres and did not appear in New York. This is hardly surprising as the season was virtually over. As Ivan Narodny noted in *Musical America*:

> Jean Sibelius's unnoticed visit to these shores was to New England rather than New York since we in our metropolis showed less public interest in so outstanding a musical guest than we should have done. But this was due to the fact that the great Finnish master came as the guest of Carl Stoeckel . . . Nevertheless his visit did not go wholly unnoticed.

On the credit side Sibelius could point to some extensive and splendid reviews in the *New York Herald Tribune*, the *New York Times*, the *Boston Post*, *Musical America* and other papers. The influential Henry Krehbiel was favourably disposed in spite of the fact that he still saw the Fourth Symphony as a step backwards. In Olin Downes, Sibelius had found an enthusiastic advocate, who nine years later was to occupy a key position as chief critic of the *New York Times*. It was a pity that the war disrupted his plans for a return visit and a concert tour, but by that time the Americans had other things to think about than a Finnish composer who happened to have a German publisher.

However, as far as other conductors were concerned, he had much to be thankful for. In New York, Walter Damrosch of the Symphonic Society, Josef Stransky of the Philharmonic Society and Modest Altschuler of the Russian Symphony took his works into their repertoire. The real Sibelian among them, however, was Karl Muck at the Boston Symphony who was responsible for countless performances of the Fourth, First and Second Symphonies as well as many of the tone poems before his internment in 1918. But the real Sibelius boom in America came in the second half of the 1920s.

Back in Ainola, Sibelius was enjoying the Finnish high summer as much as was possible in the menacing times that Europe was undergoing that July: 'Finland wonderful. What a beautiful and poetic country we have! I say "have"! I wonder how long.'

WAR DECLARED. AUSTRIA – SERBIA These four words leap out in red ink from a sheet, torn out of the sketchbook in which Sibelius was to work in the autumn of 1914 and the spring of 1915 on his Fifth and Sixth Symphonies. That Wednesday, 29 July 1914, dawned with heavy cloud and rain. The cool weather came as a welcome and refreshing change after the hot easterly winds and thundery heat of the preceding days. 'A wonderful theme', possibly the main idea of the Fifth Symphony, held Sibelius in its thrall, and consumed him all morning. Later on he strolled over the road to see Eero Järnefelt at Suviranta. There the two men sat and tried to assimilate the dreadful news and on his return home the war rather than the new theme dominated his thoughts. Up to that point all had seemed to be going well. In early July he had received a letter from Paul Heinecke of the New York office of Breitkopf und Härtel, promising him the fullest support in terms of publicity and promotion for the concert tour of the United States that he was planning for 1915. The project – Sibelius had spoken of some forty or fifty concerts in his letter to Christian – was by now well advanced and the generous fees quoted were an enticing prospect. Sibelius viewed with the keenest enthusiasm the prospect of being able to pay off all his own debts, which now amounted to 90,000 Finnish marks, as well as Christian's: 'America is the land of the future!'

Only a few days earlier Breitkopf und Härtel in Leipzig had written to Sibelius congratulating him on his honorary doctorate at Yale and affirming their willingness to buy *The Oceanides*, for which they offered 3,000 Reichsmarks. In his reply Sibelius was not slow to point out that he had just been given another honorary degree in Helsinki: 'the greatest token of honour that my unhappy country can confer on me'. But the next day when he opened his morning paper, *Hufvudstadbladet*, the news prompted an alarmed diary entry:

29 July. World peace more doubtful than ever. The Austrians have bombarded Belgrade and declared war on Montenegro. Massive War Demonstrations in Paris, Berlin and St Petersburg. Danger of War threatens Finland.

The international situation, of course, threatened far more than his 1915 tour: his music and his whole way of life were at stake:

30 July. The war has started. How will it affect me? My family needs money; also my children! My German publisher cannnot send anything because of the war. How shall I manage? . . . They say that German ships are cruising towards our coast. Will we remain supine because of lack of leadership? Emasculated as we are, I would set greater store by the Swedish-speaking element of the population than I do by our Finns!

That entry pinpoints a recurring fear of the Finns during the whole of the next decade: that the Germans would attempt to attack St Petersburg by the back door, as it were, through Finland. He took comfort from the thought that in such an eventuality the Finns would make common cause with the Germans and rise against the Tsarist yoke. But his doubts mount when he looks at the quality of the potential leadership of which the country can avail itself, particularly among the Finnish-speaking politicians, 'wet hats' as his friend Gallén-Kallela called them, after the wily herdsman with a wet hat in the *Kalevala*. Sibelius's reference to emasculation is prompted more by some of the over-cautious Finnish politicians of the day; he regarded the Swedish-speaking part of the political community as being far more positive.

He continues confiding his thoughts to the sketchbook:

31 July. In Helsinki: waiting. War is in the air. Impossible for me to negotiate a loan. Rebuffs from all sides! Strange. It is almost as if I no longer mattered.
1 August. Wired Breitkopf und Härtel. But uncertain if the telegram reached them. Must make an approach to M. M. and get off my high horse. The new symphony is beginning to move! Why does it always have to be me whose work is disrupted, never able to get on with what my soul is created to do. A wonderfully understanding letter from Axel! He is unique. But does not know that my money problems (nearly 90,000 in debt) weigh on me.

Like most people Sibelius felt a horror of war, and realized that once it engulfed Europe, Finland would inevitably be drawn into the conflict. She was a Russian dependancy and therefore officially in a state of war with the Central Powers. Naturally the thought that Germany and the Austro-Hungarian Empire were 'enemy powers' was, for him, an absurdity. He had known Berlin and Vienna as a student; it was from Germany that his fame had spread throughout the world; Breitkopf und Härtel and Lienau had been steadfast in their support of him on the Continent. Now he saw Germany being encircled.

Sixty years before, during the Crimean war, Sibelius's father had served as a doctor in one of the Imperial warships that had guarded Finnish waters against the enemies of the Tsar. The difference in attitude between father and son pinpoints the collapse in confidence between the two countries. Mutual trust had given way to mutual suspicion. In the eyes of the Tsarist regime, the Grand Duchy represented a dangerous military and political vacuum with a population that in time of war could be expected to side with the enemies of the Tsar. Steps must be taken to erode such little autonomy as it still possessed. One side-effect of the increasing policy of 'Russification' was welcome: because special Finnish regiments in the Russian army had been disbanded, in response to the growing wave of nationalism, there was no mobilization in Finland. And even in 1914, in spite of the perfidious Nicholas II, the Duma and the anti-Finnish lobby in St Petersburg, some vestiges of the trust that had predominated before the 1890s still remained. Indeed, at the outbreak of war, a small number of Finns even volunteered for service in the Imperial Army! Not enough, however, to calm the fears and suspicions of the Tsarist authorities, who poured troops into key areas, particularly along the coast. From the windows of Ainola, Sibelius watched the Russian troops defile the Järvenpää highway, 'our cross', he called them. Even if he could not wish them victory, neither did he wish them ill: never did he succumb to any generalized hatred of the Russians.

Indeed the war led to a strengthening of contacts between Russian and Finnish artists, particularly as young musicians were no longer able to study in Germany and Austria. The new generation of composers like Aarre Merikanto and Väinö Raitio went to Moscow instead of Vienna, the pianists Ilmari Hannikainen and Ernst Linko studied in St Petersburg. Glazunov and other Russian musical notabilities continued to make guest appearances in Finland. In his own family circle Sibelius experienced no interruption of his connections with Russia: Aino's Russian relatives, the painter, Mikhail von Clodt and her Aunt Olga had stayed at Ainola, and some years later his son-in-law, Arvi Paloheimo, like so many other Finnish businessmen, established himself in Petrograd as a representative of the expanding Finnish paper industry. Even less did he bear any enmity towards Russia's western allies – unlike Axel Carpelan, who allowed his hatred of the Russians to encompass the whole Entente:

What has happened is ghastly: Italy's transparent breach of its treaty obligations and England's ignominious attack on culture . . . But it is unthinkable to conceive of the fall of Germany, Luther's, Kant's, Goethe's and Beethoven's country crushed by the Muscovite juggernaut. Russia is the aggressor . . . God! Help Germany.[1]

For all his German sympathies, Sibelius in no way shared Carpelan's Anglophobia. He corresponded with Rosa Newmarch, who gave him to understand that she regarded the war as 'cruel but necessary': 'I think that you and I have long shared the same view of Berlin's so-called "Kultur".' In that, however, she was mistaken. Even if Sibelius had been repelled by one or two examples of 'ungraciousness' in Wilhelmine Berlin, he set great store by their 'Kultur' – which did not prevent him from admiring English culture and their reticence as well as the generosity they had shown him and his music. Otherwise Sibelius could glimpse from Mrs Newmarch's letter something of the unshakeable determination of the English and their will for victory. He understood her feelings, when she sat and knitted socks for the Tommies or taught them French – in the expectation that her own son would be posted as a doctor to a warship. He replied: 'You are often in my thoughts, you with your patriotic heart which must beat more strongly than ever.' Sibelius suffered both as a pan-European and a composer. Mrs Newmarch was frightened that his scores published in Germany would be covered by the wartime regulations against the products from enemy countries. Fortunately the situation was improved by the fact that the London offices of Breitkopf und Härtel were managed by the Swiss. *Valse triste* and *Finlandia* could still be played but the symphonies, alas, had no place in the wartime repertory.

Rather more quickly than expected, the Russian grip on Finland quickly hardened, and in November the Tsarist regime was unwise enough to allow news of further Russianization to seep out in the press. This, and news of the Russian defeats in East Prussia, revived Finnish spirits and hopes. The so-called 'Jaeger' movement came into being: young men, 2,000 in number, enlisted in the German Army and became the 27th Imperial Prussian Light Infantry ('Jaeger') Division. Sibelius presumably learned of the movement at an early stage, in February 1915, when he was visited by one of their organizers, Dr V. O. Sivén. Sibelius's own diary records on 6 February: 'Sivén – a most manly character – was here yesterday' and this perhaps gives us a clue that he was initiated into the secret. On his own admission he 'was always a warm supporter of this movement', even before the autumn of 1917 when he was asked to compose a March for the Finnish Light Infantry Division. He was even to dignify it with an opus number (Op. 91a).

Finnish opinion embraced a wide spectrum, and its diversity ranged from the officer class, who were more or less Russian in outlook, to the 'Jaeger' movement; from industrialists, whose business contacts were with Russia, to revolutionary workers, whose sympathies lay with Russian radical

---

[1] Letter of 7 August 1914.

movements; from career civil servants to the loyal opposition, which was confined to Kretsy Prison, St Petersburg, or even – like Pehr Evind Svinhufvud – banished to Siberia; from pro-Germans, who were by no means rabidly anti-Russian, to Anglophiles and Francophiles with many differing attitudes to Russia. Sibelius did not possess the same keen political instinct or interest as many others of his circle – such as Gallén-Kallela, Bertel Gripenberg and Werner Söderhjelm – nor was he a salon strategist like Axel Carpelan. He maintained a certain distance from any active involvement. But because he had travelled widely and made so many contacts, he had developed a certain awareness of and feeling for international affairs. However intense his absorption in his own creative world, he still was unswerving in his concern and care for Finland. He shared the feelings of despair and impotence of most thinking Finns at the growing pace of Russianization and perhaps some realization that the outbreak of war might open up hitherto unseen possibilities. In his most optimistic moments he could probably conceive the attainment of some form of Finnish autonomy but we would be deceiving ourselves if we imagined that he was sufficiently far-sighted to have even dimly envisaged the collapse of the Tsarist order, the October Revolution and Finland's Declaration of Independence in 1917 as being within the realms of possibility.

On the contrary, he lived life one day at a time in a state of anxiety and uncertainty, plagued by false rumours – 'Hangö is in flames, the Emperor Franz Joseph is dead' – irritated by guests and, in particular, Aino's Russian relatives, who admired all sorts of people 'nur nicht Jean Sibelius'; still cursing his innate reticence and 'esprit d'escalier, which allows anybody to elbow him aside', worried by the fact that his income from Breitkopf und Härtel had been cut off, relieved by his good relations with his Helsinki publishers. Yet behind all these personal problems was the awareness of the dark forces unleashed on to the world: 'I fear that all the bitter conflicts that are in the air will not resolve themselves only in war. Humanity's hatred and wrath has frightening depths.' He was frightened – and not without good reason – that the forces now raging would spell the end of civilization.

Select Bibliography

Abraham, Gerald (ed.), *Sibelius, A Symposium*, London, 1947.
Ekman, Karl, *Jean Sibelius, En konstnärs liv och personlighet*, (tr. *Jean Sibelius: his Life and Personality*), Helsinki, 1935, and London, 1936.
Furuhjelm, Erik, *Jean Sibelius. Hans tondiktning och drag ur hans liv*, Borgå, 1916.
Gray, Cecil, *Sibelius*, London, 1931.
Johnson, Harold, *Jean Sibelius*, New York, 1959, London, 1960.
Krohn, Ilmari, *Der Stimmungsgehalf der Symphonien von Jean Sibelius*, Vol. I, Helsinki, 1945; Vol. II, Helsinki, 1946.
Layton, Robert, *Sibelius* (Master Musicians), London, 1965, 1977.
Layton, Robert, *Sibelius and his World*, London, 1970.
Levas, Santeri, *Nuori Sibelius*, Helsinki, 1957.
Levas, Santeri, *Järvenpään mestari*, Helsinki, 1960.
Niemann, Walter, *Jean Sibelius*, Leipzig, 1917.
Parmet, Simon, *Sibeliuksen sinfoniat* (The Symphonies of Sibelius), Helsinki, 1955, and London, 1959.
Pike, Lionel, *Beethoven, Sibelius and 'The Profound Logic': Studies in Symphonic Analysis*, London, 1978.
Ringbom, Nils-Eric, *Jean Sibelius*, Stockholm, 1948, and University of Oklahoma, 1954.
Roiha, Eino, *Die Symphonien von Jean Sibelius. Eine formanalytische Studie*, Jyväskylä, 1941.
von Törne, Bengt, *Sibelius i närbild och samtal*, (tr. *Sibelius: A Close-up*), Helsinki, 1935, and London, 1937.
Tammaro, Ferrucio, *Jean Sibelius*, Turin, 1984.
Tanzberger, Ernst, *Jean Sibelius*, Wiesbaden, 1962.
Vestdijk, Simon, *De symfonieën van Jean Sibelius*, Amsterdam, 1962.
Vignal, Marc, *Jean Sibelius*, Paris, 1965.

Index of Sibelius's Works

General Index

References in *italic* refer to illustration numbers.